From
Strategic Planning
To
Strategic Management

From
Strategic Planning
To
Strategic Management

Edited by
H. Igor Ansoff

*European Institute for Advanced Studies in Management,
Brussels, Belgium*

Roger P. Declerck

*Lecturer, Economic Development Institute,
World Bank, Washington, D.C., U.S.A.*

Robert L. Hayes

*Associate Professor, Graduate School of Management,
Vanderbilt University, Nashville, Tennessee, U.S.A.*

A Wiley—Interscience Publication

JOHN WILEY & SONS
London · New York · Sydney · Toronto

Library of Congress Cataloging in Publication Data:

Main entry under title:

From strategic planning to strategic management

   'A Wiley—Interscience publication'.
   Chiefly presents the proceedings of the first
International Conference on Strategic Management, 1973.
   1. Management — Congresses. 2. Planning — Congresses.
3. Problem solving — Congresses. I. Ansoff, H. Igor,
ed. II. Declerck, Roger P., ed. III. Hayes, Robert
L., ed.IV. International Conference on Strategic
Management, 1st, Vanderbilt University, 1973.
HD29.F76   658.4   74—20598
ISBN 0 471 03223 9

Typeset by Preface Limited, Salisbury, Wilts, and printed
by The Pitman Press, Bath

Contributing Authors

H. Igor Ansoff

Justin Potter Professor, Graduate School of Management, Vanderbilt University, Nashville, Tennessee, and Professor, European Institute for Advanced Studies in Management, Brussels, Belgium.

Edwin M. Bartee

Professor of Management, Graduate School of Management, Vanderbilt University, Nashville, Tennessee, U.S.A.

Willard T. Carleton

Professor of Finance and Economics, Amos Tuck School of Business Administration, Dartmouth College, New Hampshire, U.S.A.

James V. Davis

Associate Professor and Associate Dean, Graduate School of Management, Vanderbilt University, Nashville, Tennessee, U.S.A.

Pierre Davous

Deputy General Manager, Société Eurequip, Vaucresson, France.

James Deas

Director of Marketing, Roux S.A., Paris, France.

Roger P. Declerck

Lecturer, Economic Development Institute, World Bank, Washington, D.C., U.S.A.

William R. Dill

Dean of the Faculty of Business Education, New York University, U.S.A.

Frits Haselhoff

Assistant Professor of Business Administration, Free University, Amsterdam, Netherlands.

Robert L. Hayes

Associate Professor, Graduate School of Management, Vanderbilt University, Nashville, Tennessee, U.S.A.

László Horvath

Karl Marx University, Budapest, Hungary.

Pierre Jarniou

Professor, University of Paris IX (Dauphine), France.

Kenneth O. Michel

Program Manager, General Management Programs, Executive Education Operation, General Electric Company, U.S.A.

H. Raymond Radosevich

Associate Professor, Graduate School of Management, Vanderbilt University, Nashville, Tennessee, U.S.A.

James R. Rawls

Associate Professor, Graduate School of Management, Vanderbilt University, Nashville, Tennessee, U.S.A.

Donna J. Rawls

Assistant Professor, Department of Psychology, Fisk University, Nashville, Tennessee, U.S.A.

Pierre Tabatoni

Professor, University of Paris IX (Dauphine), France.

Robert A. Ullrich

Associate Professor and Associate Dean, Graduate School of Management, Vanderbilt University, Nashville, Tennessee, U.S.A.

Hideki Yoshihara

Associate Professor, Kobe University, Japan.

Lajos Zelkó

Associate Professor, Chair of Political Economy, Karl Marx University, Budapest, Hungary.

Contents

INTRODUCTION

H. IGOR ANSOFF and ROBERT L. HAYES

1. Evolution of the Strategic Problem

Starting in the 1950's, first business firms and later other types of product/ service-producing organizations increasingly became concerned with their maladjustment to the environment. The cause, which became known as the *strategic problem*, was then perceived to lie in a techno-economic mismatch between the products of the firm on the one hand and the demands of the marketplace on the other. The solution was seen to lie in *strategic planning* — a rational analysis of the opportunities offered by environment and of the strengths and weaknesses of the firm and selection of a match (strategy) between the two which best satisfied the objectives of the firm. Once the strategy was chosen, the critical part of the solution was over and the firm could proceed to implement it.

In the intervening years the perception of the strategic problem has been undergoing drastic and rapid changes. In part this has been due to improved understanding of the real nature of the mismatch with the environment and of the processes involved in redressing it. As a result, the problem now appears a good deal more complex than it did 20 years ago. This complexity is illustrated in Figure 1.

The figure brings together three principal aspects of the strategic problem: the managerial problems which it poses, the processes by which these are resolved and the variables which they encompass. In this perspective strategic planning is seen as a limited attack on a part of the total problem. It focuses attention on the problem of external linkages under a basic assumption that the internal configuration of the organization will remain essentially unchanged (in strategic planning language: 'strengths of the firm will be emphasized and weaknesses minimized'). It concerns itself primarily with problem-solving, determining the new preferred linkages with the environment under the assumption that implementation and control will follow as secondary activities. The variables included in the analysis are exclusively technological—economic— informational. The social and political dynamics both within and outside the organizations are assumed to be irrelevant and unaffected. Thus, strategic

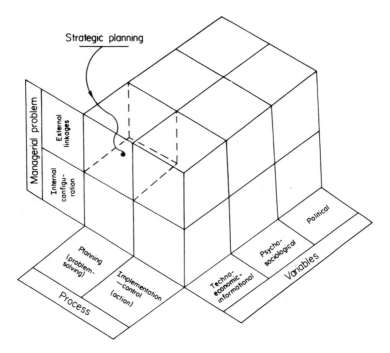

Figure 1. Dimensions of strategic problem.

planning is essentially Cartesian in its approach. To paraphrase the great philosopher: 'I plan therefore I do'.

Over the past 20 years it became increasingly clear through lessons of successes and failures, as well as through continuing research, that the Cartesian conception of the strategic problem suffers from two major deficiencies. First, in the language of management science, it is an 'improper optimization' – the excluded variables have major impact on the preferred solution. Second, strategic planning solves only a part of the total problem concerned with maintenance of a viable and effective relationship between the organization and the environment. Figure 1 attempts to encompass the total scope of the problem, which increasingly is being referred to as *strategic management*.

A distinctive and difficult aspect of the strategic problem has been the very rapid change and expansion of its content during the past 20 years. As a result, new conceptual frameworks and problem-solving technologies have tended to lag behind the real-world problems encountered by management. Thus, for example, today's literature on strategic planning offers little enlightenment on how to cope with major surprises such as the recent petroleum crisis. Thus the challenges, threats and opportunities which have confronted many organizations, particularly the business firms, have been changing and expanding faster than the understanding of the problem. And they show evidence of continuing to do so.

The pattern of these changes is shown in Table 1. As the first line shows, the

Table 1. Evolution of Strategic Problem

Dimension	Time period			
	1960	1975	1980	1985
External linkages Techno-economic-informational	Strategic imbalance	Continual change	Surprises	Constraints
Internal configuration Techno-economic-informational	Utilization of strengths avoidance of weaknesses	Capability transformation	Multi-capability	Flexible capability
Internal configuration Psycho-socio-political		Societal participation	Redefinition of norms and objectives	Responsiveness to participants' needs
External linkages Psycho-socio-political	Pressures for social respon-sibility	Societal-ecological constraints	Conflict with national sovereignty	NEW RAISON D'ÊTRE

strategic planning problem itself has undergone significant changes in emphasis. From an instrument for correcting a partial strategic imbalance with the environment, it is coming to concern itself with the changeability of *all* economic and social linkages with the environment, with increasing incidence of major surprises and with ecological and resource constraints.

As the second line indicates, internal configuration of resources is evolving from the problem of essential preservation of the firm's strengths into a problem of fundamental redesign of the internal capability of the firm in order to preserve harmony with its internal linkages. This requires the already observable emergence of multiple capabilities (cultures) within the envelope of a single organization and eventually emergence of flexible designs, capable of coping with major surprises.

The last two lines of Table 1 show the emerging importance of psychological—sociological—political variables, aspects which by the mid-1980's bid fair to become the dominant aspect of the strategic problem, both internally and externally to the firm. The fundamental cause of this trend is the 'crisis of identity' caused by loss of the social centrality historically enjoyed by the firm.

As a result, new patterns of power and influence are emerging within the firm, basic norms and values are being challenged, the image of the firm as an instrument of national economic progress is no longer clear, and ultimately the basic concept of the firm's legitimacy and social utility will have to be redefined.

Changes of this magnitude inevitably produce changes in the technology: the methods and procedures by which management tackles its problems. The continuing shift in technology needed for coping with the strategic problem is shown in Table 2. As all of the dimensions show, the thrust is towards broader

Table 2. Evolution of technology of strategic management

Dimension	Time period			
	1960	1975	1980	1985
Subproblem	├─→─ Interface with environment ──→			
		├─→─ Organizational capability ──→		
			├─→─ Entrepreneurial action ──→	
			├─→─ Integrated action ──→	
Activity	├─→─ Planning (problem-solving) ──→			
		├─→─ Social adaptation (learning) ─→		
		├─→─ Planning-learning ──→		
			├─→─ Action cycle ──→	
Variables	├─→─ Techno-economic ──→			
		├─→─ Psycho-sociological ──→		
		├─→─ Political ──→		
			├─→─ Multi-disciplinary ──→	
Uncertainty	├─→─ Probable future ─→─ Identifiable contingencies			
			└─ Surprises ──→	
Design approach	├─→─ Correction of dissonance			
		└─ Redesign		
		└── De novo design ──→		
	├─→─ Improving organizational anticipation ──→			
	─→─ Improvement of organizational responsiveness			
		─→─ Design of flexible organizations		

and more comprehensive technology: in the scope of the problem tackled, in the managerial activities treated, in the variables included.

An overview of Tables 1 and 2 suggests a fundamental underlying trend: from a technology designed to correct partial deficiencies in an organization to a technology of 'design to order' — an ability to define, structure and put into action a new organization which is responsive to a specific social need.

The emergence of a holistic design technology is a distant goal. An early and essential step is development of a multi-disciplinary community of researchers who share a perception of the problem, who understand the value of contributions by others, who participate in joint research and who, above all, are prepared to take the risk of venturing into an unknown territory.

As a step in this direction, the Graduate School of Management at Vanderbilt University organized in May 1973 the first International Conference on Strategic Management. With the generous help of IBM Corporation, IBM World Trade

Corporation and the General Electric Foundation, the Conference brought management students of different nationalities and disciplines together with business practitioners of strategic management. This book, with one exception, is based on the Conference.

2. Content of the Book

2.1. *Concepts and Frameworks*

The major expansion of technological perspective suggested in the preceding pages requires a comparable broadening of conceptual, theoretical perspective. In the first chapter in this volume *Haselhoff* suggests that such a perspective does not now exist.

Asserting that 'there is nothing so practical as a good theory', Haselhoff attempts to construct a broad conceptual framework which accommodates partial theoretical insights now available and which is broad enough for the strategic problem. The scope is 'a complex and dynamic economic—technical—social open system operating in a complex and dynamic environment'. Within this scope Haselhoff identifies four 'paradigmic' dilemmas: (a) decision *versus* system, (b) holistic *versus* elementaristic, (c) inside *versus* outside and (d) closedness *versus* openness.

The four dilemmas are examined in the light of a 'threefold criterion of organizational health and rationality: ... efficiency, survival and meaningfulness'. Practical conclusions are drawn with respect to the 'strategy—structure issue' and to the 'environmental issue'. Haselhoff concludes that the 'expansion of the strategic management problem from an organizational to social level' is 'one of the most startling challenges ... today'.

Tabatoni and *Jarniou*, in a chapter whose length belies its depth, basically accept the scope of the problem defined by Haselhoff's four dilemmas. Within it, they develop the idea that 'any strategy depends on a system of norms which are felt by people in the organization ... (and that) ... on the other hand, the (strategy) implementation reveals the fitness of the norms'.

Three types of management subsystems are postulated which guide interaction between norms and policy: (1) planning systems, which define foundations for collective action, (2) organizational structure, which expresses 'adequacy of means to paths', and (3) social control system, which tries to obtain conformity to norms expressed through structure.

From analysis of the interaction of these subsystems, Tabatoni and Jarniou suggest that strategic management be defined as a system which emphasizes its own flexibility, or a 'critical appraisal of its own conception and practice'. Thus, strategic management is basically a culture. The authors make specific the elements of such a culture and the types of planning, information and control systems necessary to support such a culture.

2.2 *Strategic Posture Transformation*

In terms of the preceding Figure 1 the first two chapters address the total cube. The chapter by Ansoff, Declerck and Hayes confines itself to the 'commercial' linkages to the environment concerned with products—markets—technology.

The authors review the historical development of American management technology and conclude that both its strengths and shortcomings stemmed from its pragmatic 'medicine man' approach to curing symptoms rather than causes. They suggest that strategic planning suffered from these same short-comings and that an improved approach is to be sought in improved understanding of the underlying problem.

The strategic problem is shown to be more than a problem of selecting attractive external linkages. On the one hand, selections must be married with implementation; on the other, external change implies far-reaching internal readjustment. The entire pattern of the internal capability (Tabatoni and Jarinou's 'culture') must also be changed.

The authors separate the firm's behaviour into two basic modes, competitive and entrepreneurial, and describe for each several levels of intensity in a way useable for diagnostic purposes. A diagnostic procedure is developed first for the firm's behaviour relative to environment and second for the firm's internal capability. The diagnostic procedures are married to planning procedures for the total strategic posture transformations.

Recognizing that a mere extension of planning will not solve psycho-socio-political problems of implementation, the authors next turn to a comparison of planned and adaptive approaches to organizational change. They suggest that the two have complementary merits and deficiencies, and that a *planned-learning* approach offers a desirable and probable paradigm for the future. The planned-learning process is described in some detail.

In a companion chapter, *Davous and Deas* provide a concrete illustration of planning-learning by describing the design and conduct of a consulting intervention in strategic management. Drawing from their own experience in France, the authors first identify characteristics which they feel are typical of the French management culture. These include the previously widespread use of MBO, the sensitivity to semantic meaning of planning terminology and the tendency towards dissatisfaction with partially formalized systems.

The basic design of the intervention is a 'spiralling process' of several iterations of the strategic plan. Earlier iterations are focused on development of the internal strategic culture; in later stages the emphasis shifts to 'real' plans. Each stage is designed to produce concrete spinoffs for strategic action, so that planning and action proceed in parallel. In terms of hierarchical levels, the intervention is designed to proceed from 'top to bottom', progressively involving lower types of management.

Conceptually, the intervention is based on a well-known environment-strengths weaknesses-objectives ('finalities') dialectic. Specific illustrations of its application are provided.

The philosophy of the intervention follows closely the Tabatoni and Jarniou concept by focusing on producing a cultural change which moves the firm to strategic management. The process is designed to bypass psychological obstacles and to bring about capability change and management development by solving real problems.

2.3. Strategy and Structure

Yoshihara opens a series of four related chapters by discussing the basic modes of strategic adaptation to the environment. He separates exploitative adaptation, which occurs while preserving historical linkages to the environment, from strategic adaptation, which seeks to change the linkages, and then relates the strategic adaptation to the concept of an industry life-cycle.

Focusing on strategic adaptation, he discusses the causes of the recent domestic 'diversification rush' in Japan, as well as the evolution of Japan's foreign investment strategy. Yoshihara cites as major weaknesses the low relative level of Japanese R & D and the peculiarities of the Japanese management system.

The last part of the chapter is devoted to 'socio-political linkage relationship' to the environment. The rising public and governmental anti-business sentiment leads the author to propose a 'socio-political transition' through which the firm can develop and maintain viable and defensible relationships with the environment. The urgent need for 'societal' strategy is emphasized.

While Yoshihara advocates societal strategy applicable across the boundaries of the firm, William Dill advocates a fundamental revision of the boundaries themselves. He discusses the 'challenge of coping with an active, intrusive environment' which is represented by external 'stakeholders' who can be 'quite specific in advice and demands'. Dill argues that the move today is from stakeholder influence to stakeholder participation. The chapter is devoted to the advantages, perils and mechanisms for such participation.

The author argues that the newly required openness is not a matter of choice but of necessity for management; but he also suggests that 'active and decentralized kibitzing on strategic issues . . . will lessen . . . reliance on rules and laws'.

He next undertakes the task of mapping the world of stakeholders, first by identifying 'the dimensions of the whole citizen', then his relationship with the enterprise, and lastly the role choice vis-à-vis strategic management.

'Successful intervention requires talent, resources and power . . . thus intermediaries between the stakeholder and the enterprise are an important part of the equation'. These represent either 'representative kibitzers' or 'opportunistic kibitzers' and thus have different roles to play.

Dill suggests that concern with the kibitzing problem has far-ranging implications for the strategic management paradigm. One of these is the need for 'preparatory work' by management to gain public understanding and awareness of strategic issues before specific decisions arise. This would reduce the present level of disenchantment with business in general and resistance to specific strategic moves in particular and 'repersonalize' the image of the corporation. These outcomes, in Dill's opinion, are worth the inevitable loss of privacy which will result.

Horvath and Zelko turn the reader's attention from Japan to Hungary and from societal to commercial aspects of strategy. According to the authors, the 'division of the decision-making powers or rights between government organs . . . and companies . . . is expressed by the relation between the national plans and the activities . . . of the economic units . . .'. While '. . . the most important investment projects are decided upon and financed by the state . . .', management of companies 'may be able to influence the main directions' by having 'good relations with higher political and government organs'.

The time horizon of plans has received considerable attention in Hungary from the early 1960's. Data were developed for employees' average stay with a company (12 years), expected lifetime of equipment (14 years), product life-cycle of the enterprises in the machine industry (11.2 years) and expected time period of changing technologies (9.1 years). The conclusion was that for a typical enterprise a decade should be the period for which 'realistic long-range plans can be prepared'.

The authors suggest that 'long-range plans in the socialist countries usually apply for longer time periods than in the capitalist countries'. The national plans define the scope of the enterprise but leave the management to make strategic decisions about the concrete product mix in the future. A system of 'strategic aims' needs to be worked out before long-range planning can take place. These aims are (a) 'aims connected with the existence of the company'; (b) positional aims: cadres of management and employees, size of enterprise relative to industry, position in technics and technology, position in the economic potential; (c) 'aims of a social and human nature'.

Commenting on the state of current practice, the authors state that 'at this time (enterprises) make long-range plans but (they) are not really based on strategic decisions yet'.

Carleton and Davis concern themselves with the problem of estimating the financial consequences of strategic action. They start by saying that 'strategic management and financial resources management do not bear a close enough relationship to one another — either in theory or practice' and that 'contemporary . . . financial theory can be made operational for the needs of strategic planning'.

Their point of departure is a criticism that often there is no attempt to integrate individual financial objectives into a coherent whole. After pointing to the limitations of the use of targets such as ROI, EPS and P/E ratio, the authors also criticize the current practice of integrating them through simulation. They are critical of budget compilers because they 'only trace out . . . the financial and operating consequences of choices already made' and go to considerable pains to substantiate their point.

Carleton and Davis next turn to a new framework designed to 'preserve the essential features of financial statement simulators, but (to broaden them) so as to permit multiple interactions between financial goals and constraints'.

The model incorporates the following features. (a) 'The structure of balance sheets, income and funds flow statements remains at the heart of the model.' (b)

'Outputs of the model are the major financial decisions.' (c) 'The inputs are of three kinds: forecasts of the economic environment, legal restrictions on financial decisions, and management policy requirements such as growth in EPS, limits on debt, etc.' (d) The corporate objective maximization of the present value of the owner. (e) The model is programmed on time-sharing with a conversational mode.

Practical experience with the model showed three major benefits: responsiveness to major prospective changes in the environment, usefulness for probing of simultaneous changes in policy, the occasional finding that whatever corporate objective is employed *no* plan is feasible.

Radosevich shifts attention from strategy to structure, from external linkages and strategic action to the internal configuration of the firm. He suggests that writers about organizational innovation virtually ignore the necessity for combining the change in the strategic posture with the efficient exploitation of current 'businesses' of the organization. He recognizes a dichotomy between 'strategic posture' (S-P) innovation, which results in fundamentally new linkages to the environment, and 'exploitation potential' (E-P), where the innovation is used not to change linkages but to increase efficiency. Since in many large industrial firms in the U.S. large portions of resources are invested in mature industries, the S-P type of innovation is essential, but the author points out that it is necessarily on both the investment (new linkages) as well as the divestment side (discontinuance of linkages).

The author next presents a detailed comparison of the differences in attributes between innovative and operating units and suggests that, for successful coexistence, they must be structurally separated. An example is presented and discussed in detail. The 'dichotomy is established at a very high level' right below the chief executive officer. The innovation group has a fluid structure which includes R & D, market analysis, new ventures and acquisition analysis. There are permanent and rotating staffs and a cadre of new venture managers and future operations managers, as well as outside 'nominal groups'. The operations group is structured along appropriate conventional lines.

Radosevich briefly presents an alternative structure which consists of three differentiated parts, new business development, new business strategy and current business operations, and then takes up the subject of integrative mechanisms. A number of mechanisms for the transfer of new ventures between innovative and operating groups include written proposals, transfer agents, coordinating committee, physical transfer of personnel and facilities and equipment.

In conclusion, Radosevich suggests that 'as the breadth and rate of diversification of resources increases, the trends may well be to the innovative forms'.

2.4. *The Strategic Manager*

Ansoff's chapter opens this section by attempting to predict the future shape of the business manager. This is done in a converging series of steps: from the impact of turbulent environment on social structure, to the consequent business trends, to the transition of the firm to a new shape, to the impact on the job of management, and finally to a prognosis for the future manager.

Next the historical development of the manager's profile is married to the prognosis. Several scenario alternatives emerge for the future. Ansoff opts for a scenario which visualizes not one but a number of different management profiles, each built through matching individual talents and personality to the distinctive tasks which managers will have to perform. Strategic management will thus become a team effort requiring several 'differentiated managers' to cope with the full complexity of the job. All differentiated managers will have certain key commonalities: (1) skills in social relations, communications, social influence, planning and ill-structured problem-solving, expertise in using experts, suboptimizing in relation to the total enterprise; (2) knowledge of the behaviour of complex organizations in complex societies, general problems of management and general processes of management. The dimensions of specialization among managers may be among one of the following: type of problem, type of process, cognitive profile, management technology, productive work, scientific discipline, professional technology.

Ullrich summarizes the work of the key researches on motivation by saying that 'underlying each of the organizational prescriptions is the . . . assumption that . . . an organization will (perform better) if employees are provided with opportunities to fulfill their needs for achievement, responsibility, recognition' . . . and that this will occur 'regardless of the technology or organizational system . . . and the mental processes whereby the organization goals are derived'.

He next raises questions about this undifferentiated assumption by describing significant differences in organizational behaviour along four principal dimensions: the types of solution employed (construct, judgement, programme, vote); the coordination processes employed (planning, feedback); the means for problem simplification (control over environment, modelling, differentiation); existence of agreement on goals and means (leading to inspiration, judgement, compromise, computation).

Ullrich next questions the prevalent assumption that human needs are basically insatiable, and suggests, instead, a model of behaviour that allows for satiation as well as increase in goals. He then uses this model to suggest ways to reduce resistance to organizational change.

Ullrich suggests that individuals typically become involved in planning in one of two dominant work roles: a role which involves dealing with constructs and a role dealing with vote rote. Using previous arguments, Ullrich advances propositions for different types of participation in planning indicated for individuals in the respective work roles.

Bartee turns attention from motivation on systems for the manager to helping him become self-motivated. His basic proposition is that 'it is one thing to think strategically and . . . another to . . . *act strategically*'. He argues that the current 'legitimate' learning experiences induce passive change-absorbing behaviour and that the development of strategic managers is a problem of reeducation. He visualizes this as proceeding in steps of a threat hierarchy which progressively increases the managers' adventuresomeness and environmental orientation.

The key concept in this progress is 'to cope with greater future ambiguity by changing personal expectations' and 'the strategy for learning how to learn'.

Bartee next presents a pedagogy for the reeducative process which follows the sequence conceptual orientation, immersion, feedback, internalization of experience, new cognitive concepts, new cycle of experience. Implementation of this cycle is difficult because 'legitimate' learning environments are not structured to accommodate them.

2.5. *Education, Selection and Training of the Strategic Manager*

Rawls and *Rawls* concern themselves with the problem of identifying the strategic manager from a population of his peers. Since no empirical work has been directed specifically to this problem, the authors review studies which have sought to identify successful managers, individual entrepreneurs, change managers and organizational entrepreneurs. On the basis of these findings, they suggest a list of criteria which appear to be applicable to the identification of the strategic manager and which need to be tested empirically.

They then review current trends in management selection and make suggestions on how different approaches can be made useful in selection and placement of strategic managers. These include self-selection, multi-dimension—multirater approaches, new selection instruments and emphasis on development, placement and career learning.

In the final chapter *Michel* describes how a very large corporation converts theory into practice in its management development programmes. 'Although in the General Electric Company many avenues (of learning) are (used) at various stages of . . . careers . . . the intrafirm education programmes are the pre-dominant education sources'. . . . These programmes are built on a highly articulated rationale for strategic management used by the firm. Michel describes this rationale in some detail. The total programme is built around three curricula: the professional curriculum which focuses on knowhow, skills and art; the general curriculum dealing with personal attitudes, awareness, human relationships, etc.; and the managerial curriculum focused on business and management of resources.

The approach to educational offerings is career-coordinated, responding to the different knowledge, skills and perspective needs which occur on the different levels of a manager's career. Generally, 'having earned his spurs as a specialist, the manager is given a new drastically different challenge, that of excelling as a generalist'.

It is at this latter level in the General Management Course that managers are exposed to strategic management. A curriculum for the course is appended.

3. A Bird's Eye View

In a book which ranges 'from cabbages to kings', from the philosophical perception of organizational behaviour to management selection, it is not easy to

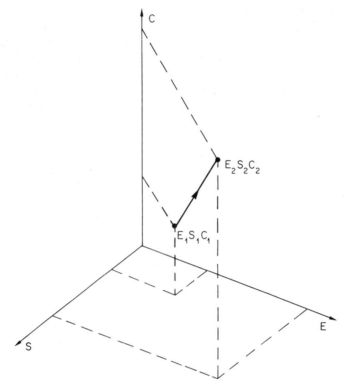

Figure 2. Strategic posture transformation. E, environmental turbulence; S, intensity of external linkages; C, responsiveness of internal configuration.

keep to the common thread. This thread is a real managerial problem which, for better or worse, encompasses the full range of complexity.

It may be useful to restate and illustrate this problem simply. The problem is maintenance of a productive and viable relationship between an organization and its environment. It can be visualized simply, as in Figure 2, along three dimensions: (1) the changing environment; (2) the linkages between the firm and the environment; (3) the internal configuration of the firm's resources. As environment changes from E_1 to E_2, the firm needs to find and carry out a *strategic posture transformation*: from S_1 to S_2 and from C_1 to C_2. It is in the problem of effecting this transformation in a deliberate and planned way that all the chapters in this volume find a common theme.

Papers by Haselhoff, Tabatoni and Jarniou and Ansoff, Declerck and Hayes deal with the total transformation vector; Yoshihara, Dill, Horvath and Zelko and Carleton and Davis with the external linkage component; and Ansoff, Radosevich, Ullrich, Bartee, Rawls and Rawls and Michel confront the problem of internal configuration.

1

Conceptual Framework

A NEW PARADIGM FOR THE STUDY
OF ORGANIZATIONAL GOALS

Both the study and the practice of setting organizational goals have become a very hot potato to many students and practitioners of management. The management consultant in particular, the middleman between the theorist and the practitioners, suddenly some years ago was confronted with this tremendous problem of strategic management. According to my personal experience as a full-time management consultant, he was not very well prepared for this new and glamorous job. When this strategic issue came my way, I could not do better than develop my knowledge, skills and attitude through doing the consulting job itself, a sort of craft way of learning and doing things.

In doing so, I gradually became aware of two things. First, I soon discovered that, if anywhere, the phrase 'There is nothing so practical as good theory' could be applied to top-floor decision-making. A sound theoretical structure expressed in a conceptual scheme, in short what Kuhn called a paradigm, apparently was very useful for top-management problem-solving. The practice of consulting made me also aware of another fact, namely that a paradigm that only reflects part of the picture would not work. Even worse, this particular shortcoming, this lack of generality, could be very dysfunctional to the quality of organizational life when the consultant or the manager himself tried to work with it. For instance, it could happen, depending on the consultant's background, that his paradigm was only fit for dreaming up some well-formulated corporate strategies by using techniques of ill-structured problem-solving. At the same time it could be that his frame of reference was not turned to the problem of getting one of these strategies off the ground. Or vice versa his approach could be more or less adapted to dealing with action within and by human groups, so effective on a suborganizational level, but could be useless in handling problems of adapting total organizations to their environments.

These two facts bothered me very much when I was trying to do a good job in management consulting in business firms several years ago. I felt that I was equipped with half-theories, while nonetheless being invited to solve comprehensive problems of organizational survival and growth.

Attempting to accept these challenges, it came to me that there were two additional survival problems to solve, both concerning my own survival. The one was related to my survival as a person while being around in corridors of power. The other had to do with the economic survival of my consulting work as a business. The latter forced me to work within very narrow constraints of time and money. Although these economical constraints can be a heavy burden on the outside consultant, I shall leave this problem aside. The other, personal survival issue is more relevant here.

Being in the executive suite culture forms for consultants a strong temptation, namely to look at problems from the apex of the hierarchical pyramid. This can have a drug-like effect on the consultants mind, because things look so different from there, from above. From there reality looks to much like manipulable black boxes. The reason is that detailed information will, on its way to the top, very much be aggregated to almost dead facts and figures. One needs all one's imaginative powers to keep alive that vivid sense of the real organizational world behind these facts and figures. Avoiding that distortion of view which the client is sometimes caught in has to be the very strength of the consultant. I believe strongly that this psychological survival problem has much to do with the intellectual powers of the consultant. But because he is a man of flesh and blood, this is only part of the story. He has not only to take care of his intellectual, but also his emotional and moral survival.

This is true if he appears to be influenced by two parts of the organization, by top management and by the technostructure. In practice it frequently works out that one of these two influences is more effective than the other. The management-oriented consultant tries to identify with the man in power. But we may expect that, unexperienced as he will be, he understands what it feels like to wield power; does he really understand how effective — and often how ineffective — authority can be? The average management consultant is an intellectual type of person. He has mostly achieved his high-ranking position within the boundaries of a protected environment. Will he not be an easy prey of manipulation on the part of top management? Will he not be in real danger of becoming a servant of power, losing thereby the support of the technostructure? And if he avoids that, will he still be able to effect any differences for his client-system?

On the other hand, is it not the technostructure-oriented consultant who is drifting away from the management part of the organization? Is it not he who will himself become another whiz kid with so many of them already around? Is it not he who is another stubborn intellectual governed more by ideas than by realities, at least as far as the managers see it? Many consultants, however, feel more at home in this intellectually more exciting technostructure than in the power-ridden world-at-the-top of bargaining, persuasion and compromise.

A conclusion I can draw from my own experience is that the outside consultant has to be a real middleman, concerned with abstractions between theory and practice, more concrete and also more existential between top management and the technostructure, and also between people. In other words, in order to be effective he has to protect his outsideness. This quality has to be his most important asset. It is even his very legitimation of being hired, because it keeps him objective and impartial. It provides him with an undistorted view. Above all, a top management consultant cannot afford to take sides, becoming part of the client's organization. All this is a prerequisite for developing a true professionalism of consultancy, the capstone of which has to be the intellectual power he is able to control. The role of the top management consultant in modern society makes him the very bearer of the intellectual credentials that are expressed in good theory, in a sound and effective paradigm.

Paradigms have always played an important role in the development of theory, especially in the field of natural science. Kuhn even says that

The developmental pattern of natural science is usually from paradigm to paradigm (Kuhn, 1972, p. 91)

What he then takes a paradigm to be is, and I quote again,

. . . in the first place, a fundamental scientific achievement and one which includes both a theory and some exemplary applications to the results of experiment and observation. More important, it is an open-ended achievement, one which leaves all sorts of research still to be done. And, finally, it is an accepted achievement in the sense that it is received by a group whose members no longer try to rival it or to create alternates for it. Instead they attempt to extend and exploit it in a variety of ways. (Kuhn, 1972, p. 91)

So, in short, a paradigm is a scientific achievement that is both open-ended and accepted.

Asserting that a paradigm is something practical, one may ask where that practicality comes from as far as the study of organizational goals is concerned. Kuhn again says

. . . nature (we would rather say reality, FH) is vastly too complex to be explored even approximately at random. Something must tell the scientist where to look and what to look for and that something, though it may not last beyond his generation, is the paradigm with which his education as a scientist has supplied him. (Kuhn, 1972, p. 96)

Consequently a paradigm is at the same time both a stepping stone for dealing with problems and a set of constraints in doing so. In a way,

The scientist largely ceases to be an explorer at all, or at least to be an explorer of the unknown. Instead, he struggles to articulate and concretize the known, designing much special-purpose apparatus and many special-purpose adaptations of theory for that task. (Kuhn, 1972, p. 96-7)

A consultant needs this in order to do his work adequately. The difference in what Kuhn is describing here is that while Kuhn focuses on discipline-oriented problems we worry about interdisciplinary problems. It is exactly here that many organizational theories are in real trouble. Struggling with strategic issues in business firms, I found most existing theories too restricted. By using them I could not escape from a kind of myopic vision of organizational reality upon which they were so often built. I became gradually convinced that a theoretical breakthrough was very much required. It appeared to me that the main focus of that conceptual breakthrough had to be a theory of the formulation of organizational goals.

Organization science is a science both of human artifacts and of human reality; it is both normative and explanatory. Therefore we have to escape from the deterministic, mostly economic theories in this field that deal with means for accomplishing certain preformulated goals. In fact, these theories could only solve the efficiency problem. As a consequence of social change, many organizations ended up in serious identity crises with respect to their environments. The overarching strategic issue came up and the self-evident way of producing wealth had to be abandoned. Change and complexity of the environment became a threat as never before, and the all-time predetermined goals formulated in earlier days no longer worked as a reliable criterion. Insight into what is behind that magic word profitability, a more generalized criterion not only for efficiency but more for viability, asked for new and further-going knowledge about the working of business firms. The economic theories of the firm could not offer this; they took too much of these internal operations for granted. We had to adapt a new construct that could represent the business more adequately. It had to be something like a complex and dynamic economic—technical—social open system operating in a complex and dynamic environment. So complexity, dynamics, and openness had to become the catchwords of the new paradigm of the science of organizations.

This new construct and its characteristics had to redirect the development of new knowledge, new skills and new attitudes in order to handle new problems. First of all, I have to confess that the paradigm I constructed is not a brand-new thing. It is more of a super-paradigm that comprises several other paradigms each with smaller ranges of applications. One might ask, why this super-paradigm? The answer is very decisive; because I do not believe that there exists one paradigm that will do the whole job. Even traditional theories and concepts cannot be discarded. They can be still very useful, albeit on the condition that they need a new context. And it is particularly this context that coincides with the super-paradigm. Therefore this paradigm does not exclude older ones; it is more of an elaboration, an expansion of them. On first sight, this very characteristic of the new paradigm looks rather complex. But that is exactly what is intended. The reality of management, particularly of top management, is complex indeed; it is of a completely dilemmatic nature. We cannot even say of it that we really solve problems at all. Sometimes we get rid of them at the cost of creating other ones; sometimes we hardly succeed in reducing to bearable proportions the threats and the dangers that go with them; and in very rare cases we are extremely lucky to solve them.

Is this a sceptical theory? Yes and no. Yes, insofar as we have to acknowledge that much of our so-called problem-solving is no more than move them away from our territory, from our department and from our organization as a whole. In doing so we do not really solve problems; we only succeed in transferring them. This is sceptical indeed. But our theory is not sceptical insofar as it is a realistic theory, which teaches us what kind of dysfunctions our behaviour creates and where it does so. This is important because those places can easily become sources of new problems.

So in organizational life we have to live with dilemmas on the one hand, but on the other hand we have to make decisions all the time. We cannot afford academic doubt; action is forced upon us. If we do not accept the existence of these dilemmas of decision making, we shall lose sight of reality. If, however, we do accept these dilemmas too easily, we shall forget them later on and simplify things too much. We could say that plugging holes is a concomitant of organizational action, but doing so consciously asks for a kind of paradigm without which we shall live at the mercy of half-theories tuned to half-problems.

It will be understood now that the structure of the new paradigm will be adapted to the dilemmas of organizational problem-solving, that is problem-solving through, by and within organizations. This can be best exemplified by four paradigmatic dimensions:

(1) the decision *versus* system dilemma;
(2) the holistic *versus* elementaristic dilemma;
(3) the inside *versus* outside dilemma, and
(4) the closedness *versus* openness dilemma.

I have tried to visualize this fourfold pair of extremes on four axes of a wheel (Figure 1).

According to the demands of the real organizational situation, one has to compromise between these extremes. An organization science such as I have in mind has first a material object. This is both the organization itself and its environment. Secondly, there is a formal object, which I call organizational problem-solving, that is, reducing complexity and inconsistency of the environment in order to allow meaningful and feasible human action. Our super-paradigm achieves this by a threefold integration of the more classical organizational doctrines, namely doctrines concerning the future, doctrines concerning the environment and doctrines about the human being. This expanded paradigm is able not only to conceptualize the problem of adapting

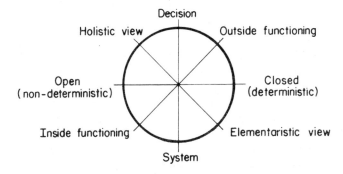

Figure 1

means to given goals, but also how much flexibility and how much consensus are required in order to have a healthy organization — a healthy organization being one that is directed to the right goals. Therefore goals have to be problematized by looking at them as means, means for survival and meaningfulness. Only after the selection of goals has taken place can efficiency play its role as a criterion. Efficiency is a concept that can only be filled with content after having available a clear-cut goal; efficiency is goal-dependent. Within an efficiency paradigm the problem of formulating the goals cannot possibly be solved. This seems to me to be the drawback of older theories.

We came up here with a paradigm that provides a threefold criterion of organizational health and rationality, namely efficiency, survival and meaningfulness. The first is goal- and future-dependent, the second is environment-dependent and the third is dependent on man himself. How does this construct of a dilemma-ridden organization as the empirical object of organization science look?

1. Decision Versus System

The fact that every organization is more or less a coherent whole that gets its dynamics from the decision-making and problem-solving of actors made of flesh and blood shows clearly how closely interwoven the decision concept and the system concept are. In my view this implies that the science of organizations has to be based on two theoretical accomplishments, that is, on a decision theory and on a system theory. However, so far most conceptualization in the field of strategic management has been developed either from the act-of-decision or from the open-system notion.

The act-of-decision model of the economic theory of the firm with its linear input-throughput-output concept has always used a machine model in which the inputs are the means of production and in which the outputs are products and services. This popular model is far from what we would call an open-system model. The latter is instead more of a circular nature. Linearity combined with efficiency, that is, maximization of profitability as a decisive rule of choice, is again goal-dependent. If we would cling to profit as a goal, the sky would be the limit. It is no use to resort to profit as a goal of business. This does not solve anything in this respect. Profit, particularly long-term profit, is a survival criterion of a much too vague and abstract nature. It may serve as a strong motive for organizational action: theoretically it cannot offer enough clues to finding relevant alternatives of action. The act-of-decision model is far too narrow for that. Moreover, it is too rationalistic, too cognitive, a reason why the links to organizational behaviour can hardly be made. Only one person, or at best a homogeneous decision group, can make the overall decisions of strategic management. So the decision model even when the act of decision is considered to be sophisticated, ill-structured, strategic problem-solving, is strongly linked to the omniscient rational manager, albeit he is in most cases assisted by a professional technostructure. This model represents too exclusively managerial problem-solving; it cannot go beyond that; it cannot visualize organizational problem-solving. The latter asks for the circular open-system view. While the linear system was of an input-throughput-output kind, the circular system can be represented by the interface concept. Simon has defined the interface as a meeting point between an 'inner' environment, the substance and the organization of the artifact itself, and an 'outer' environment, the surroundings in which it operates. If we turn now to the social version of the systems concept, those two environments are represented by the so-called stakeholders. These environments have materialized in 'objective' things or 'thing'-like structures of more or less hazy type like social structures, knowledge systems, moral systems, technical structures and economical systems. Behind these 'things' stand people who decide about the rigidity, about the changeability of these structures. So the interface is ultimately surrounded by human beings and their norms, their intentions, their feelings, their patterns of behaviour, their 'artifacts,' etc.

But how can that interface concept be brought down to earth? What does it mean in reality? Where is it located? Particularly when one wants to move managerial to organizational problem solving, this appears to be an almost insoluble question. So the systems concept has to be completed with other notions that will be partly found in the other three dimensions of our paradigm.

What have we accomplished so far by putting side by side the two concepts of decision and system? On the one hand, the decision model is now embedded in a much wider and more comprehensive model, namely that of the open system. Goal formulation now can be problematized, and that must be considered very important progress with respect to strategic problem-solving. On the other hand, we have paradoxically also created an irreconcilable tension, or maybe even conflict, between the two. The decision model points to managers who make decisions but at the cost of too much simplifying of the model of organization itself. However, as Hall says,

A total acceptance of the open-system approach ... would make it appear that there is actually little need for organizations at all, since things just seem to happen. (Hall, 1972, p. 26)

And he goes on with

The very nature of organizations signifies that they do accomplish certain things. They do alter their input and produce outputs and make decisions, and these things are done on a relatively predictable and relatively stable basis. (Hall, 1972, p. 26)

By adopting the notion of an open system as a model for modern organizations we cannot exclude the decision model. Means and ends are the triggers of action, input and outputs towards and from the various stakeholders in the context in which those decisions have to be placed. Organizational action is more of a stream of events; it implies a fluctuating attention to the interests of the different stakeholders in reducing them to a meaningful cooperation that serves the viability of the organization as a whole. The interface is the localization of where decisions are made, like a chess player that has to play games simultaneously on different boards.

2. Holism Versus Elementarism

The interface, however, continues to be a vague notion. It did not sufficiently describe the problem-solving agency itself. I have complicated things very much by insisting on something that I called organizational problem-solving. That means, in fact, that the organization itself is the decision-making agency. It has to decide on itself. The idea we have to expand on now is that of a system of subsystems. If we stress, on the contrary, the autonomy of the subsystems like organization members, group departments and divisions, our viewpoint is more or less elementaristic. Here can be seen the dilemma of harmony and conflict. Many theories so far have been made a definite choice between the harmony and the conflict model. Consequently, they were only able to solve special problems. Within this subparadigm of holism *versus* elementarism, however, we are able to face dilemmas such as: how much consensus do we need and how much non-consensus, that is conflict, can we afford? In reality we cannot assume full harmony, but we cannot afford open conflict either, at least not for a long time. The question is now: what are the levers of producing consensus — are they power and authority, are they common interests, are they common values, or something else, or even a combination of these?

In older theories the solution of these problems was often made logically feasible by accepting a harmony bias. In our modern culture we have to deal more and more with the phenomenon of dissensus, even with on-first-sight disruptive actions that try to revolutionize our system. That means definitely that we must go into moral issues, in particular when organizational goals are more to be formulated than implemented. We cannot shy away from ethical judgements if the humanization of the modern organization is at stake. And that is exactly what is the case here. There is a definite strong tension between the viability of an organization and its significance, its meaningfulness to its members. Any organization is the product of a mixture of manipulation and participation. We have to acknowledge that fact in our theories and paradigms. To people who think that we are already doing our best, I would say that it is my conviction that we must bring to bear more imagination, that we must take more risks in trying to humanize our organizational systems, much more than we did in the past, in spite of the many results that have been accomplished up to now.

3. Inside Versus Outside Functioning

In supposing that there is a dilemma between decision and system, the notion of internalities and externalities is very complicated. From the point of view of decision-making or problem-solving, organizational action, as we mentioned earlier, is located on a so-called interface. This interface, however, remains a very hazy concept because we do refrain from identifying the activity of the interface with managerial problem-solving. We decide to try to use this interface notion in order to conceptualize organizational problem-solving. So the idea of the open system in order to visualize the distinction between system and the environment turned from a linear to a circular concept of the organization. This concept consists of two layers.

First, it is focused on the stakeholders; a very important consequence for strategic management goes with it. In some strategic theories there is too much asymmetry in this respect, for instance by stressing product-market strategy. Even in a business firm there is much more than product-market strategy. Strategy defined as the business the firm is in is a too shortsighted concept. A business firm is not only a kind of production machine on behalf of customers, it is at the same time also trying to get support from other stakeholders. The survival of the system depends on dealing with those different stakeholders separately and unrelatedly.

Between their actions, between their separate and unrelated decisions, an organization has to find the margin of its viability. Coordinated action between stakeholders will relate inputs and outputs in such a way that the organization will lose its autonomy. And if that happens to be the case, we can say that it has become part of another organization. The structure of the marketplace, or in other words of the environment, is very decisive for organizational autonomy and survival. Organizations that are not able to operate separately in different markets will definitely lose their relative freedom, and with it their fitness to react adequately to the needs of society. Besides this somewhat unclear concept of the interface that coincides with the location of problem-solving and is surrounded by an environment that embraces all relevant stakeholders, there is another more clear-cut concept of 'linear' and 'outer' as far as environment is concerned. This distinction uses another notion of a system, not so much a system of problem-solving, of action, but more of a real, concrete system of people and things, of organization members and investments the organization wields power over, again embedded in an environment. This on-first-sight concrete distinction between organization and environment that goes with this concept will give us clues about the role and the place of organizations in society, and the manner it has to be managed to play that role adequately. But this appearance of concreteness is deceptive. It is a kind of trap following on from the mistake that organizations are analogous to mechanisms and organisms. This cannot be true because in organizational life the fight for survival can impossibly be only a fight to maintain the *status quo*. And here again another dilemma appears, namely that of adaptability of the organization to its environment. The two horns of the dilemma are exercising power, that is, generating change, and accepting influence, that is, absorbing change. It is a matter of an inside—out or outside—in approach of organizational decision-making.

Emery and Trist have analysed how an organization is able to maintain its viability in today's world, that is going to become an increasingly turbulent field. It seems to me that one of their most important conclusions is that this very environmental development has created a situation that is difficult to stabilize. This stabilization can no longer be done by the individual organizations themselves. This is also what we hear so many futurologists say: the momentum of society is on the way to killing us. What Emery and Trist try to point out is that the actions of organizations on their own are completely unable to cure this situation of instability and to redirect existing trends. It could be that the cause of this impotence is that the organizations do not have enough flexibility to redirect their own momentum. This is what I would call the dilemma between anticipation and flexibility — a dilemma that cannot be evaded by exercising sheer power or by the threat to do so. This is in my view a traditional strategic philosophy, a kind of cold war philosophy we have to get rid of. I do not see a clear-cut solution myself, but I an inclined to conclude from the observations of Emery and Trist that egotistic power-based strategy is very outmoded now.

Is the world going to be overruled by a few mega-organizations because of all those organizational momentums? Can we go on with the destructive power play that those organizations in so many ways are invited to engage in? I doubt very much so, because we cannot afford to let this go on. If we continue to permit the development of the growth of organizations — and why should it stop itself? — then we shall enter indeed a *terra incognita* of which we can only say with Emery and Trist: the ground is moving. Every business firm doing its own thing means too much of a build-up of uncertainty in society. This polarization of external behaviour does much harm to modern society and its future by creating too much organizational momentum and rigidity.

So evidently we have no choice, and I would say that two things are needed. First we have to dream up a philosophy of strategy that creates a *modus vivendi*, a kind of peaceful symbiosis between organizations. Strategy formulation has to go beyond the immediate interests of the organization itself. That means that the strategist has to look upon his opponent, upon his competitor, as part of the solution of his problems. Second we have to trade in hard power for soft power, that is, sheer power for flexibility and intelligence. In fact, this has something to do with non-violent action. I know that there is some speculation in what I say. However, many futurologists keep telling us that we are heading for a post-industrial society in which cultural norms and values will be quite different from what we consider to be normal at this moment.

4. Deterministic Versus Indeterministic Action

The last dilemma I wanted to present is related to the question: do we have a sufficient amount of degree of freedom of action? I have previously stressed that we actually need a mode of thinking that enhances the imagination of the decision-maker. We badly need a theory that really starts enterprising decisions that will produce relevant change. Both extrapolation and muddling through will capture the decision-maker repeatedly in the narrow boundaries of so-called reality. If we cling to what is and call it realism, if we do not make a real difference, if we allow ourselves to be caught in a closed, deterministic model of decision-making in which we think available information is pretty reliable, then we shall not succeed. If we want to defend reality instead of challenge it, we shall at some time have to act out of fear. The muddling-through kind of way of doing things will paradoxically be an enormous risk in the long run, because the momentum that goes with it will become increasingly threatening to both the organization itself and its environment. But fear is the most dangerous adviser of action we can think of. So in many regards we cannot have a postponement of creative action. What seems impossible today hopefully will appear possible tomorrow by trying it.

Also here is a dilemma that makes it difficult to find the right solutions. A lot of so-called problem-solving is, in fact, no more than pushing constraints. As Simon said, there is no clear distinction to be drawn between goals and constraints. What is a constraint at one point in time is a goal at another. However, it is very hard to say how much change we can accomplish in a world where more and more constraints are put upon us by participation and democratization. This is what I call the dilemma of determinism and indeterminism. For the sake of humanizing social relations within organizations, this participation is badly needed. But at the same time and for the same reason much change is required, change that is blocked by this very participation.

5. Practical Implications

The dimensions of my kind of super-paradigm of the organization as a dynamic and complex open system will teach us where theorizing about strategic management so far went astray. I did not dwell on it, but anybody can easily bring to mind where older theories placed their stress marks. Our paradigm is one of an economic—technical—social open system, in which an interchange of means and ends directed by decision-making and problem-solving processes has to bring about the adequate function that has to be fulfilled by the organization, namely efficiency, viability and meaningfulness. There are two central issues for which our paradigm has some practical implications.

First there is the *strategy—structure issue*. The one-sided manipulative managerial decision outlook has to be discarded, or at least it has to be expanded to the organizational problem-solving vision. This expansion challenges the idea that the strategy of a complex organization is a conscious plan constructed by a more or less homogeneous decision-making agency. This naive picture of the internal operations of an organization has too many shortcomings. Strategy is more of an organizational outcome, a result of cooperation between the several subsystems of which an organization consists. The top management perspective is not decisive any more. Strategy is also the result of checks and balances from within the organization. There is surely a role for top management that is much more than rubber-stamping. I am strongly convinced of that fact. But I also believe that though the external strategy is still very important, the internal strategy will become more critical. In order to create the possibility of quick action in an organization as far as implementation of the mostly temporal external strategy, more attention has to be drawn to the internal set-up of that organization. At the same time a certain amount of flexibility that allows for rapid shifts from one external strategy to another is indispensible. Organizations will have to develop themselves as general-purpose devices instead of being a special-purpose machine that can only earn a reasonable profit by building up a kind of one-dimensional power. The latter, as we said before, will in the long run do much damage to its environment. So external organizational behaviour, and consequently strategy formulation, has to refrain from selfishness; competitive action has to drop the zero-sum game of philosophy of what-I-win-will-be-lost-by-my-opponent. The opponent has to be looked upon as part of the solution of my problem.

Internal organizational behaviour and strategy formulations has to be guided by new notions, notions that are more complicated than Chandler's adagium structure-follows-strategy, which says that the internal structure of an organization will mainly be dictated by the external strategy. There has to be a redirection of priorities in the sense that formulating a more generalized system strategy will become a more important job of management. A system strategy

(1) that allows an organization to go from the environmental situation as it is toward decisions that, in fact, are based on a subjective interpretation of that situation;

(2) that keeps alive an adequate institutionalization of values in order to come up with a certain consensus about what to do;

(3) that preselects what part of the potential environment is relevant for the time being;

(4) that differentiates the internal system in order to come up with stability by building different sorts of thresholds between the subsystems;

(5) that gives flexibility to enable the organization to shift quickly from one strategy to another.

From these five system strategies the more concrete organizational goals have to be derived. But even this will not be sufficient. There is also an *environmental issue*. Organizational survival in an environment that carries the characteristics of turbulent fields cannot be based on organizational action alone. If it is not up to the individual organization to solve this environmental issue on its own, who has to do it? Can we hand that hot potato to our political institutions? I am afraid not. I would prefer a stimulating cooperation between political and organizational strategists. Theorests and practitioners of general management within organizations have to go beyond their immediate field of study and try to contact the theorists and practitioners of political management. If they fail to do so they will one day find out that politicians have taken the initiative and that they have set the pace. But on the societal level of strategic management also, we cannot rely on a technocratic elitist approach from the top down. It has to be complemented by efforts to involve the relevant stakeholder in that decision process in order to find really workable solutions.

This expansion of the strategic management problem from an organizational to a societal level seems to me one of the most startling challenges to the experienced and trained strategists in today's profit and non-profit organizations.

References

Ansoff, H. I. (1965). *Corporate Strategy*. New York, McGraw-Hill.

Bennis, W. G. (1966). *Changing Organizations: Essays on the Development and Evolution of Human Organization*. New York, McGraw-Hill.

Chandler, A. D., Jr. (1966). *Strategy and Structure*, Chapters in the History of the industrial Enterprise. New York, Anchor.

Emery, F. E., and Trist, E. L. (1965). The causal texture of organizational environments, *Human Relations* (February), No. 1.

Galbraith, J. K. (1968). *The New Industrial State*, New York, Signet.

Hall, R. H. (1972). *Organizations, Structure and Processes*, Englewood Cliffs, Prentice-Hall.

Kuhn, T. S. (1972). 'Scientific Paradigms,' In B. Barnes (Ed.), *Sociology of Science*. Harmondsworth, Penguin, pp. 80—104.

Luhmann, N. (1966). *Theorie der Verwantungswissenschaft. Bestansaufnahme und Entwurf*. Kiln, Grote.

Luhmann, N. (1968). *Zweckbegriff und Systemrationalitat. Ueber die Funktion von Zwecken in sozialen Systemen*. Tubingen, Mohr.

Luhmann, N. (1971). *Politische Planung. Aufsatze zur Sociologie von Politik und Verwaltung*, Opladen, Westeutscher Verlag.

Simon, H. A. (1969). *The Sciences of the Artificial*, Cambridge, Mass., MIT Press.

Thompson, J. D. (1967). *Organizations in Action, Social Science Bases of Administrative Theory*, New York, McGraw-Hill.

THE DYNAMICS OF NORMS IN STRATEGIC MANAGEMENT

PIERRE TABATONI – PIERRE JARNIOU

This study illustrates an analytical as well as a pedagogical tool which we use in France to underline the normative aspects of strategic planning and strategic management. It emphasizes the idea that any strategy depends on a system of norms which are felt by people in the organization to be its basic policy or its specific type of management. On the other hand, the implementation, through the strategic programmes, reveals the 'fitness' of that policy, so that it can either reinforce the existing norms of management or call for change in them.

The analysis of that system of norms and of its dynamics appears central to the problem of strategic planning and management.

The argument will be presented in four sections.

1. *'Management Systems'* are presented as a particular configuration of three subsystems: planning, organization and social control.

2. In *'Rationality, Policy and Management Systems'* we see 'Policy' as the specific 'rationality' which generates a particular configuration of the management system or a particular system of norms of management.

3. *'Dynamics of Policy'* emphasizes the two main components of any policy: the rationality of 'Production' by the organization and its 'Social recognition'. It relates the constraints resulting from a policy to the conflicts resulting from its implementation through the 'social control' subsystem and it visualizes the dynamic of policy-making through the dynamic of the relations between the three subsystems.

4. *'Strategic Management'* is seen as a particular form of 'management system' where 'Policy' is expressing a rationality of innovation involving the change of 'Policy' itself, the working of dialetical relations between policy and strategies, and finally the development of a 'strategic culture' throughout the organization. It needs new types of management models which take account of socio-political and cultural norms as well as of technico-economic potential.

1. Management Systems

Management processes are social processes which permit a voluntary collective action in the organization for its survival and development within a broader social system. They are based on:

(a) The practice of *'planning systems'* in a broad sense, which include the rules of information choice and control. They determine the structure of operational aims, the allocation of resources to implement them and the methods of implementation.

(b) The design of *'organizational structure'* which identifies the different organs according to their specific missions, sets the corresponding roles of people working in these organs and determines the communication and control relations between these organs, and more generally the objective modes of coordination between their particular activities.

(c) The methods of *'social control'*, which deal with the interpersonal relations systems. They aim at the efficiency of collective action. They permit establishment of the social boundaries between the organization and its environment and the build-up of a corresponding feeling of belonging within the organization. They therefore establish some specific 'potential' of collective action which can be mobilized within the organization structure to plan and implement its plan. They relate to the personal aspects of communication, leadership and enforcement methods, learning and teaching systems, motivating and participative processes.

'Management systems' express the types of interrelations between these three subsystems; we should talk of these interrelations as they are felt and lived by the people within the organization.

A major problem relates to the degree of *coherence* between these three subsystems. The ideal of perfect coherence is of course difficult to realize in practice. Proper management systems should at least avoid the most significant dysfunctions, as these dysfunctions involve economic, 'inside' psycho-social and therefore political costs when they are strongly resented by people. There is no doubt meanwhile some state of equilibrium which permits the organization to define and implement its objectives at the minimum 'total' cost and to reinforce its identity within its environment.

2. Rationality, Policy and Management Systems

Social processes, as practised by the participants are to a large degree determined by the 'organization structure'. 'Structural norms' induce the essential relations within the organization (hierarchical, delegation and co-ordination, interconnection between activities . . .).

The norms which characterize these relations are not only 'structural norms': they express the processes of negotiation between the social groups within and outside the organization.

We can therefore consider that system of 'structural' and 'relational norms' as *the* 'organization structure'.

The principles which command the design of that system of norms can be seen as its *rationality*.

It is well known that, due to the multiplicity of the objectives and constraints, in the process of time, or at a given moment of history, different 'rationalities' can be superseded and/or coexist. But the essential utility of strategy is to try to redesign the total system along some dominant rationality which corresponds to the basic choices and constraints selected and perceived by the 'political' system of the organization.

That political system, for tactical reasons, might not like to make clear its dominant rationality, or might choose not to pay the 'cost' of making it really a dominant one. The study of the relations between the constraints, the basic choices and the degrees of freedom of political manoeuvring in designing the major norms of the organization should be a prominent part of management science.

These phenomena appear still more complex if we take account of the fact that 'political systems' within an organization do not choose and act in isolation from the broader socio-political environment, which itself is based on some societal rationalizing model.

It follows that unless the 'survival' constraint appears strong and obvious, the 'rationality' within an organization will be a complex one. We can assume, however, that the participants in the organization, who have to live with its normative expressions, will — right or wrong — build up some image of it, and take it as a system of action models.

A main function of the 'social control system' is to 'teach' these 'action models' according to the rationality preferences of the political system of the organization. The efficiency of the social control system thereby reinforces the 'organization structure' and in fact gives to it its practical and operational significance. This is done within *some overall rationality which is really the 'policy' of the political system of the organization.*

'Policy' is, therefore, a chosen 'system of management' expressed by a particular system of norms of management which at the same time expresses and determines the vision of the environment, the identity of the organization, the intelligence of the problem, the conception of the strategies and structure and the social control (Tabatoni, 1972).

3. The Dynamics of 'Policy'

Any organization is at the same time:

> an agent of production;
> a concrete social structure.

As a 'production agent' it works in competitive and cooperative relationships with other production agents. It has to cope with the production constraints of its activities and to design and implement some competitive strategies within its specific strategic degrees of freedom (Tabatoni, 1968).

As a 'concrete social structure' it has a need for recognition by society at large and it must therefore comply with, as well as reinforce, the broader social demands, norms, and values of society. Serious deviations should normally imply costs for the organization, either for reinforcing the specific boundaries of the organization in a close-in strategy or for compensation.

Survival and development of the organization as a production agent, as well as its recognition as a social structure, are so intimately linked together that their specificities identify the organization. But each of those needs must be related to different reference systems. 'Survival needs' must cope with technico-economic systems and be satisfied through some rational model of the adequacy of the structure to the objectives. 'Recognition' needs must be referred to the broader system of social cohesion and social reproduction, which permit the functioning of society under conditions acceptable to people.

It is the role of 'policy' as a choice of a specific management system, to define its specific way within these two reference systems and to trace, therefore, an 'identity path' for the organization. Cost-benefit analysis of policy must be conducted along these two components. The horizon of policy-making cannot be determined without consideration of the appropriate level of policy-making, because on that level depends the feasibility of that policy. This means that some 'policies' cannot be implemented within the boundaries of a specific organization and depend on cooperative strategies of different organizations or on prerequisite arbitrages by higher levels.

We can now redefine the management system in more precise terms.

(a) The *planning system* of the organization, *on the basis of a specific and combined interpretation of 'survival' and 'recognition needs'*, identifies the level of policy-making, the admissible constraints to be coped with, the degrees of freedom to exploit and the different models which will be the foundation of collective action.

(b) The *organization structure* is the expression of the adequation of means to plans. It depends on a set of 'structural and relation norms' which will generate organs, roles, procedures and their interrelations.

(c) The *social control* system tries to obtain the higher-level conformity to those norms from the participants, which implies that they will reproduce by their own initiative the rational models of their collective action. This is done by *compensating devices* (compliance and retribution systems . . .), which help to compensate the constraining effect of the organization norms, and by *learning-teaching systems*, which help them to understand those norms and, if possible to 'internalize' them, therefore reducing their constraining effects. Obviously, these social control devices will not suppress *conflicts and frustration, which will have to be managed* in certain ways which are also part of the social control system.

The 'admissible' constraints (designed by planning) will strongly influence the organization norms, which will themselves influence the functioning of the social control system with the usual dynamic interactions between the three subsystems. All significant dysfunctions within that total management system, as they appear in its dynamic functioning, will create cost (expressed in 'survival' and/or 'recognition' performances). The planning system must be able to monitor those dysfunctions, appreciate these 'costs', redesign plans and/or organization norms and/or social control systems, or even to change rational models so that the significant dysfunctions are reduced. Where to start and how to implement change will depend on the dynamic properties of that management system, which themselves depend on:

the political system of the organization, and more specifically its own flexibility and capacity for conceiving and implementing needed change, including its own rationality models;

the degrees of constraints and conflicts, their localization;

the amount and nature of slack resources of the organization (in its broad sense);

the efficiency of the planning (and, of course, of the information) systems;

the leverage effects of specific conflicts or dysfunctions on the overall performance of the management system;

the short-term feasibility of certain types of reforms, i.e. the ones which incur least cost (economic as well as socio-political).

4. Strategic Management

Is any 'policy', understood as a particular 'system of management', completely identical with 'strategic management'? By making more explicit the proposed meaning of 'strategies' as compared with 'policies', one can specify more clearly the idea of 'strategic management'.

'Strategies', as we see them, are the operational expressions of policies in the sense that, within a system of management, they define operational criteria on the basis of which 'strategic programmes' can be conceived, selected and implemented. These programmes can concern the activities portfolio ('external strategies') as well as the 'internal strategies' which deal with the organization structure and the activities of social control.

In that sense, the couple 'policy—strategy' is non-dissociable as long as policies are implemented. But if we look now from the point of view of 'policy dynamics', as defined in Section 3, we are conducted into the dynamic relations between policies and strategies which are the essence of 'strategic management'.

'Strategic management' is understood here as a chosen system of management which emphasizes its own flexibility, i.e. which induces innovative strategic programmes, which looks for changes in policy itself, which praises the development of potential for future changes more than short-term performances, and which understands the fundamentals of power and cultural characteristics within the organization because these are the main generators of its own flexibility.

In other words, there is no 'strategic management' unless the organization is *willing* and *able* to develop a *critical appraisal of its own management conception and practice, through the search for and the implementation of innovative strategies.* Planning systems, structures and social control practices must be such that they permit and even promote that critical attitude and that will for policy changes. This implies a political system of the organization willing and able to go in that direction, and that might be called the dominance of a 'strategic culture' or 'strategic language' within the organization. Again, that 'strategic culture' is essentially composed of such elements as:

awareness of change as a *normal state*, and not as a pathological one;

readiness to search for forms of actions in uncertain and risky conditions;

readiness to launch experiences whose results are difficult to control in the short run;

readiness to accept new methods of management with their socio-political implications;

capacity to manage conflicts so as to minimize the 'costs' of change;

interest in accumulation of potential, more than in immediate income, and praise of 'potential for change';

thorough awareness of the value of learning processes;

acceptance of working in multicultural environment and ambiguous political structures;

capacity to redesign management methods so that planning, structure and social control practices reinforce each other and contribute to a cumulative learning and diffusion of that strategic language.

There is not much doubt that 'learning' and 'teaching' such 'languages' will be based less on formal pedagogical schemes than on the launching of innovative strategies and 'controlling' part of their performances in terms of their contributions to more flexible policies and more innovative aptitudes and attitudes throughout the organization. The managerial dysfunctions to look for should be the ones that go against these lines. And, as it has been described by the scientific literature on innovative organizations, that type of management can reveal as non-significant a number of the classical 'rational management methods'. The 'rational mode' here is a 'strategic rationality' which can go along perfectly with classical managerial dysfunctions and even exploit such dysfunctions as a resource.

'Strategic rationality' as generator of 'strategic management systems' obviously calls for new strategic planning, information and control systems within the organization. Such models, in broad terms, would include socio-cultural indicators and attempt to appraise the interaction of technico-economic constraints with these other components of policy design.

(a) Scenarios of pertinent changes in the environment which could specify the nature and degrees of 'survival' and 'social recognition' risks for the organization and prognose *probable changes or possibilities of contributing to the realization of potential changes.*

(b) Socio-cultural diagnosis of the organization, i.e. of its political and cultural capacities to incur specific types of changes in its external and internal strategies.

(c) Prognosis of the feasibility of new 'strategic programmes' (external as well as internal).

(d) Overall multicriteria cost-benefit analysis for selection of 'programmes' which can satisfy some desirable and feasible set of 'survival' and 'social recognition' needs.

(e) Estimation of the 'overall costs of the inertias of the management system, i.e. of the presently unchangeable items in the feasible policy strategies. Special strategies to cope with the most significant inertias should be designed and included in revised version of (d).

(f) Models of 'strategic information systems', which will be the core of the new management system, to plan and monitor operations under (a), (b), (c), (d) and (e).

Such models would articulate in a dialectical way policy formation and strategy implementation and organize the learning of strategic management practices, thereby normalizing change in the organization. In that sense strategic management is a proper 'normative management of change', as its strategic specificities depend on the diagnosis of these internal and external norms which generate management practice and on learning—teaching systems capable of changing these norms in an organized way.

References

English Texts

Ansoff, I. (1972). 'The concept of strategic management', *JPB,* **2**, No. 4.

Ansoff, I. and Declerck, R. P. (1973). 'From strategic planning to strategic management', (Report at International Conference on Strategic Management, May 1973).

Argyris, C. (1965). *Organization and Innovation*, New York, Irwin.

Bauer, R. A. and Gergen, K. J. (1968). *The Study of Policy Formation*, London, Collier-Macmillan.

Buckley, W. (1967). *Sociology and Modern Systems Theory*, Prentice Hall.

Chandler, A. D. (1969). *Strategy and Structure*, Cambridge, Mass., MIT Press.

Etzioni, A. (1961). *A Comparative Analysis of Complex Organizations*, New York, Free Press.

Guth, W. D. (1971). 'Formulating organizational objectives and strategy', *JBP,* **2**, No.1.

Newman, W. H. (1971). 'Strategy and management structure', *JBP,* **2**, No.1.

Ozebekhan, H. (1969). 'Towards a general theory of planning', In E. Jantsch, *Perspectives of Planning*, OECD.

Pugh, D. S. (1971). *Organization Theory*, Harmondsworth, Penguin.

Simon, H. A. (1964). 'On the concept of organization goal', *ASR,* **9**, June.

Thomas, J. M., and Bennis, W. G. (Ed.) (1972). *Management of Change and Conflict,* Harmondsworth, Penguin.

French Texts

Barel, Y. (1971). 'Prospective et analyse de système', *Documentation Française.*

Bourdieu, P. (1970). 'Reproduction culturelle et reproduction sociale', *Inform. Sciences Sociales* (10-2).

Grozier, M. (1963). *Le Phenomène Bureaucratique,* Paris, Seuil.

Grozier, M. (1970). *La Société Bloquée*, Paris, Seuil.

de Jouvenel, M. (1972). *Du Pouvoir — Histoire Naturelle de sa Croissance,* Hachette.

Rocher, G. (1963). *Introduction a la Sociologie Generale* (I.II.III) (id. HNH).

Tabatoni, T. (1972). 'Le plan strategique face aux contraintes socio-politiques, *Le Management*, April.

Tabatoni, P. (1968). 'Etude empirique des contraintes strategiques de l'Entreprise', ISEA Economie et Societe, March.

Touraine, A. (1972). *Sociologie de l'Action*, Paris, Seuil.

Touraine, A. (1971). 'Systemes et conflits', Seminaire de Courmayeur, Roneote.

Touraine, A. (1969). *Le Societe Post-Industrielle*, Paris, Denoel.

II

Strategic Posture Transformation

FROM STRATEGIC PLANNING TO STRATEGIC MANAGEMENT

H. IGOR ANSOFF, ROGER P. DECLERCK
and ROBERT L. HAYES

1. A Historical Perspective

1.1 *The Problem*

In the middle fifties many American firms were confronted with disturbing symptoms which could not be readily remedied by available management techniques and which had no precedent in recent experience. For some firms the market demand began to level off and could not be restimulated by even the most energetic marketing and promotion. For others the demand began to decline in the face of substitute products offered by new technologies. Still others saw their traditional markets invaded by vigorous foreign competitors (Ansoff, 1973a).

The managerial techniques of long-term budgeting, financial control, even the then popular long-term planning, appeared inadequate for dealing with the new symptoms. In the inventive tradition of American business, firms turned their energies to development of new management approaches to the new perplexing problems. A number of leading firms and consulting companies, working independently, found themselves converging on a new approach towards the end of the fifties. The result, which developed through trial, error and exchange of experiences, became known as *strategic planning*.

The technology of strategic planning has now been around for some 15 years. Its actual application to practice has lagged. Today only a handful of leading firms employ genuine strategic planning to manage their forward growth thrusts. A majority still employ the simpler and earlier long-range planning techniques based on extrapolation of the past and lacking the systematic generation and analysis of alternatives required in strategic planning (Ansoff, 1970; Ringbok, 1969).

Experience in companies has shown that precepts of strategic planning are difficult to translate into practice. Not only is the translation difficult, but attempts to install rigorous strategic discipline typically run into 'resistance to planning' — an organizational inertia which appears to frustrate the efforts, reject planning efforts as a 'foreign antibody'.[1]

Again, in its typical inventive fashion, management started a search for an antidote to organizational resistance which would make strategic planning acceptable and palatable. The answer was found in the commitment of top management: strategic planning should work if it originates with top management and if it receives continuing attention and support from the corporate office.

Experience has shown this to be a workable, but a temporary, solution. Indeed, in some recorded cases, the initial enthusiasm of the chief executive has been instrumental in launching a firm on the road to strategic planning. But, more frequently, organization-wide involvement waned as soon as the chief executive shifted his interest to other priorities.

The impermanence of the antidote was dramatically illustrated by Robert McNamara's efforts to install PPBS (an advanced version of the strategic planning system) in the Department of Defense. So long as Mr McNamara was able to overcome resistance to planning by force of his personality and enthusiastic support from Presidents Kennedy and Johnson, PPBS was used, albeit reluctantly, throughout the Department. As soon as Mr McNamara departed, the pent-up inertia and resistance began to transform planning into the previous political, incremental process, which does not even vaguely resemble strategic planning (Schick, 1969; 1973).

In any case, use of coercive top management authority is paradoxical. In the first place, the technology of strategic planning was developed to help organizations do their work better. The technology was not perceived as helpful, as evidenced by resistance to planning. The next step was to coerce the organization into using it. This is reminiscent of a famous line from 'You Can't Take It With You' . . . 'comes the revolution we (will) all eat strawberries and cream *and like it!*'.

The paradox can be illustrated through a manufacturing analogy. If an industrial engineer had designed an automotive assembly line which produced cars with a 'resistance to running', the obvious solution would have been to redesign the technology. Only in an extreme emergency would anyone think of building a shack at the end of the line dedicated towards 'overcoming resistance to running'. But, when a planning technologist finds his system socially malfunctioning, he reaches for help from the top manager at the end of the planning assembly line! An understanding of this apparently strange behaviour can be gained from the history of American management technology.

1.2 Perspective on Management Technology

The history of American business is one of a succession of new challenges, problems, and opportunities. As these arose, thoughtful managers continuously experimented with new responses; some failed and some repeatedly succeeded. The latter became recognized as good practice, were imitated by other managers and became codified as standard management techniques. Out of this trial and error grew a body of approaches to managerial problems: financial ratio analysis, management by objectives, capital budgeting, profit planning, long-range planning, strategic planning, PPBS, issue analysis and, most recently, strategic portfolio analysis. Each approach emerged in response to specific needs: growing complexity of operations led the DuPont company to invent financial ratio analysis; the need for coordination and motivation in complex organizations led to management by objectives; increasing lead times and size of fixed asset investments gave rise to capital budgeting; inadequacy of extrapolation used in long-range planning created a demand for strategic planning. Characteristically, each of the approaches was heralded as a definitive and complete solution superseding all others.

In retrospect, it is now clear that the respective approaches were neither mutually exclusive nor comprehensive. Each addressed a particular facet of managerial problems, each complemented the other, and their development followed a logical historical sequence (Ansoff, 1973b).

All of the approaches shared a shortcoming of experience-derived technology. They sought to remedy specific symptoms rather than the problems which created them. When each remedy was proposed, an understanding of the underlying problems was typically missing (Ansoff, 1969). The solutions were like 'medicine man' potions aimed at alleviating superficial aches and pains caused by a mysterious illness.

If the cure removed the symptoms, superficially all was well again until the next symptoms appeared. Until they did, the management technique could claim cure-all properties. Thus, budgeting was the cure for the firm's problems until profit planning came along, only to be succeeded by long-range planning, which, in turn, was succeeded by strategic planning, etc., etc.

If the cure did not work, lack of an understanding of the underlying problems left no alternative but to try another cure. If strategic planning encountered resistance, a technique was needed for overcoming resistance (coercion from top management); if even with management support strategic planning still remained a disembodied set of documents, the 'total system' PPBS approach was invented and tried.

Without doubt, the trial and error method of experientially based technology produced results. It was a natural method to flourish in the pragmatic environment of American management culture, and for a period of time it gave American managements a commanding advantage over their European competitors, who lacked the frontier-like spirit for bold learning from successes and failures. It was the only route to progress in the absence of deeper knowledge of the problems and their underlying causes. But, as management developed its own technology through trial and error, the systematic method of science began to contribute insights into behaviour of firms and managers (Ansoff and Hayes, 1972). These insights made possible potentially more efficient approaches which seek to understand the underlying problems before treating the symptoms. In place of experiential trial and error, the method examines the effect produced by different solutions and selects the solution which promises the best results. Thus science expedites, improves and reduces the cost of solution.

In this chapter, we shall apply this method to identifying the problem which caused strategic planning to come into being. We shall then show that strategic planning is only one, and frequently not the first, of a series of steps which need to be taken to enable a firm to respond to the new challenges. As a first step, we need to establish some concepts and definitions.

1.3 A Perspective on Interaction with Environment

The firm relates to its environment in two distinctive ways. (1) Through *competitive* (or operating) behaviour in which it seeks to make profitable the goods/rewards exchange with the environment. It does this by attempting to produce as efficiently as possible and to secure the highest possible price and market share. (2) Through *entrepreneurial* (or *strategic*) behaviour in which it replaces obsolete products/markets with new ones which offer higher potential for future profits. The firm does this by identifying areas of new demand, developing responsive products, developing appropriate manufacturing and marketing capabilities, market testing and introducing new products to the markets.

Since the competitive mode is profit-producing and the entrepreneurial profit-absorbing, it is to be expected that the firm would gravitate towards the former, so long as the potential of its existing markets is perceived adequate for satisfying growth and profit objectives.

Analysis of historical behaviour confirms this expectation. The period from 1820 until roughly 1900, the Industrial Revolution, witnessed the birth of the firm. Farsighted entrepreneurs linked new technologies to the emerging demands. The linking body was a new social entity – the business firm. The emphasis of the Industrial Revolution was entrepreneurial activity – creation of profit potential where none existed before.

By the 1900's firms had staked out their technological and product positions and established linkages with profitable and growing national markets. For the time being, the entrepreneurial work was substantially done, and focus began to shift to competitive behaviour, where it remained for the next 50 years. The entrepreneurial behaviour did not disappear, but it substantially changed its shape and importance. Early in the century 56 leading firms, notably The Bell System, General Electric, Dupont and Westinghouse, *internalized* technological innovation by establishing research and development laboratories. These began to spawn new products and processes which enabled firms to better satisfy customers and extend market horizons. But even in the most active firms this remained a secondary activity. In a majority of firms competitive behaviour dominated the entrepreneurial. The environmental linkages changed slowly through logical extrapolation of the past position. The original basic linkages were viewed as the natural boundaries on the firm's relation with the environment. Steel companies were in the 'steel business', petroleum ones in 'petroleum', etc. The growth prospects and opportunities seemed bright enough to justify this position.

The focus on competitive behaviour was enhanced by neglect of other linkages with environment. As modern industry grew in the second half of the nineteenth century, society's attitudes towards the private sector evolved in parallel. The goal of national wealth and affluence loomed attractive and compelling, and the private sector promised to lead society to this goal. The political philosophy of the founding fathers, a philosophy of self-reliance and individual freedoms, found a congenial companion in the contemporary 'invisible hand' theory of Adam Smith. The result was social acceptance of the '*laisser faire*' doctrine: the hypothesis that the greatest social good will ultimately result if independent entrepreneurs are allowed to maximize their profits under minimal constraints from society. Thus, it was possible for a leading industrialist to say that 'what is good for General Motors is good for the country'. It was also possible for firms to focus single-mindedly on competitive exploitation of their market linkages. The result was the American 'economic miracle' which, within the short space of a half-century, helped win two major wars and placed affluence within the reach of every citizen.

As suggested in the opening paragraph of this chapter, by the mid-fifties difficulties began to accumulate on two distinctive fronts. (1) Aggressive pursuit of competition could not arrest slowdown of growth in some industries and decline in others. Industrial leadership began to shift from 'first-generation' industries to technology and affluence-born newcomers: computers, Xerography, pharmaceuticals, etc. (2) Single-minded pursuit of profit caused a multitude of undesirable side-effects. Neglect by the firm of the environment and of changing social values became progressively unacceptable to society. Anti-trust legislation, safety legislation, consumer pressures, pollution constraints, price and wage controls — all increasingly showed that the firm was losing both its immunity from outside influence and its privileged position as the principal instrument of social progress.

The first set of symptoms was the first one to be diagnosed. As early as in the mid-fifties, sometimes through foresight and more often through crisis, many firms realized that the problem lay in the impending exhaustion and vulnerability of their traditional product-markets, that competitive behaviour, no matter how aggressive, could not cure this inadequacy. It was increasingly recognized that focus must shift to large-scale entrepreneurial behaviour — to development of major new commercial linkages with the environment.

The second set of symptoms was slower to coalesce and to be recognized. The increasing disenchantment with the firm has left some managements puzzled, but convinced that 'explaining' the firm to the public will resolve the problem (Cordtz, 1966). More widely, the problem of 'social responsibility' of the firm became of major concern to both outside observers and insiders. Assumption of 'social objectives', conflict between profitability and contribution to social welfare, the 'enlightened self-interest' doctrine, the interaction between internal and societal values and culture — all were analysed and debated (see preceding chapter by Tabatoni and Jarniou). The specific resolution is not yet clear; it is clear that a redefinition of the firm's role in society is under way and that the

)new definition will replace the *'laisser faire'* doctrine. It will also lead to the activation of new types of linkages between the firm and the environment: legal, cultural, and informational. The understanding and the technology for even thinking about these linkages constructively is yet to develop.

Thus, today not only must the firm shift its attention to realignment of its business posture, but it must also cope with the new dimensions of cross-impact and interdependence with the larger society. Attention must shift from the competitive mode to the entrepreneurial mode, but the latter needs to be much wider in scope than the historical business entrepreneurship. It is because of the need for such drastic reorientation that the emerging era has been called the 'Age of Discontinuity' (Drucker, 1969) or the Post-Industrial Era (Ansoff, 1973a; Toffler, 1970).

1.4 *The Strategic Problem*

The technology invented for dealing with the newly important entrepreneurial problem was strategic planning. It is a rational approach to redefining the firm's strategic posture: it entails an identification of the firm's objectives and analysis of adequacy of the current product markets for meeting them. Then, determination of the firm's capabilities, search for alternative growth thrusts and evaluation of the latters' potential for objectives, as well as of the firm's capabilities for taking advantage of potential. The result is a proposed new strategic posture. It is assumed in strategic planning that, given the new posture, the firm would muster and allocate its energies to effecting the realignment from old to new. At the time of its invention, this seemed a perfectly reasonable and adequate assumption (Ansoff, 1965).

In the test of the last 20 years, the strategic planning process continued reasonable. No new logic has been advanced for deciding 'What business we want to be in'. But time and again the following mustering of energy proved inadequate for moving the firm to a new posture *vis-à-vis* the environment. It is to this element of the problems that we must now turn.

2. Diagnosis of Strategic Posture

2.1 *Modes of Organizational Behaviour*

At first glance the problem appears to require a transition of emphasis from the competitive to the entrepreneurial mode of behaviour. To gain insight into the inherent difficulties, we need a definition of the respective modes.

(1) Through existing linkages to the environment, *competitive behaviour* conducts advertising, selling, distributing and purchasing. Internally it is focused on the efficient production of goods/services.

(2) *Entrepreneurial* behaviour changes the pattern of environmental linkages. It identifies areas of opportunity, develops product/services, measures the market potential, tests markets, introduces new products to the customers and divests obsolete products. In the future it will increasingly involve concern with non-business societal linkage to the environment: surveillance of social and political trends, assessment of their impact on the firm, selection of areas of

societal opportunities and development of programmes for relating to societies and of programmes of social service.

While the concern of competitive behaviour is with extracting profits from the existing environmental linkages, entrepreneurial behaviour seeks to build up and maintain profitable linkages. As the definitions suggest, the two modes pose distinctive and different challenges to the firm. These differences have been explored in detail elsewhere (Ansoff, 1973a,b).

We shall summarize them briefly through a series of tables.

Table 1 illustrates the principal dimensions of the respective challenges. Competitive challenges are seen to relate to the historical experience of the firm, while the entrepreneurial introduce novelties, discontinuities and greater risks.

The challenges, to be successfully met, require distinctive managerial behaviours within the firm. These are illustrated in Table 2. The table suggests that an organization committed to one mode would look and act differently from an organization engaged in the other. The table also suggests that the skills, the knowledge, the attitudes and the values of managers would also differ. This is further illustrated in Table 3.

The overall impression to be gained from the tables is that, when a firm transforms itself from a focus on competitive behaviour to an emphasis on the entrepreneurial, a fundamental transformation takes place in each of its major characteristics: its objectives, its value systems, its managers, its processes, its systems, its structures. It is not an exaggeration to call this a *cultural transformation*.

Viewed in this perspective, strategic planning can be seen as only one, and not necessarily the most important, element of the cultural transformation. It is a rational approach to assessing and redefining the linkages of the firm with both

Table 1. Competitive Entrepreneurial Challenges

Attribute	Competitive	Entrepreneurial
Occurrence	Serial and continual	Random and episodic
Shift in objectives	Magnitude	New objectives and new priorities
Direction of change	Continuation of history	Discontinuity
Size of change relative to asset	Small	Large
Duration of negative cash flow	$\simeq$ Budget cycle	$\gg$ Budget cycle
Relevance of capabilities	High	Small
Nature of problem		
Familiarity	Related to experience	Novel
Cost of information	Low	High
Structurability	Well structured	Ill structured
Variability	Risk and uncertainty	Partial and total ignorance
Probability of catastrophe	Low—medium	Medium—very high
Outcome	Increased efficiency	Enhanced potential effectiveness

Table 2. Comparison of response challenges

Mode Attribute	Competitive	Entrepreneurial
Objective	Optimize profitability	Optimize profitability potential
Goals	Extrapolation of past goals modulated	Determined through interaction of opportunities and capabilities
Constraints	(1) Environmental	(1) Limitations on ability to affect change in environment
	(2) Internal capability	(2) Ability to acquire or develop requisite skills
		(3) Ability to accommodate differing modes of behaviour
Reward and penalty system	(1) Rewards for stability, efficiency	(1) Rewards for creativity and initiative
	(2) Rewards for past performance	(2) Penalties for lack of initiative
	(3) Penalties for deviance	
Information space	(1) Internal: performance	(1) Internal: capabilities
	(2) External: historical opportunity space	(2) Global opportunity space
Problem space	Repetitive, familiar	Non-repetitive, novel
Leadership style	(1) Popularity	(1) Charisma
	(2) Skill to develop consensus	(2) Skill to inspire people to accept change
Organizational structure	(1) Stable or expanding	(1) Fluid, structurally changing
	(2) Activities grouped according to resource conversion process	(2) Activities grouped according to problems
	(3) Search for economies of scale	(3) Activities closely coupled
	(4) Activities loosely coupled	
Managment problem-solving		
(a) Recognition of action need	(1) Reactive in response to problems	(1) Active search for opportunities
	(2) Time-lagged behind occurrence of problems	(2) Anticipatory
(b) Search for alternatives	(1) Reliance on past experience	(1) Creative search
	(2) Increment departures from *status quo*	(2) Wide ranging from *status quo*
	(3) Single alternative generate generated	(3) Multiple alternative generated
(c) Evaluation of alternatives	(1) Satisficing — first satisfactory accepted	(1) Optimizing — best of a set of alternatives is selected
(d) Risk attitude	(1) Minimize risk	(1) Risk propensive
	(2) Consistency with past experience	(2) Risk portfolio

Table 3. Comparison of the managers' profiles

Competitive	Entrepreneurial
World outlook	
Intra-film	→ Environmental
Intra-industry	→ Multi-industry
Intra-national (regional)	→ Multi-national
Intra-cultural	→ Cross-cultural
Economic	→ Economic
Technological	→ Technological
	Social
	Political
Social values	
Surrogate owner	→ Professional
Committed to *laissez faire*	→ Committed to social value of free enterprise
Profit optimizer	→ Social value optimizer
Personal values	
Economic rewards + power	+ Self-actualization
Stability	+ Change
Conformity	+ Deviance
Skills	
Experientially required	+ Acquired through career-long education
Popular leader	+ Charismatic + political leader
Participative	+ Political + charismatic
Goal-setter	+ Objectives-setter
Familiar problem-solver	+ Novel problem-solver
Intuitive problem-solver	+ Analytic problem-solver
Conservative risk-taker	+ Entrepreneurial risk-taker
Convergent diagnostician	+ Divergent diagnostician
Lag-controller	+ Lead-controller
Extrapolative planner	+ Entrepreneurial planner
Skill profile	
Generalist	→ Generalist-specialist + professional-specialist
World perspective	
Surrounding environment	Global environment
Semi-open system	Open system

its business and societal environments. It systematizes the managerial problem-solving approach essential to entrepreneurial behaviour and can be seen, therefore, as a systematic treatment of the lower right-hand part of Table 2.

But the outcome of strategic planning is only a set of plans and intentions. By itself, strategic planning produces no actions, no visible changes in the firm. To effect the changes the firm needs appropriated capabilities: trained and motivated managers, strategic information, fluid and responsive systems and structure. Lacking these, the firm will appear to resist implementation of the plans. The resistance will be real enough, but it will not be due to some inner perversities, but rather due to a lack of requisite capabilities and motivations, reluctance of people to abandon tried and familiar activities in favour of unknown and risky ones. This resistance will be reinforced because, when strategic crises arise, the competitive activity typically doesn't slacken, but becomes more intense. People who previously were trained, succeeded in and rewarded for competitive activity will feel justified and more secure in pursuing it in lieu of entrepreneurial work.

Thus, it is reasonable to predict that strategic planning will evoke all the symptoms of a foreign organ transplant. The individuals will lack the motivation, the skills and the risk propensities not only to plan but to follow planning with appropriate actions. The system and the structure will be geared for competitive activities and not capable of rapid entrepepreneurial response. The available information will be totally inadequate for generating the needed strategic alternatives. The reward and value system will actually punish, rather than reward, entrepreneurial risk tactics.

In this perspective, the wonder is not that competitively competent organizations will resist strategic planning; the wonder is that top management coercion can sometimes force planning to take root in the organization. More likely is the stubborn resistance encountered by Mr McNamara.

2.2 *Intensities of Behaviour*

So far we have discussed the entrepreneurial and the competitive behaviour, as if they were clear alternatives. However, in practice one finds variation of behaviour within each mode: competitive behaviour varies from no-holds-barred, all-out, aggressive competition to bureaucratic unresponsiveness to customers of established monopolies; entrepreneurial behaviour ranges from reluctant imitation of competitors' new products to a continuing stream of innovations.

The average *intensity* of behaviour of firms in an industry is basically determined by the turbulence of the environment: the threats, the opportunities, the vigour of competition, the pressures and demands from customers, public and government. But around the average there is usually found a distribution of behaviour. Some firms take full advantage of available opportunities, others lag behind. Thus in a given industry, for either the competitive, or entrepreneurial mode, one would expect to find a range of *intensities* of behaviour, as illustrated in Figure 1. The factors which contribute to the differentiation among firms are their past history, size, the accumulated organizational inertia, the relevance of their skills to the environmental needs and, particularly, the ambitions, the drive and the capabilities of management.

It is reasonable to expect to find a relationship between the intensity with which the firm is responding in the marketplace and the capabilities found inside the firm. This is illustrated in Figure 2, where the horizontal axis is the same as that of Figure 1 but the vertical axis measures the *internal capability* within the firm. We are now dealing with two related dimensions. The first is the intensity with which the firm can be observed to behave: its aggressiveness in competition,

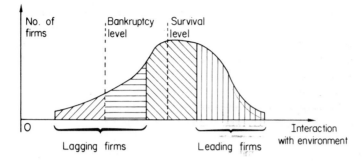

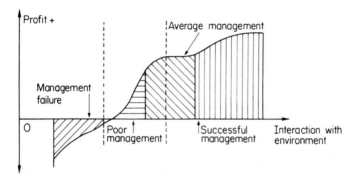

Figure 1. Typical distribution of behaviour.

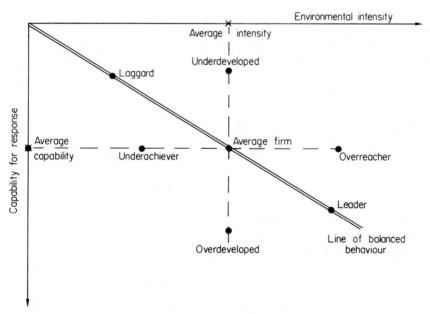

Figure 2. Capability and environment.

its responsiveness to customers, its product leadership, its penetration of new markets. The second, the internal responsiveness, is determined by the time perspective of decision-making, the skills of managers and workers, by the capacities of the organization, by responsiveness to problems, the flexibility of structure, etc., etc.

Figure 2 is constructed to illustrate a wide variety of observable situations. The vertical broken line identifies the average environmental intensity in a given industry and corresponds to the survival level of Figure 1. Firms which respond on this level will enjoy average growth and average profit.

The 'line of balanced behaviour' suggests that, whatever behaviour the firm chooses to pursue, there is a level of internal capability adequate to support this behaviour. Thus, for example, the 'laggard' firm, which invests less in promotion, selling and advertising, does not need as strong or well-trained a marketing department as the 'leader' firm, which seeks to be the aggressive innovator.

On the other hand, a firm which is seen as an average competitor/innovator by others in the industry may be 'overdeveloped': it has the potential for being much more aggressive, but the potential is not realized and 'locked in the firm' by the complacent management. The opposite description applies to 'underdeveloped' firms in which the management and the organization are stretched in an effort to behave above their means.

The horizontal broken line illustrates another type of unbalanced behaviour in which the market place activity is either below or above average, but the capabilities are adequate for balanced average success.

The varieties of behaviour illustrated in Figure 2 suggest both an explanation and an approach to the strategic problem. When a firm finds itself 'out of tune' with the environment one possible explanation is in the intensity of its environmental behaviour: it needs to become more aggressive, either to catch up with competition (when the environment is still potentially promising) or align the firm with more promising fields of opportunity (when the present fields of opportunity are in the process of becoming unpromising, like an exhausted oil-well). This is the problem which has been tackled by strategic planning.

But another explanation of the maladjustment may lie inside the firm. The environment may still be promising but the firm's capabilities are out of tune with the opportunities.

A third explanation is the furthest reaching: both the strategic position in the environment *and* the capabilities need to change. When this occurs and the firm focuses on strategic planning alone, it is neglecting the potentially more important need to change the internal culture in a way which prepares it to live in the new type of environment.

While the planning of the external strategic position has been extensively explored both in theory and practice, the planning of the *capability transformation* has received minimal attention. In fact in most conceptual approaches the assumption is made that the capability is essentially to be preserved: that in the process of strategic change the positive aspects of the existing capability ('strengths') are to be emphasized and the negative ('weaknesses') minimized.

What is now needed is a methodology for a deliberate redesign of both strategy and capability of the firm in response to the demands of a strategic posture transformation. In the following pages we shall develop such a methodology.

2.3. *Environmental Diagnosis*

We shall develop such an approach in several steps. First we shall turn our attention to the environment. For diagnostic purposes we shall deal separately with the competitive and the entrepreneurial modes. This is to say that the firm's position in Figure 2 would look differently depending on whether we deal with its ability to innovate. The firm's capabilities to behave in the respective mode will also differ.

The columns of Table 4 show four distinctive types of the competitive environment, which correspond to four selected points on the horizontal axis of Figure 2. The lines identify 11 key attributes which in general correlate with different levels of competitive intensity. But, in individual cases, they will not necessarily vary together. Therefore a diagnostic procedure for establishing intensity would be to circle the values of attributes which apply to a particular competitive environment and then determine a mean position on the intensity scale which averages the circled estimates.[2]

This procedure needs to be followed twice for two distinctive purposes.

(1) To determine the *competitive climate* in the firm's environment.

(2) To determine the firm's *own competitive behaviour*. For example, how does it react to customer pressures, what is its profitability, its product differentiation, frequency of new product introduction, etc., etc.

Line four of Table 4 refers to industry life-cycle, which is becoming an increasingly useful tool in management decision-making. A detailed discussion of life-cycles is beyond the scope of this paper. However, for purposes of analysis, we are showing in Table 5 typical characteristics of industrial life-cycles which can serve as an aid in making decisions about the competitive climate of the firm.

Table 5 becomes central in the use of Table 6. Attention now shifts from the competitive diagnosis of Table 4 to a diagnosis of the entrepreneurial environment. The same four levels of intensity are used, but the lines identify the characteristics which describe strategic change in the environment. In addition to life-cycle stage, the determinants of entrepreneurial intensity include technological rates of change, societal pressures and growth rates. Again, in order to diagnose an environment, the applicable intensities of the line items are circled with the expectation that in general they will all tend to fall in one or, at most, two adjacent columns. The firm's environment is then labelled appropriately.

Again, a dual diagnosis should be performed, first of the entrepreneurial climate of the firm's environment and, secondarily, of the firm's own entrepreneurial behaviour.

The results of the competitive and entrepreneurial diagnoses can now be

Table 4. Types of competitive environment

Attributes	Environmental Intensity Scale			
	Stable (1)	Reactive (2)	Anticipatory (3)	Initiative (4)
(1) Market structure	Monopoly	Oligopoly	Oligopoly	Multi-compet.
(2) Customer pressure	None	Weak	Strong	Very strong
(3) Growth rate	Slow and stable	Increasing/stable	Declining/oscillating	Fast/oscillating
(4) Stages in industry life-cycle	Maturity	Early growth	Late growth	Emergence
(5) Profitability	High	High	Moderate	Low
(6) Product differentiation	None	Low	Moderate	High
(7) Product life-cycles	Long	Long	Short	Short
(8) Frequency of new products	Very low	Low	Moderate	High
(9) Economies of scale	High	High	Moderate	Low
(10) Capital intensity	High	High	Moderate	Low
(11) Critical success factors	Market control	Market share	Customer perception	Anticipation of needs and opportunities
		Production costs	Distribution service	

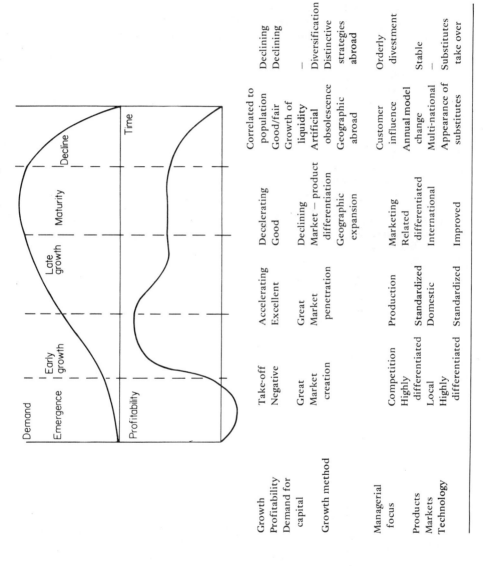

Table 3. Typical characteristics of life-cycle stages

Growth	Take-off	Accelerating	Decelerating	Correlated to population	Declining
Profitability	Negative	Excellent	Good	Good/fair	Declining
Demand for capital	Great	Great	Declining	Growth of liquidity	–
Growth method	Market creation	Market penetration	Market – product differentiation; Geographic expansion	Artificial obsolescence; Geographic abroad	Diversification; Distinctive strategies abroad
Managerial focus	Competition	Production	Marketing	Customer influence	Orderly divestment
Products	Highly differentiated	Standardized	Related differentiated	Annual model change	Stable
Markets	Local	Domestic	International	Multi-national	–
Technology	Highly differentiated	Standardized	Improved	Appearance of substitutes	Substitutes take over

Table 6. Types of Entrepreneurial Environment

Attributes \ Environmental Intensity scale	Stable (1)	Reactive (2)	Anticipatory (3)	Initiative (4)
(1) Stage in life-cycle	Late growth or maturity	Early growth	Late growth	Emergence or decline
(2) Growth rate	Slow	Accelerating	Decelerating	Fast (±) acceleration
(3) Change in technology	Slow	Slow	Fast	Discontinuous
(4) Change in market structure	Slow	Moderate	Slow	Discontinuous
(5) Likelihood of breakthroughs	Low	Low	Moderate	High
(6) Societal pressures	None	Moderate	Strong	Very strong
(7) Diversity of technologies	None	Low	Moderate	High
(8) Demand for growth capital	Low	High	Moderate	Very high
(9) Profitability	High	High	Moderate	Low
(10) Rate of technological obsolescence	Low	Low	High	Discontinuous
(11) Technological intensity	Low	Low	High	High

Figure 3. Diagnosis of environment.

consolidated as illustrated in Figure 3. The firm's behaviour is shown at point S_1, point E identifies the environmental climate. The shaded area is significant for managerial purposes, because it defines the *region of managerial discretion* within which management is free to position the firm and still assure continued survival. If, on the other hand, the management tries to position the firm outside the region, it will place the firm in danger of falling behind competition. At best, this will lead to below-average performance; at worst, as Figure 1 suggests, the firm may be courting bankruptcy.

The decision on where the firm wishes to be within the region may be arrived at by judgement, reflecting preferences of influential managers, or it may be determined by analysis. There is now a considerable literature on strategy formulation and strategy planning which addresses this task (see, for example, Toffler (1970)). Rather than repeat it here, we proceed to the much less explored problem of internal capability.

2.4 *Capability Diagnosis*

Tables 7(a) and 7(b) are offered as a means for diagnosing the firm's internal capabilities for response. Table 7(a) approaches the diagnosis through observation of internal attributes of behaviour: the values that prevail, the focus of management attention, reaction to change, etc. These are shown to vary from the least responsive *stable* mode, which is found in many bureaucracies, to the active *initiative* mode, observed in the behaviour of entrepreneurs. It should be noted that, for later purposes, we are using in Table 7 the same column headings as we did in assessing the environment, but the labels now apply to the *internal* characteristics of the firm.

Lines (8), (9) and (10) are of considerable importance. They show the effectiveness of the respective modes along three common measures of performance:

(1) The cost-efficiency of its purchasing, production and distribution activities

(2) The efficiency of marketing in generating sales and

(3) The effectiveness of the innovative organs in generating continuously promising profit potential: new profitable products, markets and technology.

As Table 7(a) shows, the different types of performance are best attained in different modes. Best unit costs are obtained in the stable mode, which permits economies of scale, benefits of learning and automation of processes. Best competitive efficiency lies in the region of reactive—anticipating modes, where marketing does not 'oversell', where it responds to existing and emerging needs but does not undertake excessive risks and costs of continual changes. On the other hand, where the criterion is the development of profit potential of the future, continuously generated forward-looking attention to the environment provided by the initiative mode will produce best results.

Table 7(b) offers an alternative and complementary approach to diagnosis of capabilities through analysis of the various elements of structure and systems, such as distribution of power, organizational structure, management systems,

Table 7 (a) Types of organizational capability

Types of organizational behaviour	Stable	Reactive	Anticipatory	Initiative
(1) Management values	'Don't rock the boat'	'Roll with the punches'	'Plan ahead'	'Dream ahead'
(2) Focus of behaviour	On repetitive operations	On the efficiency	On synergistic effectiveness	On global effectiveness
(3) Trigger for organizational response to change	Crisis	Unsatisfactory history of performance	Anticipation of threats and opportunities	Continued search
(4) Reaction to change	Reject	Adapt	Anticipate	Seek
(5) Source of alternatives	Random	Past experience	Past experience and extrapolation into the future	Totality of future opportunities including those unrelated to past experience
(6) Risk preference	Reject	Accept familiar risk	Seek familiar risk	Seek tradeoff between risk and gain
(7) Goals of response	Restore status quo	Minimize disturbance of organizational efficiency	Improve on past performance	Best possible performance potential
(8) Productive efficiency	High	Medium	Medium	Low
(9) Competitive efficiency	Low	High	Medium	Low
(10) Entrepreneurial effectiveness	Low	Low	Medium	High

Table 7 (b)   Types of organizational capability

Types of organizational capability	Stable	Reactive	Anticipatory	Initiative
(a) Problem solving	Problem triggered trial and error	Problem triggered diagnostic	Anticipatory well-structured optimization	Ill-structured creativity
(b) Power focus	Production	Production-marketing	Marketing – R & D	Entrepreneurial managers
(c) Organization structure	Functional	Functional	Divisional Multi-national	Divisional, multi-national project structure, new ventures
(d) Management system	Policy and procedure manuals	Control, capital budgeting	Long-range planning Budgeting	Strategic planning PPBS, venture planning
(e) Management information system	Informal precedents	Formal, based on past performance	Potential future in the historical environment	Global future potential
(f) Environmental surveillance	None	None	Extrapolative forecasting	Trend analysis, techno-socio-demographic forecasts
(g) Management technology	Industrial engineering	Ratio analysis Capital investment analysis	Operations research Computerized transaction analysis	'What if modelling'. acquisition analysis, impact analysis, Delphi, scenarios

etc. It is intended to be used together with Table 7(a) to accumulate the weight of evidence on the type of organizational capabilities found in the firm.

Typically, the average level of capability will not be the same for the competitive and entrepreneurial modes. For example, the firm may have highly developed and responsive marketing and manufacturing capabilities which qualify it as a competitive initiator, but it may have a poor R & D department and lack new-venture skills.

Therefore, for the purposes of analysis, Tables 7(a) and 7(b) should be used at least twice: once to assess the responsiveness in the competitive mode and once again in the entrepreneurial mode.

2.5 Consolidated Diagnosis

It will be recalled that unless the firm is 'balanced' (See Figure 2) the results of internal capability analysis will not fall into the same columns as did the environmental intensity analysis. Therefore, when the respective evaluations are added in Figure 3, the result is likely to look like Figure 4. The figure can be intrepreted as follows.

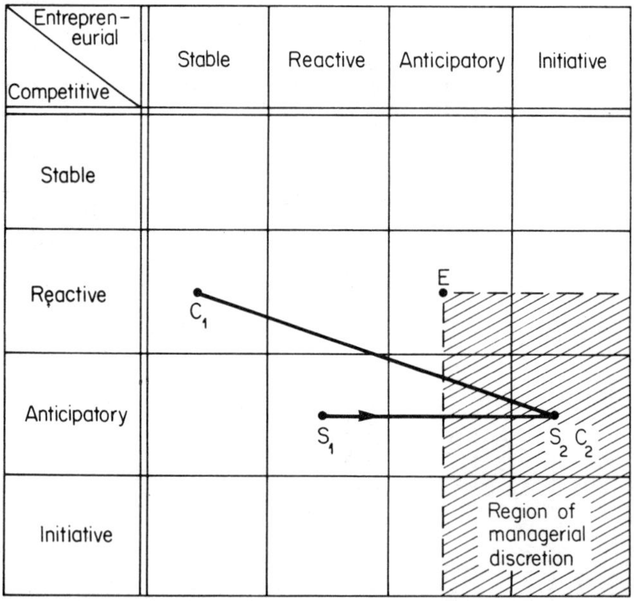

Figure 4. Diagnosis of strategic posture. C_1, current responsiveness; S_1, current behaviour; E. environmental climate; $S_2 C_2$, target posture.

This firm is reactive innovatively but has a history of being vigorous, if not the leading, competitor. Thus, its current strategy places it at point S_1. The capabilities for competition are underdeveloped (the firm lives on 'nervous energy') and virtually non-existent for innovation (Point C_1).

An analysis of the environment shows that the firm is safe in its competitive behaviour, because the bulk of its competitors are reactive — the industry is competitively quiescent. On the other hand, the strategic intensity is high. Apparently, rapid technological and/or structural changes are taking place in the industry. Either firms are introducing new products, or new technology is emerging, or there is an exodus from the industry because of impending stagnation (point E).

It is suggested in Figure 4 that the firm, through a process of strategy formulation, decides to move to point $S_2 C_2$. There is no clear way to preserve

Table 8. Diagnosis of managerial capability

Component (Mode)	Stable	Reaction	Anticipation	Initiative
A. *Organizational values*	①	②		③
1. Objectives and goals	●	*—————	——————	—►*
2. Norms	●	*—————	——————	—►*
3. Individual and group norms	●	*—————	——————	—►*
4. Rewards and penalties	●	*—————	——————	—►*
B. *Managers*				
5. Skills	●	*————		——►*
6. Aptitudes	●		*————	—► *
7. Knowledge	●	*◄——		—► *
8. Risk propensity	●	*◄——		—► *
9. Depth of management	●		*————	——►*
C. *Structure*				
10. Responsibility-authority	●	*—————	——————	——►*
11. Job definition	●	*—————	——————	—►*
12. Informal power	●	*—————	——————	—►*
13. Content of information	●	*—————	——————	—►*
14. Capacity for self-renewal	●	*—————	——————	—►*

Table 8 — Continued

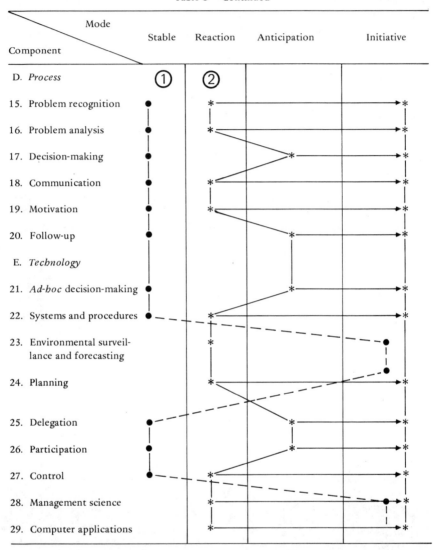

Mode / Component	Stable	Reaction	Anticipation	Initiative
D. *Process*	①	②		
15. Problem recognition	●	*		*
16. Problem analysis	●	*		*
17. Decision-making	●		*	*
18. Communication	●	*		*
19. Motivation	●	*		*
20. Follow-up	●		*	*
E. *Technology*				
21. *Ad-hoc* decision-making	●		*	*
22. Systems and procedures	●	*		*
23. Environmental surveillance and forecasting		*		●
24. Planning		*		*
25. Delegation	●		*	*
26. Participation	●		*	*
27. Control	●	*		*
28. Management science		*		● *
29. Computer applications		*		*

Illustrative examples: (1) dots indicate the capability profile of the Department of Defense after introduction of PPBS; (2) crosses indicate a frequently encountered profile of a firm in a first-generation industry.

'strengths' and minimize 'weaknesses' because the capabilities are too far out of tune with the environment. Thus a dual strategic posture transformation is in the offing. Two questions arise: (1) How to effect the transformation from C_1 to C_2 and (2) how to coordinate this with the change in strategy from S_1 to S_2. We turn to these questions next.

3. Planning of Strategic Posture Transformation

3.1. *Capability Transformation*

Reference to Table 8 shows that the transformation of capability is a complex process involving mutually consistent changes in a number of attributes of the firm's culture. The five attributes which we have chosen for this discussion are:

Organizational values and norms;
Managerial skills, knowledge and risk propensities.
Structural relationships: authority, responsibility, information, power, task.
Process relationships: problem-solving, communication, motivation, control.
Technology: formalized systems, information acquisition, decision analysis, computer applications.

These attributes apply equally to managerial work and to the work of the 'doers' on the 'shop floor'. For purposes of this chapter we focus attention on managerial capabilities. The same analysis is applicable (more simply) to the transformation of the logistic capabilities of the firm.

In Table 8 each of the above attributes is further subdivided into a number of controllable components, a total of 29. It is through changing these components that management can bring about change in its own capability.

The first step is to determine the change needed in each individual component. Although Figure 4 has diagnosed the overall state of the capability, individual components will be in different states. Thus, for example, a firm which is on the whole reactive, may have, as a result of recent personnel turnover, a cadre of managers capable of doing work in the anticipation ('long-range planning') mode.

Thus, the first step is to construct a profile of the current capabilities, using the results of the diagnosis in Tables 7(a) and 7(b). The next step, using point C_2 in Figure 4, is to construct the desired profile. The two profiles thus describe C_1 and C_2 in detail.

The results are illustrated in Table 8 for two different cases. The first, denoted by dots, describes the condition in the U.S. Department of Defense after Mr McNamara introduced PPBS. It suggests the analogy of a rubber band firmly anchored in the stable bureaucratic mode and stretched in four or five points to the extreme of the initiative mode by the force of Mr McNamara's authority. It also suggests that the band will snap back (as it did) once the coercive authority is removed.

The second example shows a profile of a firm which could be typically encountered in the late 1960's, in which we called 'first-generation industries'. In the example shown, the firm needs to make a transition to entrepreneurial initiative. The terminal profile is indicated by the vertical line in the last column of Table 8. The amount of movement for the various components is indicated by the horizontal lines.

A firm analysing its own capability transformation would of course start with a blank set of forms. The diagnosis in Figure 4 will be performed first to determine the *average* values of the starting and of the terminal capability will have been determined. The next step would be to analyse the capability components, one by one, determining their present status and the desirable terminal points. The result would be very similar to our two examples shown in Table 8.

3.2. *Phasing of Strategies and Capability Transformation*

We now turn to the second of two questions posed earlier: how to relate the processes of change in strategy (changes in the industries, countries and technologies in which the firm competes, and in the manner in which it competes) to the change in capability (in values, systems, structure, skills, power and technology). It will be recalled from the opening part of this chapter that in the earlier conceptions of strategic planning this was not a serious problem, because the emphasis was on preserving the capability intact and using its applicable attributes (strengths) to support strategic action. Thus the bulk of the concern was with strategy change. In the present conception we provide for the more likely possibility that *both* inside configuration and outside linkages have to undergo substantial changes. Both will be costly and both will lay claim on the same organizational resources, particularly in the typically score management. Therefore an orderly set of priorities is needed.

Determination of priorities is illustrated in Figure 5. The analysis presented in Figure 4 leads to one of the three outcomes indicated: need for strategic change alone (STRATEGY NOK), need for capability transformation alone (CAPABILITY NOK) or need for both (BOTH NOK). Procedures to be followed

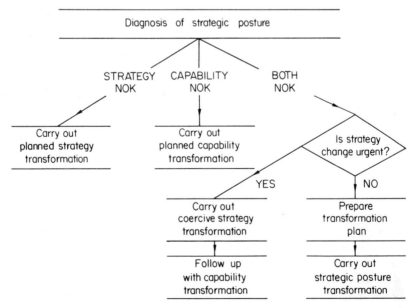

Figure 5. Alternatives for strategic posture transformation.

Table 9. Capability development plan

YEARS	1	2	3	4	5	6	7	8	9	10
1. Development of plan	———									
2. Organizational development		———————————————								
3. Reward system		———		———						
4. Training		——————————————————————								
5. *Ad hoc* planning		—————————————————————								
6. Information system	—————————————————————————									
7. Structure		———		———						
8. Plan planning	———									
9. Operation plans		——————————————————————————								
10. Control system			—————————————————————							
11. Strategic plans		——————————————————————————								

in the first case have been described elsewhere (Toffler, 1970). In the second case, if the transformation is of some magnitude, the procedure of Table 8 needs to be carried out and then transformed into a plan which will phase the change over time.

The phasing is of particular importance, since there is a certain *natural precedence* among components which, if observed, will assure efficient transition. Thus motivation and information are natural precedents to all other change activities, managerial skills should precede installation of formal systems requiring the skills, etc. An example of a plan-phased capability transformation (constructed with a realistic timetable) is shown in Table 9.

Turning to the third alternative, in which both strategy and capability need change, the first question is one about urgency. Frequently, the need for a transformation is recognized late, in reaction to an impending crisis. Therefore the first question confronting the firm is whether there is the time needed to effect an orderly capability transformation before the profitability deteriorates beyond repair.

If the answer is that there is not sufficient time, a coercive (McNamara's type) transformation is indicated which puts total emphasis on strategy. Capabilities will change adaptively in response to different patterns of work but no special effort or delays for orderly development can be made. Frequently missing capabilities will be sought from outside, say by engaging a consulting firm. Unavoidably, the work of changing strategy will require strong support and guidance from top management. Certain vital capabilities such as strategic planning will be implanted coercively, against resistance. As in DOD positive but temporary results will be obtained unless top management continues to contribute its energies and authority until the organizational culture has become stabilized at a higher level.

The coercive transformation is likely to be costly, inefficient and disruptive, but it responds to the pressing need. Frustrations, dissatisfactions, outward and covert resistance must be anticipcated and coped with. As the new strategy takes

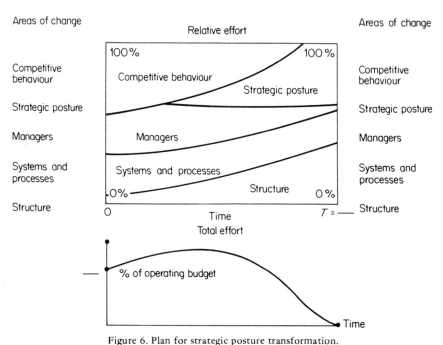

Figure 6. Plan for strategic posture transformation.

shape, however, it is possible to turn attention to matters of capability, as indicated in Table 8.

The final alternative shown in Table 5 calls for simultaneous and parallel attack on both strategic position and capability. A sample plan for the strategic posture transformation is presented in Figure 6 and shows changing priorities over time. In the lower part, the total posture transformation effort is given as a percentage of the annual operating budget of the firm, to give an idea of the relative magnitude of the effort. The upper part illustrates time-phased division of effort among strategy-changing (competitive behaviour plus strategy posture) and capability-changing activities (managers plus systems and processes plus technology plus structure).

A major emphasis in the transformation plan must be on the interrelation of the strategy and capability processes. Certain elements of the transformation can be the natural outcome of strategy-changing activities (personal skill, team work, information). Thus an approach of changing capabilities by doing strategic work is attractive, particularly since it combines and interrelates the cognitive process of planning with the socio-dynamics of 'implementation'.

We shall deal with the dynamics of this approach in the last part of this chapter on a somewhat theoretical level, and Davous and Deas will discuss it in a practical setting in the following chapter. In both chapters a key feature of a successful planned-learning transformation is emphasized. This is the need to deal with the frustrations which are typically set up when a planning process goes on for too long a period of time without producing concrete organizational results. Therefore, the strategic posture transformation needs to be carried out in phases, with each phase 'throwing off' projects which lead to immediate action.

In contrast to the Davous—Deas paper, we need to emphasize that while 'changing by doing' can affect a number of important capability components, it does not address them all. Thus a formal planning system, new rewards and new structure will not be automatically spun off by strategy formulation and implementation activities. They need therefore to be provided in the overall plan, over and above the 'changing by doing' activities.

3.3 Conflict of Cultures

In the example shown in Table 8, we chose the initiative mode as the terminal culture for the entire firm. But reference to the example illustrated in Figure 4 shows that generally the terminal condition of the competitive mode will be different from the entrepreneurial mode. Thus, ideally, different parts of the firm should have different terminal capabilities, depending on whether their mission is to support competitive or entrepreneurial activities.

This is further supported by the last three lines of Table 7(a), which show that different modes of behaviour result in different performance on the respective criteria of effectiveness and efficiency. As we defined them earlier, the competitive mode is focused on *efficient* (profitable) exploitation of existing linkages to the environment while the entrepreneurial mode seeks *effectiveness* (profitability potential) through new linkages. From Table 7(a) it appears that maximum results will occur in different modes of behaviour.

How is the conflict between efficiency and effectiveness to be resolved? There are three possible solutions.

1. Dominant culture
2. Average culture
3. Cultural coexistence

Under the first solution the organizational capability supports a dominant culture. Thus, during the mass-production era the competitive culture dominated the entrepreneurial culture. Hence the capability has evolved in the reaction anticipation region. As illustrated in the upper half of Figure 7, optimum profitability was to be obtained by focusing organizational energies on the competitive mode. 'R & D' activities, while significant, were a minor part of the energy and budgets and had to operate in spite of (rather than because) the existing structure, systems and values. Innovation was a necessary nuisance which interfered with making profits. The problems were graphically described as 'harnessing the R & D monster' (*Fortune*, 1965).

As the post-industrial era emerged, increasing energies had to be devoted to entrepreneurial activities which would no longer be 'harnessed'. As the lower part of Figure 7 shows, the importance of entrepreneurial activity began to equal the competitive model in contribution to the firm. Thus a conflict arose: a design for optimal competitive performance would degrade entrepreneurship, and *vice versa*.

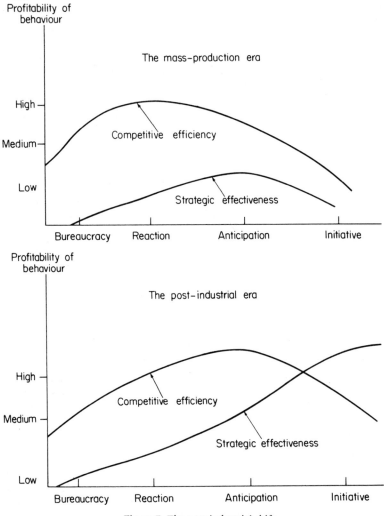

Figure 7. The post-industrial shift.

Two solutions have evolved, so far neither as yet fully developed or satisfactory. The first, referred to above as the 'average culture', is a compromise capability pattern which lies between the two maxima, say between anticipative and initiative modes. The second, 'cultural coexistence', is a new organizational form called the *innovative form* which attempts to accommodate two separate cultures within the same organization. This form has been described earlier by Ansoff and Brandenburg (1971) and will be discussed in detail by Radosevich later in this volume.

If one examines the lower part of Table 5, which describes differences in the characteristics among different phases of a life-cycle, it becomes evident that an 'ideal' solution for a multi-life-cycle firm is to have not two but a number of capability patterns each attuned to the particular needs of the environment. For example, the firm may need to have a part of the organization attuned to horizon-exploring activities which provide emerging industries, another part with aggressive market expansion capabilities, yet another with prudent management of cash-rich maturity, and another geared for effective divestment. Thus dual-culture form appears to be but a first step in the development of new organizational forms which accommodate within the envelope of a single firm, a variety of cultures (or capability patterns), each responsive to the different environment. The need for such forms already exists in multi-national, multi-industry firms (Ansoff, 1974).

In the current single-culture management such variety in internal structures, values and systems skills may appear confusing and unmanageable. But equally confusing and unmanageable must have appeared in the 1900's the prospect of the transformation from a single-product, single-market firm to the incredibly complex firms of today.

A consequence of great importance (on which we can dwell only briefly in this chapter) is the already observable emergence of a new domain of general management activity which concerns itself with a 'peaceful co-existence' of several cultural/capabilities patterns within the boundaries of a single firm. We shall call it *integrative management*.

3.4. *Integrative Management*

Anthropologists find that most cultures will tolerate the existence in their midst of small deviant sub-cultures, but when the sub-culture grows beyond a certain threshold problems of coexistence will arise. As described in this chapter, the entrepreneurial activity was a deviant subculture during the mass production era. The competitive activity dominated because the environment offered apparently boundless opportunities for competitive success with only a moderate support from product and market development. As the post-industrial era approached, entrepreneurial activity rose both in volume and importance; from a subordinate status, it began to move to the position of a coequal culture. A number of previously secondary problems moved to the forefront of managerial attention:

(a) the allocation of scare resources between on-going competitive operations and the innovative profit-generating activities;

(b) the disruption of existing on-going operations by introduction of new products;

(c) the resulting tendency to reject new ventures before they have reached a self-sustaining state;

(d) the need to redesign the organization along lines discussed at length in the preceding section;

(e) the conflicts which typically arise between manufacturing, marketing and R & D during transition of a product or technology from developmental to operational status:

(f) the problem of day-to-day management of two or more competing cultures.

The new set problems can be viewed from three complementary aspects. The first concerns the short-term dynamics of interaction between a set of competitive and entrepreneurial activities within each major industry life-cycle in which the firm participates. This is illustrated by reference to the lower part of Table 5, which shows that each major life-cycle stage calls for a special mixture of entrepreneurship and competition.

The second aspect concerns the longer term dynamics of transition between stages of a life-cycle in which emphasis on respective modes, and hence the ways of doing business, had to be changed and adjusted to suit new characteristics of the environment.

The third and the 'global' viewpoint concerns the balance among the different life-cycles in which the firm is involved and which, at a given time, are typically in different phases of growth, thus presenting the management with a life-cycle *portfolio-balancing* problem.

All three of these aspects are increasingly important to the firm's success. As a result, integrative management will become increasingly important.

4. Dynamics of Posture Transformation[3]

4.1 *Limitations of Cognitive Technology*

Having recognized early in the chapter that concern with the external linkages alone is inadequate for coping with strategic transformation, we have developed a practically useable approach to planning the total transformation which provides for both strategy and capability. Historically, capabilities (as well as strategy) developed through trial and error, a process which requires time as well as 'blood, sweat and tears' of learning. Our assertion is that the planning has become essential during the post-industrial era because neither the time delays nor the inefficiencies of trial or error are acceptable when environment changes rapidly and the firm is forced to devote major energies to entrepreneurial work.

Having said this, we have to recognize that original objections and resistance to change occurred typically not because there was not enough, but rather in cases when there was too much, planning! To be sure, planned approach to capability can anticipate certain psychological and sociological obstacles. But to anticipate is not necessarily to overcome; change is not only a cognitive-logical problem, but also a psychological-social process.

Furthermore, strategic change poses personal threats and challenges to individuals. In the historical strategy-structure adaptation the process of incremental trial and error has served as a mechanism for working out personal and interpersonal threats and problems.

It is not surprising, therefore, that replacement of this vital mechanism by the alternative of strategic planning would tend to swing the pendulum from one extreme to another. While the firm's logic was improved, its social adaptation mechanism was suppressed. The result was the 'resistance to planning'. If strategic change is to be handled effectively it is necessary to develop an approach which combines the desirable elements of both cognitive-logic and social-psychological dynamics. We next turn to the development of such an approach.

4.2 *Adaptive Learning*

Numerous observers in sociology, political science and information sciences, each forming his own disciplinary viewpoint, have reached very similar conclusions on the manner in which complex organizations have historically adapted to major changes. A model of these observations, applied to the evolution of new structural form, is illustrated in Figure 8.

The trigger for action typically comes from the environment, but not in an unambiguous directly recognizable way. The firm, as all other organizations, continuously receives both positive and negative signals from the environment which call for responses through incremental adjustments. The evidence that a major change is needed is hidden among these other voluminous signals; it is not loud, clear and unambiguous, like the voice of doom, and it is not welcome information anyway.

Thus, the initial response is to reject the voice of doom and respond to signals in traditional ways: to reduce costs, to sell more agressively, to replace an unsuccessful manager. But the new signals persist, and cumulate and stubbornly resist treatment. Gradually a conviction grows that a major response is in order. In the meantime a substantial period of time, labelled Δ_1 on Figure 8 and measured in years, has passed.

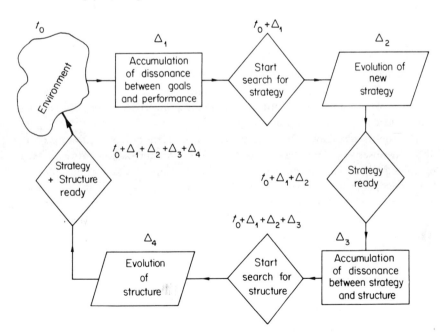

Figure 8. Adaptive-learning organization change.

Thus at time $t_0 + \Delta_1$ a decision is made to start a search for major alternatives. Figure 8 overstates the usual situation by giving the impression of discontinuous triggering events. More likely, $t_0 + \Delta_1$ signals the beginning of a period in which untraditional solutions, still frequently incremental, begin to be proposed, discussed, tried and eventually implemented. In some firms the solution is sought in the realm of structure; in others in new product-making technology (Ansoff, 1970; Chandler, 1969). In Figure 8, we have chosen to illustrate the latter case.

Another substantial period Δ_2, again measured in years, is spent in locating new fields of opportunity, developing new products and penetrating new markets. By $t_0 + \Delta_1 + \Delta_2$ the firm has established linkages to the environment, but, if the new strategic posture is significantly different from the old one, new adverse signals appear: difficulties are encountered in making the new strategy profitable. The situation is illustrated by the famous statement of the DuPont Company's management in the 1920's: 'The more paint we sell the more money we lose'.

Another time delay, Δ_3, occurs until the new signals are recognized as serious and due to the inability of the old structure to support the new strategy. At $t_0 + \Delta_1 + \Delta_2 + \Delta_3$ a search begins for a new structural form; it culminates at $t_0 + \Delta_1 + \Delta_2 + \Delta_3 + \Delta_4$, when both new strategy and new structure are in place. Seen in retrospect, the resulting shifts in both strategy and structure are significant and discontinuous: the firm has moved into competitive—technological domains which were alien to it before the shift; the new structure is based on a new organizing principle and is supported by a changed internal culture. But during the change process much step-wise cutting and filling goes on. The process still tends to be incremental, the significant difference from the past being that unfamiliar solutions are being explored. If the increments accumulate favourably, the final form emerges gradually. But more frequently the firm finds no accumulation of increments which results in the desired response. When this occurs, frustrations mount and a crisis occurs which brings about a discontinuous solution.

The merits of adaptive-learning process have been variously interpreted by different observers. Some have argued that it is a natural organic process, that it provides for learning and mutual adjustment in complex organizations, that it is 'self-designing', similarly to biological adaptation. As a result the final form meets the needs of both the organization and its participants and is, therefore, stable and accepted within the firm. It has been further argued on occasion (Lindbloom, 1970) that adaptive learning is the only feasible method for changing complex organizations.

4.3 Planned Change

An opposing point of view, held by the planning profession and by scientists whose roots are in mathematics and logic, is that adaptive learning is an evolutionary and historical accident which was the best available until rational planning technology came along. But it is inefficient, time-consuming and interferes with ongoing operations. The most telling argument offered by the proponents of planning is that the adaptive-learning method is always in danger of being too late. While the new strategy-structure is being worked out, the outside world is likely to change enough to make them obsolete even before the adaption is completed. As a result, the firm is always in an inefficient structure, trying to catch up with itself, like a squirrel in a cage.

Historical evidence supports this argument. For example, the DuPont Company had completed the development of the functional structure around 1915 only to discover the need for its successor, which took another six years to perfect. This successor, the divisional form, was responsive to the competitive climate of the 1920–1940's, and yet its adoption by other firms was gradual. It was not until the early post-war years that it was widely adopted in the U.S., and not until the 1960's in Western Europe (Chandler, 1969). But by that time, in a climate of multi-national competition, the divisional form was already close to obsolescence.

The planners' answer is to prepare structure in advance of the need. Figure 9 illustrates this answer. The diagram, which should be clear after our detailed discussion of the preceding one, shows that the key step is the anticipation of new strategy and structure at time t_0, ahead of the need. If, in fact, the time horizon is long enough, so that

$$\Delta_1 = \Delta_2 + \Delta_4 + \Delta_5,$$

the firm will always be ready in time to meet the challenges of the changing environment.

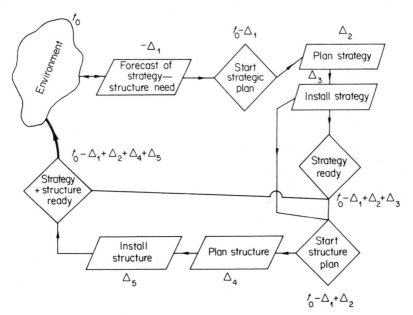

Figure 9. Planned organization change.

Since the 1950's planning has been widely applied in industry and government throughout the developed world. On the whole it appears to have had a positive and beneficial effect (Ansoff, 1970); but it has also revealed major shortcomings and failures. A Belgian newspaper correspondent who attended the recent International Congress on Long Range Planning in Brussels, in 1973, which featured a veritable 'Who is Who in Planning', captured the spirit of the meeting as one of self-doubt, a crisis of self-identity.

If one studies the record of successes and failures, one is drawn back to the assertions of the proponents of the organic evolution: planning has been most successful when it deals with extrapolation of the past dynamics of the firm and least successful when applied to non-incremental major departures from the historical growth trends of the firm. Thus, while extrapolative long-range planning is prevalent in industry today, genuine 'strategic' planning is found only in isolated instances. So long as planning merely attempted to shift the firm's attention from the familiar past—present to the familiar future, it had a reasonable record of success. Whenever it attempted to focus attention on unfamiliar, radically different future alternatives, it typically ran into the phenomenon of 'resistance to planning' (Schick, 1969).

An analysis of the origins of this resistance suggests an overswing of the pendulum between the extremes of the cognitive—rational and the socio-existential approaches to managing change. The planning philosophy swung the pendulum: from a focus on the human variables in adaptive learning to the logical prescriptions of planned change; from a philosophy that 'organizations are built by and around people' to one that 'reasonable people will implement logical designs' (once these are clearly and carefully explained to them).

4.4. *Planned Learning*

There is now growing evidence of a gradual convergence of the adaptive-existential and planned-rational approaches to organizational change. We shall refer to the merged approach as the *planning-learning* process. It is illustrated in Figure 10. The figure, which combines the philosophical viewpoints of the two preceding ones, also implies three further developments. The first is a departure from the assumption which underlies all cognitive-rational approaches to the effect to paraphrase Descartes *'Je pense donc je fais'* (I think, therefore I do), that planning must always precede action. The view of the amended approach is that excessive overplanning can be as unproductive as impulsive recourse to trial and error. Therefore a way of managing must be found which blends the two.

The ultimate shape of the learning-planning management is not clear, but examples are readily given. At one extreme, typical management by crisis, which triggers 'problemistic', 'local' search for the best historical precedent (Cyert and March, 1963), will be replaced by a thinking pause at the moment of crisis,[4] devoted to a careful weighing of a set of alternatives both familiar and novel.

At the other extreme, today's laborious planning—budgeting, which is reviewed and revised annually, will be replaced by more supple procedures which involve continual attention to planning and which are responsive to major environmental changes and to unforeseen results, whenever they occur.

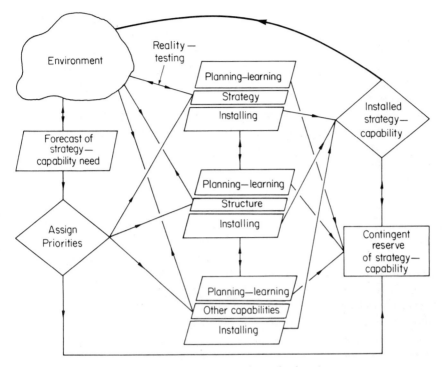

Figure 10. Planned—learned organization change.

This leads us to the second departure from current practice, which concerns the manner and the use of environmental surveillance and forecasting. Conceptually it will be recognized that the very best forecasting efforts cannot foresee all of the important events and consequences, that uncertainty about the future cannot be reduced to certainty at any cost. Further, it will be recognized that the residual uncertainty (which is sometimes ignorance) usually contains events and consequences of the greatest importance to the firm.

The responses will be dual. First, through built-in flexibility in the firm's position and structure (Ansoff, 1974). As shown in Figure 10, the firm will have a reserve of strategy-capability responses implementable of short notice.

Second, the process of design of new strategies capabilities will include testing of new designs, before installing them in the firm, or accumulating them in the contingency reserve. It is this 'reality-testing' process of deliberate closely coupled planning-trial-error-planning-etc. that is at the conceptual core of the planned-learning organizational change.

The third departure from the preceding approaches is illustrated in Figure 10 by the 'priority assignment' box. The choice of the sequence of changes in strategy-structure is neither left to chance, as in adaptive learning, nor to arbitrary priorities, as in long-range planning. A diagnosis determines both the relative needs and the relative distance which the frim has to travel. The needs are determined by the dynamics of the environment, the current capabilities of the firm and by the ambitions of the management. The 'distance' is measured by the readiness of the firm's total culture to cope with the new strategic challenges.

At one extreme, when survival is imminently threatened, the change will be paced by the needs of new strategy; at the other extreme, when the environment is benign, and strategic change is not immediately imperative, the reorganizational capability for future change in strategy. In most cases, parallel mutually interacting paths will be followed. The pacing element will be the critical barrier which must be overcome to assure orderly progress to the new form. Sometimes this may be the need for a new assignment of authority, sometimes for opening of channels of communication ('organizational development'); sometimes the next step will be to act upon the external world – to develop a product, test-market it or advertise it. Thus the sequence and relation of activities will be a part of an overall design for effective social action by the firm.

As shown in Figure 10, as the design activity proceeds, only a part of it is 'installed' and becomes a part of the on-line operating reality of the firm. Another part, in the manner described in the preceding section, becomes a part of an inventory of responses, labelled 'contingency reserve' in the Figure.

Two major forces of different origin are going to determine the shape and the pace of progress towards the planned-learning technology. The first, discussed above, is the need for efficiency in purposive societal organizations. In the firm the drive for efficient ways to deliver goods and services to society has been built in its basic terms of reference (the dependence for survival on the competitive market test) under which the firm was created in the so-called capitalist countries. As a result, with all of the historical distortions and imperfections, the firm has on the whole remained in the forefront of efficient organizations. As we discussed earlier, new complexities born of technology, geographic span, size, and turbulent environment have overtaxed the responsiveness limits of adaptive-learning organizational change. Cognitive planned change also increasingly appears limited as a change mechanism. Thus the pressure is evident for a new technology.

In other societal purposive organizations the tradition of search for effectiveness does not exist, nor was it important in the days of 'small government'. But in the era of 'big government', an evergrowing volume of social services and the threat of natural resource limitations have already given birth to a demand for effectiveness in government and this demand will continue to grow. Thus the planned-learning technology will find applications in a wide range of social structures.

But there is another force which provides a drive for new technology. This is the increasing demand for participation by organizational members and by society in the design and management of organizations. This demand, which at the moment, is much stronger in Europe than in the United States, involves approaches from the opposite levels of the firm. The first, named 'Industrial Democracy', involves 'bottom up' participation in the design of work. The second, 'Co-determination', involves sharing of power in decisions affecting the overall policies and strategies of the firm. The two trends are as yet so new that their specific purposes, nature, advantages and limitations still appear to be imperfectly understood and articulated. But it is clear that the general thrust is two-fold: (a)) to make the working life of individuals more fulfilling and satisfying; and (b) to make the firm more responsive to the values and needs of Industrial Society.

Both Co-determination and Industrial Democracy reinforce the 'learning' aspect of organizational change, because learning implies involvement and participation. It is less clear whether these concepts will evolve to accept the 'planning' as an instrument of organizational change; partly because, in very complex organizations, certain key aspects of planning (such as strategy-setting in a turbulent environment) cannot be made totally participative without becoming self-defeating and ineffective; partly because the requirement of consensus on common goals necessary in planning may not be attainable in politically polarized decision settings. (The history of the LIP watch factory in France is a dramatic example.)

This suggests that, complicated as it is, the plannned—learning approach to organizational change will only meet the needs of those organizations which remain essentially 'purposive' in the sense of having a substantial measure of common agreement on the objectives and goals of the enterprise. More complex approaches will be needed in organizations which are more 'political' than 'purposive', in which decision-making is based on bargaining and power play. But this is a subject to be treated on another occasion, outside of this already too lengthy chapter.

5. Summary

We started in search of an explanation for the failure of strategic planning to resolve the problem of the firm in the post-industrial era. We traced the problem as being one of a basic transformation of behaviour from a predominantly competitive mode to a combination of competitive and entrepreneurial modes. We then argued that transformation of the firm's linkages must be accomplished by a corresponding transformation in the firm's internal capability, particularly managerial capability, and that capability for entrepreneurial activity is distinct from that for the competitive activity. This two-phase process constitutes a strategic posture transformation as illustrated in Figure 11. Strategic planning was shown to be only a component of the total capability vector needed for entrepreneurial acitivity.

Using these conceprs, we have presented a methodology for planning the transformation of the firm's capability to a new environmentally responsive culture. We have had numerous opportunities to test this methodology in the class room with practicing managers and in consulting situations (see following chapter by Davous and Deas). A series of semi-programmed exercises was

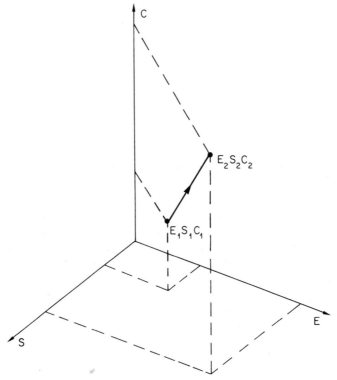

Figure 11. Strategic posture transformation. E, environmental turbulence; S, intensity of external linkages; C, responsiveness of internal configuration.

developed and tested which takes a group of managers, previously inexperienced in strategic posture analysis, through a complete strategic posture planning cycle (Ansoff, 1972). Therefore we feel comfotable in recommending this approach to managers who are confronting the strategic-change problem.

The methodology recognizes that competitive and entrepreneurial modes can have different intensities depending on the environment and on managerial objectives. We suggested an intensity classification scheme which permits a direct comparison between the two modes. Using this, we hypothesized that optimal behaviour in the two modes occur at different intensities. A firm which has to behave in both modes has to solve the problem of accommodating and reconciling two conflicting capability 'cultures'. This gives rise to a new and important top management challenge — the integration and coordination of multi-cultural 107 the multi-model operations. We suggested that the new scope of post-industrial management should be called *strategic management*. This includes:

(1) operations management of the competitive mode;

(2) entrepreneurial management of the entrepreneurial mode;

(3) integrative management of the coexistence of the two modes.

Finally, we recognized that, within strategic management the rational process of planning is only a component of a much more complex socio-dynamic process which brings about strategic change. We have argued that, to focus exclusively either on rational planning processes or on adaptive psycho-socio-political processes, as has been done in much of the literature, is to swing a pendulum between two inefficient extremes. Having examined the advantages and limitations of the purely adaptive and purely planned approaches we have suggested that the eventual approach will combine the two in a process of planned learning.

References

Ansoff, H. I. (1965). *Corporate Strategy*, New York, McGraw-Hill.

Ansoff, H. I. (1967). 'The evolution of corporate planning'. Report of the SRI Long-Range Planning Service, Palo Alto, California, September.

Ansoff, H. I. (1969). 'Managerial problem-solving'. In J. Blook, Jr. (Ed), *Management Science in Planning and Control*, The Technical Association Publication No. 5, New York.

Ansoff, H. I. (1970). 'Toward a strategic theory of firms', In H. I. Ansoff, *Business Strategy*, Harmondsworth, Penguin.

Ansoff, H. I. (1972). *Strategic Posture Analysis Exercises* (forthcoming).

Ansoff, H. I. (1973a). 'Management on the threshold of the Post-Industrial Era'. *Challenge to Leadership*, Managing in a Changing World, the Conference Board, New York, Free Press.

Ansoff, H. I. (1973b). 'The next twenty years in management education', *The Library Quarterly*, Chicago, University of Chicago Press, Vol. 43, No. 4, October 1973.

Ansoff, H. I. (1974). 'Corporate structure present and future'. Paper presented at the International Congress of Corporate Planers, Brussels.

Ansoff, H. I. et al. (1970). 'Does planning pay?, *Long Range ange Planning*, Dec., 2.

Ansoff, H. I. and Brandenburg, R. G. (1971). 'A language for organization design', *Management Sciencce*, **17**, No. 12, August.

Ansoff, H. I. and Hayes, R. L. 'Role of models in corporate decision-making', In M. Ross (Ed.), *Operational Research*, Amsterdam, North Holland.

Chandler, A. D. (1969). *Strategy and Structure*, Cambridge, Mass., MIT Press.

Cordtz, D. (1966). 'Face in the Mirror at GM', *Fortune*, **74**, August, 116.

Cyert, R., and March, J. G. (1963). *The Behavioral Theory of the Firm*, Englewood Cliffs, Prentice-Hall.

Drucker, P. (1969). *The Age of Discontinuity*, New York, Harper & Row.

'Harnessing the R & D monster' *Fortune*, **LXXXI**, (1965). No. 1.

Lindbloom, C. E. (1970). 'The science of muddling through', in H. I. Ansoff, *Business strategy*.

Ringbakk, L. A. (1969). 'Organized planning in major U.S. companies', *Long-Range Planning Journal*, **2**, No. 2, December.

Schick, A. (1969). 'Systems politics and systems budgeting', *Public Administration Review*, **29**, No. 2, March/April.

Schick, A. (1973). 'A death in the bureaucracy: the demise of Federal PPB', *Public Administration Review*, March/April, 146.

Toffler, A. (1970). *Future Shock*, New York, Random House.

Notes

1. A typical experience was encountered by one of the authors in a billion-dollar American company, which prepared some five years ago a six-inch thick Corporate Strategic Plan. The

planning Effort so exhausted the planning staff, and so depleted its goodwill with operating managers, that no effort was made at subsequent revisions. Some four years later the chairman said at a top management meeting 'I suppose we should do something about strategic planning. But, let's not revise that damned thing again'.

2. It should be made clear that for most firms there will not be one but many competitive environments. The analysis would be performed for each. This issue is discussed in a later section.

3. This section is adapted from Ansoff (1974).

4. Which is typical of successful crisis managers and which was recently described by a famous politician struggling for personal survival by the words: 'The hotter it gets the cooler I get'.

DESIGN OF A CONSULTING INTERVENTION FOR STRATEGIC MANAGEMENT

PIERRE DAVOUS and JAMES DEAS

1. The Problem

It is only very recently that the problem of strategic management has been recognized in Europe as being the solution to the firm's strategy problems. Many firms are still trying to use strategic planning as the means to solve the problem, and reasons for the 'failure of planning'[1] are frequently discussed in companies and intercompany seminars.

As the title shows, our interventions are aimed at promoting strategic management – a behavioural phenomenon – and not the production of a 'strategy' or a plan. We concern ourselves with the managers, the structure, the process and total management system of planning implementation and control. We believe that the firm's strategy is the concern of many organizational levels (Figure 1).

We believe the term 'strategic planning' is a bad and misleading one; better to distinguish strategy analysis, planning, strategic decisions and strategic behaviour, each of which is a distinguishable element.

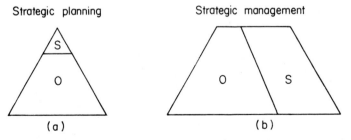

Strategic planning   Strategic management

(a)   (b)

Figure 1. Who is concerned in the strategy? (a) A top management problem with 'implementation'. (b) A behaviour at several levels of the organization.

The necessarily limited number of comments we shall make in this chapter on our manner of handling the problem of designing a consulting intervention to promote strategic management should be understood in the following context.

We are dealing with medium-sized and large firms.

We are working in France in 1973, in a given management culture and sophistication.

We are intervening in public, semi-public and private organizations.

The key points of our approach will be seen to be:

A cascade process which progressively increases the involvement of the structure and the level of sophistication of analysis.

Quick results during the cascade — flashes of analysis and decision on key strategic issues.

Planning used as a *pedagogical tool* in the process of introducing strategic management at many organizational levels.

Strategy analysis on real problems.

2. Why is the firm going to adopt strategic management?

This is the first question the consultant must ask himself. The answer will be of considerable importance in designing the intervention and in the role of the consultant with regard to the organization.

Does the stimulus come from the top management?

If so, is it as a new gadget (like O.R., EDP, MBO, etc.), or is it as a means of stimulating creativity and innovation in the firm? Is the management 'old style' sure of itself, or is it 'new style', conscious of the breakdown in continuity and the rapidity of environmental change?

Is the management defensive, seeking a coordinating and cohesion-oriented tool? Or is it aggressive, seeking to push the firm to new activities?

Is the move brought on by a change in the top management? If so, what is the power position of the new man, what is he trying to prove? Does he have influence to get the thing going and stimulate the process during its lengthy progress?

Is the desire to have strategic management (in planning) the result of the solution of another organizational problem (EDP plan, structural change, etc.), and how did the emphasis on strategy come about?

3. Diagnosing Organizational Culture

In addition to an analysis of *why* the firm is setting about the task of introducing strategic management, the consultant spends a lot of time examining the present organizational *culture*. Dr Ansoff has already presented an operational outline for this diagnosis (managers; process; structure and systems).

One very important aspect of the firm's culture in France is its past history in MBO, which is so close to many aspects of strategic management.[2] We find quite a range of situations regarding MBO history.

MBO is implemented, but as a vectorial system, insufficient and exhausting. A 'new gadget' is sought.

MBO has failed because of lack of interest or, as is often the case, because of stubborn resistance by unions.

MBO is implemented, and there exists a certain consciousness of the need to make it evolve from a system with objectives coming top-down, through a system with negotiated objectives in a fixed strategic context towards a system which allows strategy analysis as a basic element in the process.

The state of the firm's culture in MBO will be a strong determinant in intervention design.

We look also at, and it may be hard for a non-French audience to believe this, the *semantic culture* of the firm. Many words in France are taboo, for example:

Plan — connotation of state planning, dirigism, leftish tendencies and anti-liberalism;

Strategy — militarism;

Participation — political connotations; Gaullism.

These few examples illustrate the kind of *blockages* which can result from careless use of language.

Moreover, one often finds in companies that there have been battles around terminology and that a faction has won the battle. If the consultant adopts the 'defeated' terminology he is doomed to failure from the beginning.

Great care must be taken in this field. The French 'wear out' words quickly and stick political meanings on to them with startling regularity, as well as delighting in linguistic discussions.

We also look carefully at previous consulting interventions and the organizational attitude to consultants. We are going to attempt a cultural change as *change agents*, and thus, as in OD interventions, relation with the organization and its image of us are of fundamental importance.

4. The Formalization of Management Systems

(a) I shall not discuss the general tendency for management systems in Latin countries to be generally at a lower level of formalization.

Let me just mention a very interesting finding revealed in a survey of 100 French and 30 French-Canadian Firms. We reviewed the 'degree of satisfaction' with which the managers of these firms regarded their internal Information Systems. An 'index of satisfaction' was constructed according to the answers to 56 questions. (Other 'indexes' were constructed but they are not relevant to our present discussion.)

We correlated this index with the level of formalization of planning in the firm (which ranged from no formal planning at all, up to a well-structured and well-accepted planning system) (Figure 2).

Plotting the 'index of satisfaction' against the level of 'formalization of planning' produced initially a negative trend. This surprised us at first. But it can be explained by the fact that an organization operating without any formal planning may take advantage of individual creative initiatives, and these initiatives may be discouraged if the first steps in formalizing planning are not taken with due consideration.

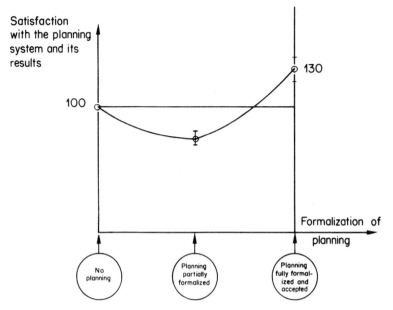

Figure 2. Efficiency of planning.

(b) This lower level of formalization of *systems* unfortunately goes hand in hand with a greater rigidity in the reporting attitudes. Many firms have started only recently to pay attention to the importance of *communicications* and the involvement of lower-level people in the decision process.

(c) An important point for French planning culture is the existence since World War II of a government organization for national planning. Whether the National Plan is a plan as such, or is really a long-range forecast, whether it is a technocratic process or not, does not concern us here.

The result is that many managers, especially in large firms, were already involved in national planning committees long before they were involved in the internal planning activities of their own firms. Or at least they had heard a lot about the National Plan before working on planning in their own firms.

In France, long-range planning developed first in the Government and only then was adapted in the firm, whereas the reverse was true in the United States.

5. The Structure of the French Economy

This is another factor governing the design of our interventions. The public sector has a much larger place in the economy and in the gross national product of France, and includes a wide range of different types of organizations.

In the last year, we have carried out interventions in strategic management in the following types of organizations:

Five medium- and large-sized private firms;
One very large transport undertaking heavily subsidized by the Government;

One regional planning board, which will manage at the end of this year its own independent budget but which is at the present time purely a coordination body;

Two Government agencies.

6. The Multi-level Strategy Process

When one speaks about the definition of strategy in the firm, everybody is ready to agree with the fuzzy statement that it is a 'multi-level process'.

Various connotations are implicit in the words 'multi-level strategy definition'. This becomes immediately obvious when people speak of a hierarchized graph of objectives'.

(1) The various levels of this graph can be described according to:

the degrees of *availability* or *accessibility* of the outcomes of the actions

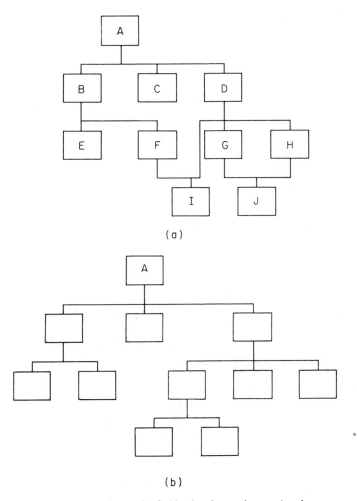

(a)

(b)

Figure 3. The graph of objectives is not always a 'tree'.

within the time-period covered by the planning process. (This has to do with semantic discussions about 'objectives, goals, ends . . .').

the degrees of *relevance* of an outcome of a given level in helping to reach an outcome of the level above (figure 3);

the degrees of *abstraction* of the purpose (from a very down-to-earth practical intent up to the more abstract levels of purely ethical motivation).

(2) Moreover, the objectives can be spelled out in such a way that the graph of objectives exhibits a kind of *correspondence with the organization chart.*

Some people will even say that this correspondence is a must, because there is no such thing as the 'organization's objectives', and, they say only people can have objectives; accordingly for each objective you must specify whose objective it is.

(3) A third element is introduced in planning the intervention. The consultant faces two practical requirements:

the intervention has to be tailored at each phase to the degree of sophistication of the people involved in the process;

the intervention has to involve progressively the different levels of the management organization.

We understand our role as designers of a strategy of change which has to start with people as they are and bring them progressively to a level where strategic management will be a well-understood, well-accepted and efficiently integrated dimension of management.

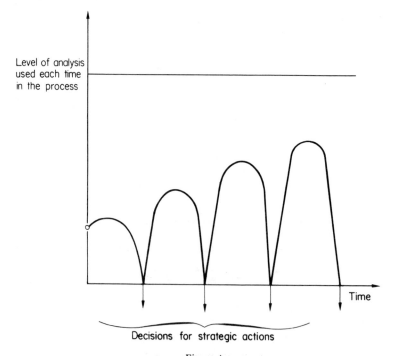

Figure 4.

7. The Structure of an Intervention

In order to reach the general objective I have just mentioned, we have deliberately adopted a strategy of change based on the principle of successive and short iterations. These always aim at two kinds of outputs:

one set of decisions for some strategic moves, which are submitted to the operational planners:

an increment in the skills of the people involved in the process, with a view to making them able to pass successfully through the next more sophisticated iteration.

This is best explained by Figure 4.

In this kind of 'spiralling' process the objective of the first cycle cannot be to arrive at a complete strategic plan, but only at a set of strategic decisions. The focus is primarily on training the management team. We can say that the objectives are 80 per cent educational, with only 20 per cent of the effort used for its own sake, and that mainly as a by-product. The second cycle will be by contrast, 50 per cent educational, 50 per cent plan, and the third phase 80 per cent plan and only 20 per cent educational These figures are given only as indications of the shift in emphasis from education to the formulation of workable strategy.

8. The Penetration of the Process of Change into the Organization

At each step of this process we accomplish several things.

(a) We involve a new layer of the organization.

(b) We work with the layers previously involved at an increased level of sophistication, following the upgrading in their abilities.

When we use this word 'layer' we do not mean one specific level in the organization chart. We find it useful to involve simultaneously in the first step people in the upper levels together with some people at the level of middle management. This process is illustrated in Figure 5.

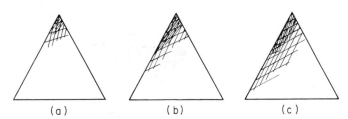

Figure 5. Penetration of strategic management into the organization. (a) After the first wave. (b) After the second wave. (c) After the third wave.

9. Structure of the Intervention within One of its Cycles

There is nothing new in the basic structure we use and readers will have already seen it dozens of times. What may be somewhat new is the way we use it. The diagram will avoid a long description (Figure 6).

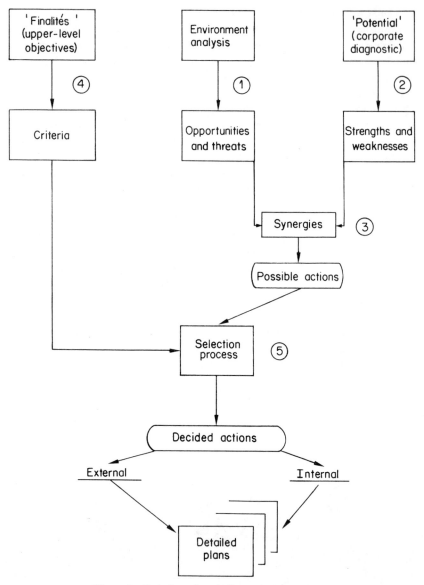

Figure 6. Circled numbers indicate time sequence.

We know that this is an oversimplification of what would be desirable. The reason why we still use it is that:

due to its simplicity, it can easily be memorized, even in an organization with a low management culture. People can more easily stay on the tracks.

due to its generality (it is only an application of general praxeologic scheme of philosophers like Piaget, Vallon, etc. It lends itself to rather quick and iterative applications, at various 'levels' of abstraction or of aggregation.

10. Iterative Use of the 'Trident'

When we apply it in a large 'multi-business' organization, the first iteration will have the limited goal of taking a broad overview of the organization and understanding clearly the various businesses it is really in (or should be in). So, rather than 'actions', one would look first at business areas'. A lot of fuzziness is still there at the end of the first cycle, but a second cycle is started, with as many groups as business areas which have been identified during the first cycle. Within each business area, the process is closer to a conventional strategic planning process. At the end of the second cycle, a third cycle is started at the overall level, taking into account the results of the second cycle (Figure 7).

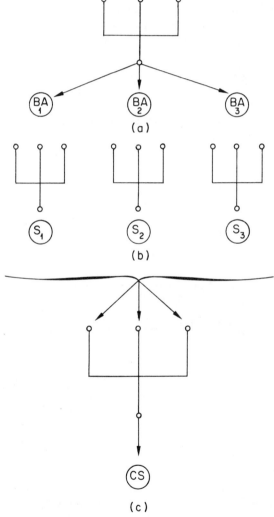

Figure 7 (a) First cycle. Identification of business areas. (b) Second cycle. Strategies for each business area. (c) Third cycle. Consolidated corporate strategy.

In this third cycle the emphasis is placed on verifying the consistency of the results of the second cycle.

It is our experience that it is not very easy to achieve this consistency by purely analytic approaches. In order to speed up the process of checking consistency, we suggested recently to one of our clients that he should introduce a carefully prepared 'scenario' between the second and third cycles. This would be constructed on the assumption that all the decisions taken in the previous cycle concerning the various strategic business areas would be implemented simultaneously.

11. Monitoring the Full Process

At each step, the consultant has to monitor carefully:

the optimal depth analysis, according to the present cultural level;

the logic of the interfaces between partial processes, establishing the right balance between logic and flexibility;

the information given to the entire organization about the planning process, and more generally the whole psychosociological climate of the intervention (Table 1).

On this last point, we help our consultants by training them to a kind of 'psychological early warning system'.

As an example we can take a look at the chart giving the various causes for lack of motivation of the management group right at the beginning of a strategic planning intervention (Figure 8).

The progress of the intervention is reviewed in special sessions with those in the organization in charge of the planning process; we focus on how the process is progressing rather than on the content of the documents generated.

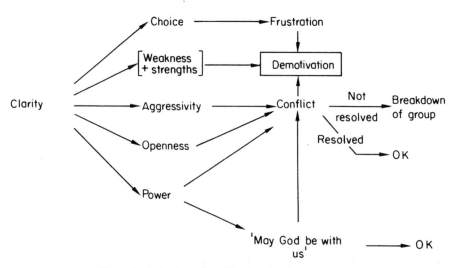

Figure 8. Attitudes induced by the planning process.

Table 1.

Phases \ Participants	General Manager	Board	Upper managt. (25)	Middle managt. (350)	Lower managt. (1,600)	Union delegates
Start						
Kick-off Meeting	X		All	Pt (35)		
Flash Report (2p.)			All	All	All	All
3 Initiation one-day Seminars			All	Pt (125)		
1st step						
3 Strat. Plg Teams			All (3 × 8)	Pt (15)		
12 Oper Plg Teams			All	Pt (120)	20	
Closing Str (2d)	X	Pt (1)	Pt (12)	Pt (12)		
Seminars Opl. (2d)	X		Pt (12)	Pt (15)		
Present To Board	X	X				
To unions	X					All
5 One-day Inf on Meet			Pt (10)	All (350)		
Plan available to					All	
2nd step						
People involved in committees	X		All	All	300	
People informed by at least 1/2 day meet					All	All
3rd step						
Presently under design						

12. Modules of the 'Trident'

A full description of all the separate modules contained in the 'trident' is beyond the scope of this short chapter.

I will take the liberty of focusing on one single 'box' rather than try to cover them all superficially, selecting the first one, 'Finalités'.

13. Attitudes and the Planning Process

An effective planning process requires *clarity* in all matters from its participating groups and their individual members. To a large extent the success of the planning effort is dependent on the fulfillment of this requirement.

However, while clarity is an essential ingredient in effective planning, it in turn poses various psychological difficulties for the planners. They are the following.

(a) In striving for clarity, the group (or the individuals) is confronted with *choices*. This confrontation requires the group to evaluate alternatives and make decisions. Frequently this selection process generates frustration, since it is necessary to abandon a number of alternative paths to walk a chosen one. This involves second doubts which are capable of heightening the frustration level.

(b) In clarifying an organization's potential, the group must necessarily analyse its particular strengths and weaknesses. Examining one's strength in most cases is ego-building and at worst painless. However, facing up to one's *weaknesses* is often distasteful and demotivating for a planning group.

(c) A successful planning process requires the planning group to define the nature and exact capabilities of its competition. Possibly for the first time, the group becomes conscious of the forcefulness of its marketplace rivals, and this, of course, heightens the anxieties and *aggressivity* of the group. If the planners feel themselves incapable of fully meeting the challenges of their competitors, conflicts may be generated followed by demotivation.

(d) *Openness* is a necessary condition for effective planning. A free flow of ideas and information is essential. However, this requirement obliges each member of the planning group to open wide the window on his particular sector of organizational activity and responsibility. Often the scrutiny which such an openness implies is distasteful or embarrassing to a group or individual and causes conflict by demotivation.

(e) Lastly, the clarification process touches upon the sensitive issue of organizational *power*. Psychologically, man is willing to exercise power to the extent that it is a response to the call of fate, 'the wishes of the Gods'. This explains why we often 'knock on wood' or 'cross our fingers' before undertaking a particular endeavour. If, however, the situation is ambiguous and results uncertain, the planner may be less than enthusiastic to accept the reins of power. Once again conflicts may surface followed by demotivation.

In summary, then, the clarification process in planning may lead to demotivation either through frustration or conflict. Moreover, if these conflicts or frustrations are not handled correctly, they can lead to the eventual breakdown of the group.

14. Definition of the Objectives

Designing the part of our interventions devoted to the definition of the objectives of the organization, we used the systematic concept of 'levels' with the two main connotations that we mentioned earlier.

14.1 *Organization (Figure 9)*

It is now a widely used concept to consider every individual in a social organization as having, like Janus, two faces:

first, he belongs to a hierarchical tree composed of his boss and his peers;

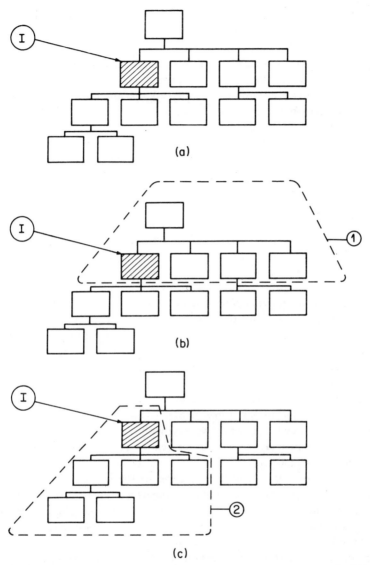

Figure 9. Every individual I in the organization belongs to a group composed of his boss and his peers (b). The individual I is also the summit of another hierarchical tree composed of all the people reporting to him (c). 1 and 2 define the well-known 'Janus effect' for I.

second, he is the summit of another hierarchical tree composed of all the people reporting to him.

the set of his objectives can usually be divided into two subsets.

Subset A. These objectives are derived from the orientations decided above him and or from the need to be consistent with the upper part of the organization. He has here only the flexibility to negotiate some improvements to the formulation of objective, or to suggest new objectives which will or will not be accepted by his boss. The objectives of 'Subset A' satisfy the need for *integration* of the individual in the hierarchy.

Subset B. This second category of objectives is derived from the requirement of the individual and the team reporting to him to exhibit some *'self-affirmation'*. It has been obvious for 20 years that the normal development of people demands that they have the possibility to express their personality through objectives selected by themselves.

An individual in an organization is a member of two overlapping but distinct groups: a group composed of equals and immediate superior (Figure 9 (b)) and a second group made up of his own subordinates (Figure 9 (c)). This phenomenon of dual membership is known as the 'Janus effect which is found in all hierarchical organizations'.

This is possible only if, starting from the upper level, there is enough room left for flexibility in the objective-setting process, and if, at each level, one or several of the objectives recognize the need to keep, for the lower levels, the required freedom margin.

14.2 *Levels of Abstraction of Objectives*

At a given moment in time, and for its present level of culture, an organization works always according to a set of more or less explicit objectives. They may be unduly limited to the short term, they may take into account a very poor set of values, their understanding may be limited to some people at the upper level, but they exist.

It is our experience that it is pure waste of time to induce a management team to generate objectives at three or four levels or abstraction above the level of the objectives they are presently working with.

This is one of the main reasons for our iterative process: we always start from an existing set of objectives, go with the team to the next upper level, look for consistency and exhaustivity of the objectives set for this new level, and look for the strategic implications of this new set of objectives (Figure 10).

We shall climb only one more level during the second phase, when those concerned will have consolidated their first step of progress and will be ready for the next level of sophistication (Figure 11).

One might object that, if we need one year for each step, this will take a long time.

Let me say, first, that it is true, it takes a long time anyhow, as for every process of improvement in strategic management. But we can say also that in some cases the steps may be shorter than one year.

In a recent intervention (for a 6,000-person firm) we discovered such a confused situation and such a low cultural level that we decided to complete a full strategic planning cycle in one month (obviously at a very superficial level of analysis). We borrowed five full days from the top management team and, with the continuous involvement of their young planners, this was enough to establish some first decisions of urgency and to start the second iteration with a much better foundation, both in understanding of the firm and in confidence of the managers. The second iteration will be completed at the end of this year.

14.3. *Preferred Methodology for the Definition of Objectives*

14.3.1. *Participants.* We have two alternatives, according to the personality of the general manager (or, more generally, of the statutory leader of the organization).

If the general manager has a broad insight, a good perception of psychosociological problems and has already established open and informal relationships

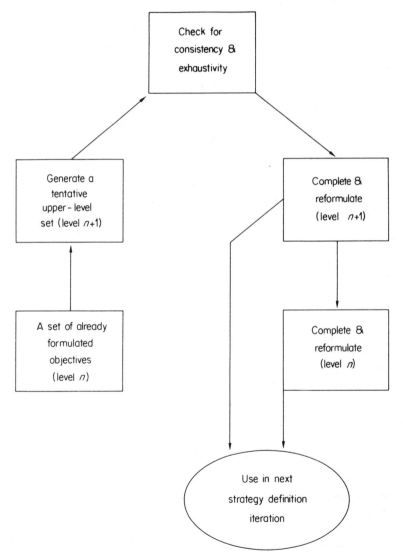

Figure 10. Tool: the 'Finalities' grid.

94

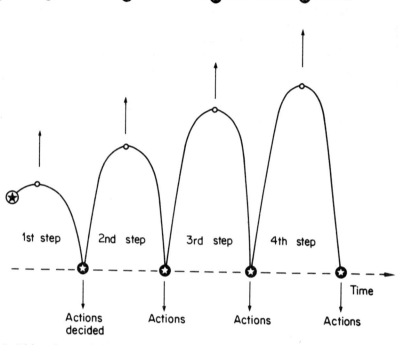

'Finalités'

1st step   2nd step   3rd step   4th step

Time

Actions
decided   Actions   Actions   Actions

Figure 11. With each step of the intervention the 'intent structure' is progressively enriched. Each step is completed by a set of decisions..

with his key managers, he can be personally present at the sessions, but he will often decide himself not to attend.

If the general manager is operating in an autocratic style, his presence would inhibit the team and the session would be limited to a dialogue between him and the consultant, a highly frustrating situation for his managers. Unfortunately it is exactly this type of man who is willing to attend the session; the consultant has to manage this problem carefully and find a way to have at least one full-day session with the team and without the general manager. Obviously the results of the session have to be reviewed afterwards with the general manager. We have not yet been in a situation where this review was stormy and destructive.

Another important point about participants. If the team is composed of people with uniformly very high seniority (as happens very frequently in France), we recommend adding some younger people of the middle management, carefully selected for their constructive creativity. In one of our interventions, the objectives were defined with a team composed of senior people and of a 'junior board'. The junior board had working sessions between the main sessions, and submitted its work to the next plenary session.

14.3.2 *Looking for the 'upper objectives'.*   (a) As we said earlier, we start from a list of existing objectives. We spend some time with the group reviewing the list, in order to make sure that everybody understands every statement in the same way. If this is not the case, we induce the group to reformulate some objectives in a way that everybody can understand. We take advantage of this review to put some flesh around the 'motherhood' statements, and we try to equalize somewhat the level of abstraction of the various objectives.

(b) We then introduce (usually this has been done before by the team!) a short discussion about the 'words': objectives, goals, ends, . . . We try to keep it short explaining that the important thing is to understand the various dimensions (availability, abstraction, relevance, . . .) involved in a graph of objectives rather than engage in linguistics.

We are helped by the existence of a word '*Finalités*', which can perhaps be translated by 'ultimate objectives', but which, clearly, has in French two connotations, a fact that helps our purpose.

(1) first connotation of '*Finalités*' is: an ultimate goal given by some higher power-owner. It is tied to the concept of 'Mission', and also of 'function'. 'You have been given the mission to . . ., you have to . . ., you must . . .'

(2) second connotation of '*Finalités*' is: an ultimate goal that emanates from myself, by a kind of internal source of purpose that I have. 'I have the freedom to . . ., I can . . ., I will . . . .'

(c) We have a short discussion with the group on a way to put some clarity into this concept of '*Finalités*'.

They soon recognize that '*Finalités*' can be put in various classes according to the social values they tend to satisfy. If we have time, we rediscover with the group an acceptable set of 'social values': truth, efficiency, usefulness, safety, self-fulfilment, integration, beauty, ...

Another dimension of '*Finalités*' is the *social group* they take into consideration. A given '*Finalité*' relates then to a given social value, and is a statement that a given social group will benefit more from this social value.

We then introduce a grid (Table 2), with social values in lines, and social groups in columns. The columns are in order of decreasing 'power' of the groups. In the middle we put the organization where we intervene, on the left the more 'powerful' social groups, on the right the groups with 'equal power', and then with 'lower power', the last column being 'individuals in the organization'.

(d) We give numbers to the objectives of the list generated earlier. Then we try to define with the group boxes of the grid where each objective should be placed; we put the number of the objective in the grid.

An objective one would like to put everywhere is generally a 'motherhood' statement. Many other statements of this kind can be made.

(e) One can usually see a structure emerging from this grid. (In one intervention, the left hand columns remained completely empty. One can understand the implication: the organization has an abnormal tendency to neglect the reactions of many groups which have in fact a lot of power over it.)

Some boxes are quite naturally empty; for some others, the group agrees that something is missing.

(f) The discussions of the group after this exercise generally result on a better

Table 2

What Value?	More powerful groups			The Firm Where We Are	Equal powerful groups			Less powerful groups	
	'Society'	Government	Banks		Competition	Unions	Supplier	Customers	Employ.
Efficiency	5	5	1; 14	1; 4; 5; 11; 14; 16; 17	5; 17	5	1	5; 18	4; 5
Usefulness	2		5	2; 4; 8; 16			8	2; 18	4; 8
Safety				1; 3; 11			7	2	4; 3; 11
Survival				1	1				10
Truth			14	14		14			13; 14
Self-accomplishment		9		2; 7; 9; 17	7; 17	7; 10; 12	7; 9; 17	7	4; 7; 10; 12; 13
Integration/Association	2			5; 14				2	4; 12

recognition of the distance between the explicit existing objective, and what a consistent set of objectives would be. The too general objectives are broken down into more specific ones, some others are regrouped according to the emphasis that the group wants to put either on a given value or on a given social group.

The lovers of quantititative statements (even in such qualitative matters!) may even on an empty grid put weights on the various boxes of the grid and define an index of relevance for the various objectives. (This we never did.)

(g) We rework a list of objectives from this analysis, and eventually come to a graph of objectives.

14.3.3 *Extracting 'Criteria' from 'Finalités'*. In addition, we always try to derive from this list of objectives a set of *criteria*, which will help to select the actions in the planning process. It is a kind of checklist of, say, 8 to 12 sentences along which all the actions decided on are checked.

Examples: Does the action contribute to growth?

move the firm from 'artisanship' to industry?

motivate people?

train people?

develop service activities *versus* production activities?

help penetration in the segment 'integrated management'?

help to stick to the present evolution of the market?

improve short-term profitability?

help a better control of medium-term situation?

Here again, many refinements are added to the quantitative aspects by defining standards of achievement and relative weights for the various criteria.

But we caution people not to abandon their decision process to a purely mechanistic process, and to bring in at each step human judgement, consistency checks, etc.

14.3.4 *Global Definition of Objectives in the Global Process.* Although the box *'Finalités'* appears in the upper left of our overall scheme, we do not recommend starting an intervention with these discussions.

The sequence that we usually follow (I repeat in 1973, in France) is:

(1) Environment appraisal

(2) *'Potential'* (internal diagnostic)

(3) Synergies appraisal (let play the concepts of 'strength weaknesses' with 'opportunities threats'). One extracts from this a structure of 'possible and realistic actions' as they emerge from a direct confrontation of the firm and its environment.

(4) *'Finalités'* and criteria

(5) Then one comes back to the list 'possible and realistic actions' and check whether they are 'desirable' and whether there are not some others to add.

There are several reasons for this choice.

(a) French firms are, generally speaking, blind to their environment, and it is essential first to open their eyes to the outside world (not only to the market, but to their competitors, to the legal and societal evolution).

(b) The discussions on *'Finalités'* are much enriched by a better understanding of the present rapid change in the value systems and in the complexity of the network of outside interactions the firm has to manage. The two dimensions of the *'Finalités'* grid are easily perceived when the group has previously gone through a good environmenent analysis.

Moreover, it is a normal biological process to:

> become conscious of the environment;
> become conscious of oneself;
> integrate both;
> become purposeful;
> act.

14.3.5 *Time Devoted to the Definition of Objectives.* The minimum time required to go through the full process of formulation of the *'Finalités'* and definition of the criteria is one full-day session.

Some work is required after that from the planners of the firm working with the consultant in order to streamline and document the information generated (let us say another full day).

In another intervention a team was assigned to this work and met for three half-day sessions, with a lot of work by junior people between the sessions (let us say six full-day meetings).

14.3.6 *Alternative Process for the Definition of 'Finalités'.* We designed another module for the same goal of definition of *'Finalités'*, for managers with a lower cultural level.

Like the first module, it is a group process that we shall not review in detail, but we will mention the main questions discussed with the group.

(a) Who are we?
    History, trends
    Image (as perceived from comments of the environment)
    Present position from various points of view:
        Business areas covered
        Technological position
        Economic position
        Sociological position
(b) What is the result of our will in the present situation?
    What is the result of outside wills?
(c) What would we like to be?
    Projection without any constraints
    Ideal picture

(d) What are we able to be?

Realistic projection, taking into account constraints (present and potential future constraints)

Summary

I have said that the goal of our intervention is not strategic planning but strategic management . . . and I have spoken about planning. It may be a good thing at the end of this presentation to summarize our rationale.

We want to move the firm towards strategic management. A cultural change has to take place raising the present cultural level of the firm. We have to design a pedagogical process, which will by-pass the psychological obstacle. We use our customary approach, the efficiency of which has been proved in our other intervention: management development by real problems approach. Strategic planning is one of the essential activities of the strategic managers and we use it as a pedagogical tool.

Notes

1. See numerous articles, for example, Ringbakk, 'Why planning fails', etc.
2. And which was introduced in many French firms after the 'events' of May 1968, piloted by personnel directors of suddenly increased importance.

III

Strategy and Structure

TOWARDS A COMPREHENSIVE CONCEPT OF STRATEGIC ADAPTIVE BEHAVIOUR OF FIRMS*

HIDEKI YOSHIHARA

1. Introduction

At the present time, which may be viewed as a period of transition from the industrial to the post-industrial society, firms in America, Japan and several countries of Western Europe are being faced with new kinds of management problems in addition to more familiar types of problems. In dealing with the new problems and securing firms' survival and growth in the new environment of the present day, their effective strategic adaptation is essential. The present chapter is an attempt to develop a conceptual framework which is capable of dealing with this strategic adaptative behaviour of firms.[1] Its primary aim is to advance an existing strategic theory of the firm developed so far mainly by H. Igor Ansoff a step further in the following directions.

First, an attempt will be in a conceptual framework to distinguish and integrate two types of adaptive behaviour of firms: (1) exploitative adaptation and (2) strategic adaptation.

Second, a comprehensive concept of strategic adaptive behaviour of firms will be presented. In his well-known book *Corporate Strategy* (1965), H. Igor Ansoff has concentrated his argument on one particular dimension of strategic adaptation, that is, a product-market linkage relationship. In addition in his recent articles and talks he has broadened his treatment further to include other dimensions such as an international dimension and a socio-political dimension. In the present chapter we shall follow his path and attempt to articulate dimensions of strategic adaptation and components of each dimension.

*I am grateful to Dr Kuniyoshi Urabe and Mr Tadao Kagono (Kobe University) for their comments on the earlier draft of this chapter. Mr Gregory G. Blackford, a special student at Kobe University from Australia, helped me in improving the English.

The method employed in this attempt is not mathematical nor empirical. The author's present interest lies in model-building at a verbal or a conceptual level. Rigorous formulation of a model and its empirical testing will be his future tasks. In terms of the normative approach, the conceptual framework developed in this chapter is expected to provide a basis for management tools which might cope with novel problems of the emerging post-industrial era.

In developing a conceptual framework which is generally applicable to the firm regardless of its nationality, examples and data are mostly drawn from Japanese situations. This kind of approach is employed partly because it is easiest for the author, but mainly because it may hopefully provide foreigners with an opportunity to get a glimpse of contemporary strategic problems facing Japanese firms.

2. Strategic and Exploitative Adaptation

2.1 A History of Strategic Adaptation of American Firms

Table 1 shows a history of adaptation of American firms in a grossly simplified form. From this table we can see what were the major environmental changes relevant to firms during the past 100 years or so and how American firms have adapted themselves to the changes to secure their survival and growth.[2]

The adaptive behaviours of firms shown in Table 1 gave one salient characteristic in common, that is, firms adapted themselves to the environmental changes by altering their environmental linkage relationships. In the case of the strategy of geographical expansion, for example, the firms', product—market linkage relationships were modified in the sense that their market was enlarged to include new regions in the United States. In the case of the strategy of diversification both products and markets of firms changed simultaneously. Other types of strategy shown in Table 1 also have the same characteristic.

Through this common characteristic this type of adaptive behaviour of firms shown in Table 1 is called 'strategic behaviour' in this chapter. This usage of the term 'strategic' is consistent with H. Igor Ansoff's usage, which we shall see soon.[3]

It is sometimes useful and necessary to make a distinction among three different stages of the strategic adaptation process. As shown in Table 1, at the first stage a new strategy is devised to cope with emerging environmental changes. Some efforts are naturally made to develop a new operating system and to make adjustment to the existing administrative structure. But, on the whole, the primary emphasis is laid upon the task of developing an excellent strategy. Thus, strategic decisions generally play a central role at the first stage.

At the next stage a new strategy is put into implementation on an extended scale. The central task is to build production facilities, devise production schedules, plan marketing policies, develop marketing channels, and so on. Thus, an emphasis shifts from the strategic decisions to the operating ones.

Implementation of a new strategy on a large scale almost always brings about unanticipated new administrative problems to the existing administrative

Table 1. A history of strategic adaptation of US firms

Year	Environmental changes	Stages of strategic adaptation		
		(1) Strategic decisions	(2) Operating decisions	(3) Administrative decisions
– 1870	Development of nation-wide market and urban market	→ Strategy of geographical expansion	→ Development of operating system for the new strategy	→ Administrative structure for managing field units
1870–1910	End of geographical expansion of US market and consequent severe competition and excess capacity	→ Strategy of acquisition and vertical integration	→ Development of operating system for the new strategy	→ Centralized, functionally departmentalized structure
1910–1960	Population growth, technological innovation and two World Wars	→ Strategy of diversification	→ Development of operating system for the new strategy	→ Decentralized, multi-divisional structure
1960 –	Comparative disadvantage of some industries, development of EEC and overall trend of internationalization	→ Strategy of foreign direct investment	→ Development of operating system for the new strategy	→ Multi-national administrative structure

structure. To restore a well-coupled relationship between the strategy of the firm and its administrative structure, a new administrative structure must be devised and installed. Thus at the third stage administrative decisions become the most dominant ones.

Although a systematic investigation into the reason why strategic adaptation often proceeds stage by stage $(S-O-A)$[4] is an interesting subject, it is well beyond the scope of the present chapter.

The concept of strategic adaptation may be appropriate for dealing with such major environmental changes and firms' adaptation to them as shown in Table 1, but it admittedly has limitations. If we look at the environment in greater detail, we should find that it never stands still but is always changing. Changes of lesser scale would be observed in almost every aspect of firms' environments: prices of raw materials and competitors' products, government economic and other relevant policies, production technology, conditions of national economy, etc.

It would also be revealed that firms respond to these incessant minor environmental changes almost continuously. This type of environmental changes and adaptation of firms to them is certainly beyond the reach of the concept of strategic adaptation. We need to have a different concept.

2.2 Concepts of 'Strategic' Behaviour

At this point it may be useful to turn our attention to a terminology problem. The same adjective 'strategic' has a different meaning to different people.

The term 'strategic' has often been used by researchers and managers of long-range planning. George A. Steiner, a leading researcher in this field, has defined strategic planning as follows (Steiner and Cannon, 1966):

In essence, we are talking about top-level corporate decisions. They are the decisions, broad in scope, which relate to the basic directions of the company and the way in which it uses its resources.

Many of those who are interested in corporate planning or long-range planning would be familiar with this usage of the term 'strategic' (Steiner, 1963, Anthony, 1965).

On the other hand, H. Igor Ansoff's usage of the term is rather special, as he himself explains in the following quotation (Ansoff, 1965, p. 5):

Here, we use the term strategic to mean 'pertaining to the relation between the firm and its environment'. This is more specific and different from a more common usage in which 'strategic' denotes 'important'. Depending on its position the firm may find operating decisions to be more important than strategic ones.

In this theoretical framework, the management decision problems are classified into three categories: (1) strategic, (2) administrative and (3) operating. The strategic decisions are concerned with establishing the linkage relationship between the firm and its environment. In other words, they are concerned with how to relate the firm to its dynamic and novel environment in order to secure its survival and growth.[5]

In the present chapter the term 'strategic' is being used in the same way as H. Igor Ansoff has used it in his theory.

2.3. *Exploitative Adaptation*

Many diverse ways of adaptations are usually available for managers of the firm which is faced with environmental changes. They may alter any one or combination of the following variables:

(1) volume or level of operating activities (purchasing, production, inventory, marketing, etc.)

(2) operating system (production schedules, inventory control system, marketing policies, R & D policies, etc.)

(3) administrative structure (organizational structure, location of facilities, reward system, leadership style, etc.)

(4) environmental linkage relationship (a product-market linkage relationship, an international linkage relationship, a socio-political linkage relationship, etc.)

The strategic adaptation we saw in the previous section represents one specific type of adaptation: the adaptation by means of alteration of the environmental linkage relationship of the firm. We know, however, that firms often adapt themselves to environmental changes differently by means of modification of such variables as (1), (2) and/or (3) but not (4) just mentioned.

In this type of adaptation the existing linkage relationship is considered to be given for the firm. What managers seek is to exploit the existing linkage relationship in order to convert its potential profitability into actual profits. This type of adaptation is called 'exploitative' adaptation in this chapter.[6]

Since the environmental linkage relationship remains the same in the case of the exploitative adaptation, strategic decisions are inactive and only operating decisions and/or administrative decisions are involved.

As a matter of fact, what management researchers have studied so far corresponds roughly to the exploitative adaptation and its related problems (Ansoff, 1972, pp. 41—55). The 'scientific management' studied the operating system of the firm, especially the production system. What the 'human relations approach' dealt with were the social-psychological problems of workers and managers at factories and offices. The school of 'principles of management' has been mainly concerned with problems of organizational structure. Operations research and management science have handled those 'well-structured problems' which are found among such operating problem areas as production schedule, inventory control, transportation and distribution system (Simon and Newell, 1958). Therefore we have a better understanding of the exploitative adaptation than the strategic one.

3. Cycle Model of Adaptation

In the previous argument two types of adaptations have been distinguished: strategic and exploitative adaptation. Our next task should be to integrate these two concepts into a coherent scheme.

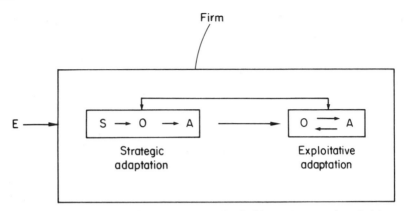

Figure 1. E, environmental changes; S, strategic decisions; O, operating decisions; A, administrative decisions.

Figure 1 represents a conceptual model for describing adaptive behaviour of firms in a changing environment. Figure 2 is a product — life-cycle (Levitt, 1965) version of Figure 1.

The conceptual model may be described by a series of propositions. Some of them have already been referred to earlier.

(1) Changes in the firm's environment bring about problems to the firm. The problems may be opportunities and/or threats to the firm.

(2) In order to secure its survival and growth the firm responds to the problem situations produced by the environmental changes. The firm's response is what we have so far called the adaptation of the firm to the environmental changes.

(3) Two types of adaptations can be distinguished: strategic and exploitative adaptation.

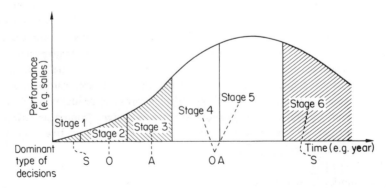

Figure 2. Stages 1, 2, 3, strategic adaptation; stages 4, 5, exploitative adaptation; stage 6, strategic adaptation.

(4) The strategic adaptation often proceeds through three distinctive stages: (a) formulation of a new strategy, (b) development of operation system for the new strategy and (c) adjustment of old administrative structure to the new strategy and operating systems. Thus, as shown in Figure 2, dominant decisions are different at each stage.

(5) In the case of the exploitative adaptation, as shown in the right-hand box inside the larger one of Figure 1, operating and administrative decisions are applied interchangeably and usually several times.

(6) There exists a coupled relationship between the type of adaptation and the nature and extent of environmental changes. Drastic, fundamental, novel or structural changes in the firm's environment are eventually responded by the strategic adaptation, though they may initially evoke the exploitative adaptation. Gradual, small, familiar or cyclical environmental changes induce the exploitative adaptation.

Figure 2 describes a situation in which some drastic changes occur in the firm's environment and are responded by the firm's strategic adaptation. The strategic adaptation proceeds through three distinctive stages. The performance position of the firm gradually improves as the new environmental linkage relationship develops and is implemented.

Stages 4 and 5, which occupy a central part in blank in Figure 2, represent a period for the exploitative adaptations. This period may last for a very long time is the basic structure or nature of the firm's environment does not change. But emergence of a new kind of environment eventually induces the strategic adaptation.

Thus, as clearly shown in Figure 1, adaptation of the firm to its environmental changes over some period of time may suitably be described as a cyclical phenomenon.

In Figure 2 it is shown that strategic adaptation takes place in stage 6, where the performance position of the firm begins to show a downward trend. This is lagged strategic adaptation, which is often observed. How to secure more rapid strategic adaptation is an important problem for managers.

Figure 3 is an attempt to present a cyclical pattern of the firm's adaptation over some period of time. Each hump corresponds to the shape of Figure 2 and shows one cycle of adaptation. Shaded areas represent the strategic adaptation and blank areas show the exploitative adaptation. E_1, E_2, E_3, depicted in the lower part of Figure 3, show those kinds of environmental changes which induce the strategic adaptation.

It is admittedly evident that Figure 3 is too simple to be considered as a sound description of the actual adaptive behaviour of firms in a real world. The conceptual model explained so far in the present chapter, however, seems to serve as a basis or a starting point from which we can proceed towards the development of a more complicated and realistic model of the firm's adaptation.

Next, let us turn our attention to various dimensions of strategic adaptation, that is, to the possible alternative ways of strategic adaptation.

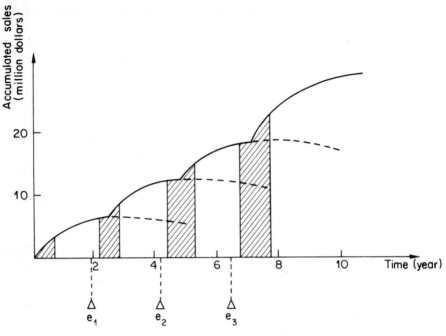

Figure 3. e_1, e_2, e_3, environmental changes.

4. Economic Linkage Relationship

4.1 *Firm and Environment*

The firm viewed as an economic organization is engaged in conversion of input resources obtained from the supply market into output products offered back to the demand market (Ansoff, 1965, Ch. 3). The conversion process is composed of several elements as shown in Figure 4.[7]

In treating the firm's environment, in this chapter a distinction is made between the two aspects (1) direct environment (demand and supply markets,

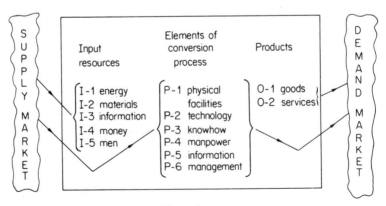

Figure 4.

and direct socio-political environment[8]) and (2) general environment (national) economy, international economy and political situation, education, technology, population, etc.[9]).

The direct environment is an aspect of the total environment which has a tangible input-output relationship with the firm. The general environment does not have such a tangible transaction relationship with the firm, though it may sometimes exert a substantial impact upon the firm's behaviour. In the argument that follows our attention will be mostly confined to the direct environment.

4.2 Input Linkage Relationship

The firm obtains 'input' from the supply market. For the industrial firm main inputs are energy through materials. These inputs are transformed into finished goods through the conversion process. Recently some firms have broadened and diversified their sphere of business activities to such an extent that industrial, trading, service and financial businesses are simultaneously conducted under a unified management control. For these firms inputs would be composed of all or many of the input resources shown in Figure 4.

The firm needs to purchase elements of the conversion process from the supply market unless it develops them inside the firm. It is a well-known fact that Japanese firms have made every possible effort to modernize their conversion process by introducing advanced technology and knowhow from US firms.

The supply market, although drawn as a homogeneous market in Figure 4, is actually composed of many different submarkets. For example, it is easy and in most cases necessary to distinguish between the supply market or raw materials and the supply market of energy. Therefore for each input resource and each element of the conversion process we can draw a line that relates it with its relevant supply market. A set of these lines would represent the possible ways to relate the firm's input resources and elements of the conversion process with their relevant supply markets. Some examples of strategic adaptation at the input linkage relationship will serve to clarify the above argument.

Example 1: alteration of materials used from natural rubber to synthetic rubber (tyre industry) from cotton and silk to nylon (apparel and fabricated textiles industry)
Example 2: alteration of the supply market of materials from US to Australia and southeast Asian countries (iron ore)
Example 3: simultaneous alteration of materials and energy resources and their supply market from domestic coal to heavy oil transported from abroad (gas supply industry, electric power industry, fertilizer industry)

4.3. Output Linkage Relationship

The firm offers its products to the demand market. This is shown by the line that relates the products of the firm to the demand market in Figure 4. This line represents the product—market linkage relationship. It has received considerable attention from researchers and practising managers interested in the diversification problem of firms (Ansoff, 1965; Gort, 1962). The point to be

Table 2

Product category	Nature and extent of 'newness'	Examples
I	Existing products	Standard-type black & white TV set
II	Different only in size, style, accessories, use, etc.	Compact TV set, portable TV set
III	Products of full-line policy	Colour TV set, radio set, tape recorder
IV	Products of the same subindustry	White goods such as vacuum cleaner, refrigerator, electric range
V	Products of the same industry	Motor, transformer, generator, computer
VI	Products of different but somewhat related industries	Oil stove, bicycle, educational equipment, machines and tools
VII	Products of unrelated industries	Foods, textile products, cosmetics, real estate

emphasized here is that managers of the firm have quite a lot of ways of combining the firm's product(s) with relevant demand market(s). This means that the alternatives for strategic adaptation in regard to the product—market linkage relationship are rather many.

However, it should be understood that all changes in the alternatives are not necessarily of equal importance for the firm. For instance, change in the product from category I of Table 2 to category VI generally has substantial impact upon the basic framework of the management and the logistic process of the firm, while change from category I to category II has relatively small impact. In the study of strategic adaptive behaviour of firms the primary attention should be focused on the former type of change. In other words, primary subject matters are found in problems of strategy or policy rather than in problems of operating procedures (See Ansoff, 1965, pp. 118—21).

4.4. *Vertical Integration and Foreign Direct Investment*

Until the 1870's nearly all American industrial firms only manufactured. They bought their raw materials and sold their products through commissioned agents, wholesalers and other middlemen. Around the turn of the century, however, many firms attained their growth by means of vertical integration. These firms, as a result of this strategy, not only produced products, but also delivered them directly to retailers or even to the ultimate customers and purchased directly or even produced their own essential materials (Chandler, 1965, pp. 24—36).

Today many large firms in such industries as chemicals, electronics, pharmaceutical and automobile industries have their own research and development departments. Even personnel-hiring and financing functions have come to be conducted directly by some firms.

The strategy of vertical integration transforms a single-function firm into a multi-function firm. We can imagine an extreme case in which a firm has pursued the strategy of vertical integration to such an extent that all of the major logistic functional activities have come to be conducted under the direct management process of the firm. Between a case of a single-function firm and this extreme case there exist several degrees or levels of vertical integration. These degrees should be regarded as representing the alternatives for strategic adaptation in regard to the linkage relationship between the firm's logistic function and their relevant environments.

The same conceptual scheme may be used to deal with the problem of foreign direct investment. As is shown in Table 1 (page 105), the strategy of foreign direct investment has played an increasingly important role in the strategic adaptation of many US firms after World War II (Vernon, 1971).

In our conceptual scheme foreign direct investment may be interpreted as overseas transplant of function(s) of the firm. We may distinguish several types of overseas transplant: Overseas transplant of (1) marketing function, (2) production function, (3) purchasing function, (4) purchasing, production and marketing functions, (5) R & D function, (6) all the major functions. Examples of each of these types can be found in the strategy of foreign direct investment followed by American and Japanese firms.

On the basis of the foregoing analysis we can easily see that the alternative ways of strategic adaptation are rather many and complex. Then which of these diverse alternatives are more important than others? Let us turn our attention from an abstract world to a real world and try to answer this question.

5. Diversification and Multi-national Expansion of Japanese Firms

5.1 *Diversification Rush*

Among the diverse strategic adaptations of Japanese firms, the following two are far more important than others: (1) diversification and (2) foreign direct investment.[10]

On the domestic front increasing numbers of Japanese firms are pursuing or planning the diversification strategy energetically, as partly shown in Table 3. Roughly speaking, a half of 517 firms which responded to the questionnaire have already entered into new industries, and a half of these same 517 firms have plans for diversification. (The latter category includes both firms extending a current diversification strategy and those planning a diversification strategy anew.) According to another investigation, during the past two years 478 firms, approximately a quarter of the firms whose securities are listed on the market, have changed their articles of incorporation so that they may enter into new industries which were not covered by the old articles (Toyokeizai Tokei Geppo, 1973).

As target industries for diversification, the following are at the top of the list: real estate, housing, amusement and tourism, pollution control, social and urban development, health and the information industry. These industries have a

Table 3. Trend of diversification of Japanese firms.

Industries \ Target industries	Housing	Social & urban development	Transportation	Retailing & services	Amusement & tourism	Information, knowledge & education	Pollution control	Health	Fashion	Others	Total
Foods	4	1	3	2	9	—	2	2	—	6	29
Textiles, pulp & paper	18	5	3	7	22	—	5	4	9	—	73
Chemicals	15	3	1	4	10	4	13	8	—	3	61
Petroleum & rubber	1	1	—	—	1	—	—	—	—	—	3
Glass and clay	4	1	1	1	5	—	3	—	—	2	17
Iron & steel, and non-ferrous metals	9	3	2	—	2	1	6	1	—	5	29
Machinery	4	2	—	—	5	—	7	1	1	4	24
Shipbuilding & other transportation equipment	6	2	3	—	4	1	4	—	—	—	20
Motor vehicles	3	—	1	—	4	—	—	1	1	1	11
Electric machinery	4	1	2	1	2	8	7	2	—	1	28
Precision machinery and other manufacturing	5	—	—	—	5	5	1	—	—	—	16
Fisheries & mining	3	3	—	1	2	—	—	—	—	1	10
Construction	15	13	—	1	10	2	7	1	—	2	51
Real estate	—	1	—	—	3	—	—	1	—	—	5
Commerce & distribution	13	5	6	5	15	5	5	6	4	—	64
Warehousing & communication	3	—	1	—	5	—	—	—	—	1	10
Transportation	10	5	5	5	11	1	2	—	—	2	41
Electricity & gas supply	—	—	—	—	—	—	—	—	—	1	1
Services	2	1	—	3	5	1	—	—	—	1	13
All industries	119	47	28	30	120	28	62	27	15	30	506

Source: *Nihonkeizai — Shinbun*, March 8, 1973.
Figures denote the numbers of firms.

common characteristic which can be described in such terms as clean, light and service.

Many reasons may be enumerated for this diversification rush, but the following seem to be distinctively important.

(1) Rapid growth of Japanese economy. Japan will soon be one of the most affluent nations in the world in terms of GNP or *per capita* income. For example, it is predicted by many economists that *per capita* income of Japan will exceed that of the US in 1980. As people become more rich, their demands for goods and services naturally show changes.

(2) Drastic change in the labour market. Japanese firms enjoyed a favourable situation of abundant supply of docile and well-educated manpower and accompanying comparatively cheap labour costs for the past 100 years since the beginning of the Meiji era. Today, they are faced with acute shortage of manpower and 15 to 20 per cent annual increase in labour costs.

(3) Growing competitive power of developing countries. Japan is rapidly and consistently losing its competitive power in those industries or products which have characteristics of labour-intensiveness, low technology, low degree of dependence upon the external economy and easy access to the world market.

(4) Huge demand on houses and land. As is dramatically shown by Figure 5,

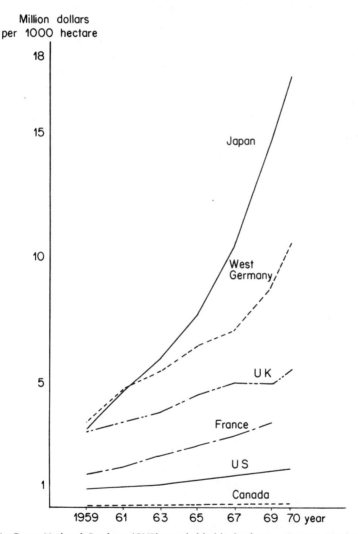

Figure 5. Gross National Product (GNP) per habitable land area. Source: Kankyo-Cho (Environment Agency). *Kankyo Hakusho* (White Paper on Environment), 1972 edition.

Japan is a truly overcrowded country in terms of economic activities. One of the most precious goods in Japan is a house with a piece of land in a city or suburban residential area. An unsatisfied huge demand for houses and land has piled up these days.

(5) Environmental deterioration and severe legislation against industrial pollution. In Japan, because of the severe legislation and the strong community feeling against industrial pollution, it is becoming increasingly hard to maintain and practically impossible to enter newly into such 'dirty' industries as chemicals, pulp, non-ferrous metals and the rubber industry.

5.2 From Export to Foreign Direct Investment

When we turn our attention to the international scene, we recognize another equally important strategic adaptation of Japanese firms. It is foreign direct investment.

For nearly 100 years since the first year of the Meiji era (1868), Japanese firms with strong government backing have made every possible effort to increase export of Japanese goods. This effort at last achieved an amazing success in the latter half of the 1960's. But this amazing success in turn has brought about new problems to Japanese firms. Since the 'Nixon Shock' that is, President Nixon's dramatic announcement of his plan to visit Peking, and the new economic policy on August 15, 1971, Japanese firms have been faced with entirely new kinds of problems: (1) revaluation of the Japanese yen[11] and (2) severe regulation on the part of foreign countries against aggressive invasion of their markets by the exports of Japanese firms. The strategy of foreign direct investment is expected to be one of the most promising solutions to the new problems.

The space limitation of the present chapter will allow us only to make a brief reference to some of the striking features of Japanese foreign direct investment.

As is shown in Table 4, the accumulated amount of investment is relatively small when compared with the case of such countries as the US, the UK, West

Table 4. International comparison of foreign direct investment

	Accumulated amount of investment at the end of 1969 (billion dollars)	Average annual growth rate of investment from 1966 to 1969 (%)
US	70.6	9.0
UK	18.7	5.2
France	4.8	6.1
West Germany	4.8	24.4
Canada	3.8	5.5
Japan	2.7	31.4

Source: Japan External Trade Organization (JETRO), *Kaigai Shijo Hakusho* (White Paper on Foreign Market), 1972 edition.
This table gives only a rough comparison because of the inconsistency of the data.

Germany and France. Japan, however, has achieved the most rapid increase in investment during the past four years (1966–1969). This high growth rate of Japanese foreign direct investment is predicted to be maintained and even accelerated in the 1970's.

The geographical dispersion of investment tells us some interesting characteristics of Japanese foreign direct investment. In the Southeast Asian area the overwhelming proportion of investment has been made in manufacturing and mining industries. An average size of investment in manufacturing industry is only $330,000. This figure is very small when compared with the counterpart figure of US investment.[12] There are two main reasons for the overseas transplant of production into the Southeast Asian area: (1) to make use of cheap local labour and (2) to deal with the severe import regulation policy of local governments.

In the US and the European areas the typical pattern of Japanese foreign direct investment is the overseas transplant or expansion of the marketing function of the parent firm. Its primary aim is to encourage the export business of the parent firm.

Investment in the mining industry occupies an important position in the overall picture of Japanese foreign direct investment. Japan's unusually high dependence upon the overseas supply in regard to most of the energy resources and raw materials will maintain and even strengthen this position.

Since the 'Nixon Shock', some new developments are recognized in the strategy of Japanese foreign direct investment. First, emphasis upon the export of goods has been distinctively decreased and foreign direct investment in turn is gaining increasingly greater importance in the overall international strategy of Japanese firms.

Second, an increasing number of firms have initiated the overseas transplant of their production as well as their marketing function in the US and the European areas.

Third, a more complex concept of international strategy is emerging. Transistor radio sets produced at the subsidiary in Taiwan are naturally sold in that country, but some of them are exported to other countries including Japan. We know of a subsidiary which specializes in purchasing essential materials for the parent firm in Japan. One company has a branch of its R & D department in the US. Development and operation of a complex network of R & D—purchasing—production—marketing on a worldwide basis is becoming increasingly important for more advanced Japanese multi-national firms.

Lastly, we observe that many firms have initiated a far-reaching change in their administrative structure in response to the greater importance of foreign direct investment. Substantial adjustments made in organizational structure and considerable effort devoted a pool of international experience and skills are conspicuous.

In the process of pursuing the strategy of foreign direct investment on an extended scale, Japanese firms would be troubled by diverse weaknesses. The following two points, however, deserve special attention.

Table 5. A comparison of R & D between the US and Japan

	US	Japan
Total R & D expenses (1969)	$26.18 billion (= 100)	$2.59 billion (10)
No. of scientists (1968)	550,000 (= 100)	160,000 (29)
Balance of technology trade (1970)		
Receipt (A)	$2.158 million	$59 million
Payment (B)	$227 million	$433 million
A/B	9.51	0.14
Average R & D expenses of the four leading firms (1967)		
Chemicals	$111.32 million (= 100)	$47.34 million (43)
Electric machinery	$146.50 million (= 100)	$28.57 million (20)
Transportation machinery	$33.08 million (= 100)	$16.66 million (50)

Source: Kagakugijustsu-cho (Science and Technology Agency), *Kagakugijutsu Yoran* (Yearly Handbook of Science and Technology), 1972 edition.

The first point is R & D weakness. One salient weakness of Japanese firms is found in R & D function. As is clearly shown in Table 5, there still exists a big gap between US and Japanese firms in regard to their R & D. The fact that strong R & D capability is a major factor contributing to the successful multi-national expansion of US firms is well established by Harvard's Multi-national Enterprise Project (Vernon, 1971). If Japanese-based multi-national firms would aspire to compete with US counterparts on an equal level, their R & D lag needs to be caught up.

The second point is an applicability of Japanese management system to foreign situations. We do not yet have a clear and common understanding of what is meant by the term 'Japanese management system'. But such expressions as 'paternalistic system', 'lifetime employment' and 'group-orientedness' have been used to characterize it. especially its social—psychological aspect.[13] The point is that the Japanese management system, which may have been an excellent one to Japanese people, may not be so to foreign employees in foreign countries. We already know some cases where Japanese-style managerial practice has met with strong suspicion and overt resistance of foreign employees.

6. Socio-Political Linkage Relationship

6.1. *Socio-Political Environment*

We are now in a postion to treat the socio-political dimension of the firm. In the highly advanced industrial society or the emerging post-industrial society of the US, Japan and several countries of Western Europe, managers of the firm have been forced to deal with difficult problems of a non-economic nature. The following are typical of such common non-economic problems of the firm, though examples are borrowed from Japanese situations.

(1) Acceleration of consumer protest. Consumerism has a long history, but it has begun to exercise a direct and tangible impact upon the firm's survival and growth, as has been evidenced in such recent cases of consumer protest as those against (1) 'unsafe' passenger cars and foods, (2) exaggerated and objectionable advertisements of cosmetics and medicines and (3) administered price policy of electric home appliances.

Managers of the firm have dealt with this sort of consumer protest by such devices as (1) grievance procedure, (2) diffusion of accurate information about products among consumers and (3) voluntary control of exaggerated advertisements and excessive packing. Managers of more progressive firms are considering the introduction of more radical devices:

(1) consumer representatives in the top management or board of directors
(2) direct discussion with consumers
(3) social auditing

(2) Environmental pollution. In Japan the court decisions of all the four big cases of environmental pollution were uniformly for the victims and against the accused industrial firms.[14] Since then a sort of national consensus has been given to the opinion that those firms which pollute our environment should not be allowed to exist unless they succeed in stopping their polluting operations. And the problem of environmental pollution in general has now become one of the most popular topics in Japan.

It is estimated that Chisso Corporation, the accused chemical company in the Minamata case, will need to pay approximately 40 million dollars to hundreds of victims of mercury pollution. And this company, which has long been one of the leading chemical companies in Japan, has its survival threatened because of this 40 million dollar compensation.[15]

As the opinion that 'pollution-spreading companies should not be allowed to exist' has gained a wide social acceptance, managers of an increasing number of firms have begun to adapt their behaviour to this new adverse situation in diverse ways. We first recognize a drastic and painful change in the managers' concept of a firm's role and responsibility in a society. A general trend in this change may be described as from (1) the traditional concept of maximum pursuit of its economic function and minimum observance of its social responsibility to (2) a newer concept of trading off of its economic and non-economic roles and even to (3) a more radical concept of carrying out its social responsibility first and then pursuing its economic function.

This emerging new concept of social responsibility is a basis for recent drastic changes in strategy, structure and operation of many Japanese firms:

(1) increasing amount of investment in pollution control (see Table 6);
(2) reallocation of factories from crowded urban to remote rural areas;
(3) closing of 'dirty' factories and entry into new cleaner industries;[16]

Table 6. Increase in pollution control investment of Japanese firms

Year	Ratio of pollution control investment to equipment investment (%)	Amount of pollution control investment (million dollars)
1965	3.1	82.50
1966	2.9	n.a.
1967	3.5	n.a.
1968	3.7	n.a.
1969	5.0	n.a.
1970	5.3	454.72
1971 (estimated)	9.1	n.a.
1972 (planned)	11.5	n.a.

Source: Kankyo-Cho (Environment Agency), *Kankyo Hakusho* (White Paper on Environment), 1972 edition.

(4) change in the input energy resources to reduce pollution;[17]

(5) creation of a special organizational unit to deal with environmental pollution problems;

(6) articulation and inclusion of an 'environmental goal' in the overall corporate goal system.

Traditional linkage relationship between the firm and its surrounding community formed by public relations policy and community relations policy is no longer effective. Managers of more progressive firms devoted serious effort to reestablishing a new linkage relationship which is more solid and direct. Such radical devices as direct discussion or confrontation with members of the community and independent inspection of the factory operation by members of the community are emerging from this effort.

Considering the fact that the content of pollution legislation has rapidly changed towards becoming more severe and comprehensive the firm must have access to accurate and completely up-to-date information in regard to pollution legislation. Thus, it is crucial that the firm has a communication channel with such authorities as are concerned with the development of pollution control policy: central government, local government and scientific research institutions.

(3) Anti-business attitude. In Japan we have observed several symptoms of a deep-seated hostile attitude of the general public towards the firm.

One of these symptoms can be seen in a sharp and widespread hostile criticism recently directed towards 'Sogo-shosha', large-scale and extensively diversified trading companies. Up to the immediate past they enjoyed a high reputation for their aggressive and opportunistic behaviour which contributed greatly to increasing Japanese exports, but are now provoking hostility from the general public by their same behaviour. The criticism says: 'their aggressive and speculative behaviour increases inflation in Japan and does not pay enough attention to the feelings and sentiments of the common people.'[18]

In Japan, as in the US and countries in Western Europe, prices of most of

Table 7. Decreasing share of votes (%) obtained by the Liberal-Democratic Party in the Lower House Elections

	May 1958	Nov. 1960	Nov. 1963	Jan. 1967	Dec. 1969	Dec. 1972
Liberal-Democratic	57.8	57.6	54.7	48.8	47.6	46.8
Socialist	32.9	27.5	29.0	27.9	21.5	21.9
Communist	2.6	2.9	4.0	4.8	6.8	10.5
Komei				5.4	10.9	8.5
Democratic-Socialist		8.8	7.4	7.4	7.7	7.0
Others	6.7	3.2	4.9	5.7	5.5	5.3

Source: *Asahi Shinbun* (the Asahi)

consumers' goods and services have shown a continuous rise in recent years. This inflational trend seems very often and too easily to be ascribed to the speculative behaviour and/or administered price policy of big firms. The point is that this type of oversimplified explanation is shared among many prople and is contributing to foster a hostile attitude towards business among them.

There exists a possibility of a drastic change in the political system of Japan in the near future. As is partly shown in Table 7, the Liberal—Democratic Party has been consistently losing its share of votes. This trend is most conspicuous in such big cities as Tokyo, Osaka and Kyoto. The recently intensified anti-business attitude among the general public may become a critical factor and eventually realize the dramatic shift of the reins of government from the hands of the Liberal—Democratic Party to the hands of the Socialist Party and the Communist Party.[19]

As there exists almost no room for compromise in regard to their policies between these two competing political powers, the change in political power would necessarily mean an abrupt and radical change. For instance, we must anticipate that the new government would carry out an extensive programme of nationalization of key industries. Thus, the political change means a real threat to the so-called free-enterprise system of Japan.

6.2 Socio-Political Transaction

In order to deepen our argument of the socio-political linkage relationship, we need to articulate in some detail what is meant by this linkage relationship. The firm cam be properly conceptualized as having two kinds of environmental linkage relationships: (1) economic (market) linkage relationship and (2) socio-political linkage relationship.

The socio-political environment may be viewed as composed of such elements or parts as (1) government (central and local), (2) consumers, (3) local community and (4) the general public.

What is the 'input' and the 'output' of this linkage relationship? The firm, to be able to exist and operate profitably in a society, needs to acquire and maintain the approval of its existence from relevant elements of the socio-political environment. Therefore the input to the firm is a set of societal behaviour rules which permits the firm to continue to operate profitably (Ansoff, 1971) in a society.

The firm acquires and maintains the necessary approval from the relevant parts of the environment:

(1) legal approval of its existence and operation from the government
(2) acceptance of its products from consumers
(3) approval of its operation from the local community
(4) social acceptance of its existence and operation from the general public.

In exchange for the input, the firm must offer output. The output to the socio-political environment is an 'image' of the firm which is socially legitimate and useful.

In the past, managers of the firm usually concentrated their attention upon the economic linkage relationship since they could take for granted, except in rare cases, the social legitimacy and usefulness of the firm. However, in an emerging new socio-political environment which is more or less hostile to the firm, the development of the image that the firm is socially legitimate and useful is the most urgent and at the same time the most difficult task that managers must carry out.

In Japan the firm enjoyed a favourable position of social centrality for almost 25 years after the end of World War II. One major contributing factor to this centrality of the firm[20] was the exclusive pursuit of the national policy of economic growth. The Japanese Government concentrated its energy on carrying out its economic-oriented national policy, since it was forced to abandon the ambition to become a big power politically and/or militarily.

In recent years the firm seems to be losing its social centrality very rapidly. Several reasons may be enumerated for this trend. The first reason is the fact that Japan has become a member of the affluent nation group from the standpoint of the GNP and *per capita* income. In the affluent society, the firm is likely to have difficulty in maintaining its importance, for many of the economic goods and services it provides are not so strongly demanded by people as in the past.

Although Japan has achieved an exceptionally rapid economic growth over the past 100 years, she is still much poorer than US and European countries in terms of the stock of capital. She is much hindered by the shortage and low quality of publicly provided goods and services such as the sewerage system, garbage-disposing facilities, parks and public recreation facilities, and public libraries. As is evident in the trend of diversification strategy of Japanese firms, more and more firms are going to be engaged in these fields. However their contributions would necessarily be restricted, and various non-profit organizations and institutions are expected to grow and gain much greater importance.

As is evident in the matter of environmental pollution by the firm, negative side-effects or external diseconomies of the operation of the firm have begun to manifest themselves sharply these days. The mere fact that Japan is a country of small size makes the situation really serious (see Figure 5, p. 115).

To sum up, the socio-political environment in Japan is no longer benevolent, and is becoming increasing hostile to the firm. Therefore development and implementation of a societal[21] strategy which works well in the new environment is one of the most urgent tasks for managers of the firm.

7. Conclusion

The basic tone of this volume is well described by its title. In strategic planning an emphasis is placed upon the task of finding out what is an appropriate shape of environmental linkage relationship for the firm. Therefore the nature of the problem-solving process is mostly cognitive and analytical. On the other hand, in the case of strategic management emphasis is shifted from making a strategic plan to implementing it. In other words, the task of strategic management is to carry out the strategic plan and actually realize the expected strategic adaptation of the firm. Therefore the problem-solving process tends to focus on behaviour variables and the bargaining or political process involved in the strategic adaption.

With respect to the product-market linkage relationship at the domestic level, we already have rather well-developed concepts and methods of strategic planning. They are generally known as diversification planning.[22] Thus, shifting research effort from strategic planning to strategic management may be valid.

However, with respect to other dimensions of linkage relationship such as an international and a socio-political dimension, our knowledge and skills of strategic planning are still poor and primitive. It is the author's opinion that strategic planning along these dimensions is among the most urgent and promising subjects for future research work. The present chapter is an attempt to make a contribution in this direction.

References

Abegglen, J. C. (1958) *The Japanese Factory*, Glencoe, Illinois, Free Press.

Ansoff, H. I. (1965). *Corporate Strategy*, New York, McGraw-Hill.

Ansoff, H. I. (1969). 'Toward a strategic theory of the firm,' In H. I. Ansoff (Ed.), *Business Strategy*, Harmondsworth, Penguin.

Ansoff, H. I. (1971). 'The concept of strategic management,' unpublished draft, February, pp. 11—12.

Ansoff, H. I. (1972). 'Management on the threshold of the post-industrial era', unpublished draft, May.

Anthony, R. N. (1965). *Planning and Control Systems. A Framework for Analysis*, Division of Research, Harvard Business School, Harvard, Mass.

Chandler, A. D., Jr. (1965). *Strategy and Structure*, Cambridge, Mass., MIT Press.

Farmer, R. N., and Richman, B. M. (1965). *Comparative Management and Economic Progress*, Homewood, Illinois, Irwin.

Gort, M. (1962). *Diversification and Integration in American Industry*, Princeton University Press.

Levitt, T. (1965). 'Exploit the product life cycle', *Harvard Business Review*, Nov.-Dec., 81.

Simon, H. A., and Newell, A. (1958). 'Heuristic problem solving: The next advance in operations research', *Operations Research*, Jan.-Feb., No. 1.

Steiner, G. A. (Ed.) (1963). *Managerial Long-Range Planning*, New York, McGraw-Hill, Chapter 2.

Steiner, G. A., and Warren, M. C. (Eds.), (1966). *Multinational Corporate Planning*, New York, Macmillan, p. 12.

Notes

1. The term 'strategic adoptive behaviour' of firms is defined in a later section.
2. This table draws heavily upon Chandler (1965) and Stopford and Nells (1972).
3. H. Igor Ansoff sometimes uses 'entrepreneurial' instead of 'strategic' (Ansoff, 1972).
4. S represents strategic decisions, O operating decisions and A administrative decisions, respectively.
5. A more complete description of Ansoff's conceptual model of firm behaviour can be found in Ansoff (1965, Ch. 11; 1969, pp. 11–14).
6. Ansoff sometimes uses 'competitive' rather than 'exploitative' (Ansoff, 1972).
7. The firm pays money to purchase input resources and receives money in exchange for products sold. In Figure 4 these counterflows of money are omitted to avoid unnecessary complexity of the figure.
8. Treated in a later part of the chapter.
9. One of the comprehensive treatments of the general environment of the firm can be found in Farmer and Richman (1965).
10. Important strategic problems of Japanese firms in regard to the socio-political linkage relationship are treated later in the chapter.
11. The Japanese Yen has practically experienced revaluation twice within the past two years and was revalued approximately 30 per cent to the US dollar. At the present time 1 US dollar is exchanged with 265 yen or so, whereas the same 1 US dollar used to be exchanged with 360 yen.
12. For example, the average size of US investment in Taiwan (Republic of China) is estimated at 2.85 million dollars, while that of Japanese investment is estimated at only 0.17 million dollars.
13. A classical work on this subject is Abegglen (1958).
14. The four cases are: (1) the Toyama case, (2) the Nitigata case, (3) the Yokkaichi case and (4) the Minamata case.
15. The financial position of this company for the recent period (Oct. 1971–Sept. 1972) is as follows:

Capital stock	$29.48 million
Sales	$173.91 million
Income after tax	$–5.12 million
(1 dollar = 265 yen)	

16. Such 'dirty' industries as the chemical and the pulp industry are among the most enthusiastic industries in pursuing the diversification strategy, while such 'clean' industries as the real estate industry, the amusement and tourism industry, the housing industry and the health industry are the popular targets for diversification as shown in Table 3 (p. 114).
17. Increasing number of firms are beginning to change their energy from heavy oil to liquid natural gas (LNG) and naphtha.
18. Representatives of the biggest 'Sogo-shosha' were summoned before a committee of the Diet and were questioned regarding their behaviour on April 11, 1973.
19. Roughly speaking, it is widely believed that the Liberal–Democratic Party serves the interest of business, and the Socialist Party and the Communist Party represent the interest of labour. The Democratic–Socialist Party and the Komei Party are heading for a more or less middle way.
20. For the term 'centrality of the firm' see Ansoff (1972, p. 10).
21. As the word 'social' seems to have a connotation of 'socialism', the word 'societal' is used.
22. An example of well-developed diversification planning can be found in Ansoff (1965).

STRATEGIC MANAGEMENT
IN A KIBITZER'S WORLD

For a company that wants to be known for strategic prowess and entrepreneurial style, there are three main challenges. First, and best explored, is the need to get management thinking in strategic, entrepreneurial ways. Attitudes must change so that those responsible for the future of the enterprise ask not only what it holds, but how it can be shaped. They must learn to search a diffuse, changing environment not only for hints of competitive threats, but for clues about new opportunities to develop. Problems and possibilities get sorted and sharpened into a concept of mission for the organization as a whole — a concept which takes into account the organization's distinctive talents, resources and potential. From the formulation of mission derive goals and strategies for action and disciplined plans that guide and focus assignments and operations to achieve the goals.

Once management has adopted a strategic perspective and built its plans, the second challenge is to assure organizational response. This means developing systems for feedback and control of progress as well as incentives to make sure that progress is made. The problems of orchestrating people and resources to carry out ongoing tasks pale in comparison with the problems of engaging people and resources for new tasks and goals. All efforts to move in new directions entail risks that important side costs and consequences will be overlooked, and that failure to consult and inform will breed resistance from those whose help is needed. However participative some kinds of planning decisions are, the essence of strategic plans calls for their endorsement and promulgation from top down, not from bottom up.

The first two challenges to strategic management have long been recognized. Many people have tried over the last decade to illuminate the issues, to interpret successes and failures from business and governmental experience, and to propose better paradigms for managing. Many organizations have invested heavily to build capabilities for strategic analysis and action. While much remains to be learned, great progress has been made. We have valuable new concepts, a growing store of transferable data and experience, some formal models useful at strategic levels, and educational programmes like Vanderbilt's that focus on building strategic perspective. We can point to increasing numbers of organizations that are committed to helping push the state of the art ahead.

The next required advance in the state of the art, the third challenge, is not yet well understood. It is the challenge of coping with an active, intrusive environment that not only presents enterprises with challenges and opportunities, but which is made up of individuals and organizations kibitzing and seeking direct influence on enterprises' strategic decisions. Each enterprise has a broad aggregation of people outside — call them *stakeholders* as Frits Haselhoff does in his paper — who have ideas about what the economic and social performance of the enterprise should include. These external constituencies — sometimes other organizations, sometimes diffuse collections of individuals, rarely a single powerful voice — are increasingly moving from such short-term concerns as product price and quality to initiatives on questions like environmental protection, overseas investment policies and employment practices which have long-range strategic implications. They can be quite specific in advice and demands about how companies set goals and how critical design and resource-allocation decisions are made.

For a long time, we have assumed that the views and initiatives of stakeholders could be dealt with as externalities to the strategic planning and management process: as data to help management shape decisions, or as legal and social constraints to limit them. We have been reluctant, though, to admit the idea that some of these outside stakeholders might seek and earn active roles with management to make decisions. The move today is from *stakeholder influence* towards *stakeholder participation*.

1. The Pressure for Strategic Intervention

A growing demand by stakeholders for strategic intervention should not be regarded as surprising. It is a corollary to the developing interest in strategic management within firms. Inside, managers have recognized that slow, steady refinement of existing policy and practice is not enough to keep pace with rapid changes in markets, technology, politics and social values. Such changes have forced probing questions about goals and difficult choices about what to emphasize as the distinctive focus or mission of the enterprise. Such questions and choices have been forced even more by the realization that no enterprise, whatever its size or rate of growth, commands unlimited resources. Strategic management, in short, has taken hold because it has seemed crucial to managers in a changing world for corporate survival.

Now consider the view from outside. There, too, people have found it inadequate to rely on a slow, steady refinement of existing patterns of influence, market response and regulation to protect themselves or improve society against the impact of corporate initiatives. They have questions about societal goals and corporate missions that they do not trust corporate managers to answer alone, and they see for themselves and society significant side-effects of what previously might have been allowed to pass as autonomous corporate decisions.

There is a new consciousness among stakeholders of the fragility of world social systems, of global resource limits, and of unanticipated outcomes of both private and public action. From this awareness come ideas and convictions about directions and limits for corporate action. Strategic intervention appeals increasingly to stakeholders because as people heretofore excluded from the management of economic enterprises they find participation in corporate decisions important for societal survival.

Much as corporations today may be dismayed by the trend, they have helped encourage it. Firms have worked hard in recent years through public relations and marketing efforts to picture themselves as sensitive, open and responsive organizations. They have invited newsmen, researchers and case writers in to look around when what they were doing seemed sure to win societal approval. They have, within employee ranks, encouraged men and women at many levels to participate in internal planning efforts.

Organizations which describe themselves as 'open' invite stakeholders to take them at their word. Organizations which like to 'rap' about what they are doing when things are going well can hardly close the door when their decisions get controversial. Organizations which train their personnel to be active and confident participants in decisions within have unwittingly helped prepare the same people to be active and confident kibitzers from outside for other organizations.

Thus, the requests from outside stakeholders for roles in making strategic decisions are not a passing fad. The requests are likely to grow in strength and variety, and planners and managers will have to adjust to a kibitzer's[1] world.

The kinds of intervention by stakeholders that firms can anticipate, it must be emphasized, are not necessarily predecessors to higher degrees of formal social regulation and control. In fact, one of the hopeful possibilities is that active and decentralized kibitzing on strategic issues, like active and decentralized responses in the markets to current products and prices, will lessen our reliance on restraining rules and laws. Regulation, even when wisely devised and sensitively administered, tends to be tied more to yesterday's problems than to tomorrow's needs. We need a behavioural theory for balancing the kibitzing process to serve societal goals that matches the economists theory which justifies preservation of competitive markets, in a way which achieves long-run social performance and, at the same time preserves kind of flexible decentralized control, provides for narrower dimensions of economic performance.

2. Mapping the World of Stakeholders

The domain of stakeholders for a corporation is difficult to map. It includes individuals, groups and organizations. It is usually described by labels such as 'customer', which imply a specific relationship to the firm. It keeps changing in composition and membership, and to the extent that events make corporations and society more interdependent, keeps growing in size and complexity.

Table 1. Ways of viewing stakeholders of the enterprise

Dimensions of the whole citizen	Relationships with the enterprise	Role choice vis-à-vis Strategic management
Sex	Owner/investor	Non-intervention
Age/generation	Customer/client	Balloting/ratifying
Race/ethnic background	Competitor	Kibitzing
Family, community, national ties	Employee	Intervening on decisions
	Supplier	'Antipreneur'
Socio-economic & educational status	Dependent on services	Referee/regulator
Professional & career identifications	Circumstantial consumer of by-products	
	Conservor	
	Taxpayer	
	Student/analyst/researcher	
↓	↓	↓
Identity, Values, Expectations, Associations Life Style	Satisfaction, Dependence, Expertise Reactive potential	Opportunities for participation Treatment in interactions

Questions of inclusion and questions of role are difficult to answer in purely objective terms because for some stakeholders, like parties concerned with the ecological impact of corporate actions, the 'stake perceived by the external claimants may not be acknowledged by the enterprise. In reverse, 'stakes' recognized by the enterprise, such as a customer's role, may not be acknowledged by supposed customers. Instead of a single, simple mapping, any effort to define the external constituencies of an enterprise is likely to produce multiple mappings from different perspectives.

Table 1 provides a framework from which some of the problems of mapping can be viewed. While we usually build maps in terms of role labels like customer, or competitor, we ought to be looking first at dimensions of the whole citizen. Few people or organizations can be confined to just one of these 'relational' roles, and it is hard for a firm to decide which of the relational roles is most important. This is not the age of the stockholder, for example, but an era when shareowners, individual or institutional, are little more than another kind of customer, buying and selling on the basis of expectations of capital gains and dividends. Neither, as some have proposed, is it the age of the consumer, a concept too specifically tied to the products and services an enterprise currently offers. It is more truly an age of the concerned citizen, of consumers and investors together in many cases looking out for themselves and their immediate selfish needs in part, but also trying in other ways to speak for broader community interests and for the well-being of future generations.

Looking at stakeholders in holistic fashion, one looks at dimensions such as sex, age, ethnic background, and community ties sociologists have long demonstrated are important. These dimensions do not tie immediately to relations with the enterprise. They do establish, though, the basic sense of identity; a life style; values, goals and aspirations; and patterns of affiliation and association that will determine specific roles and actions *vis-à-vis* business firms and other organizations.

The relational roles which develop from the more holistic dimensions of people and from contacts and experience with firms include more categories than we normally consider. Some of these categories, like supplier and employee, may be almost too comfortable and familiar, and may in fact be ambiguous categories for serious research on problems of stakeholder relations and intervention. Others, though, like involuntary consumers of by-products, express relationships of which we are newly conscious in an age when pollution has become one of the main topics for strategic challenges from outside the firm.

Stakeholders often relate to organizations in multiple ways: the owner-conservor, such as stockholders who start proxy battles to force greater investment in pollution control; the customer-regulator, such as the federal government which has tried to shape competition in the computer industry both by purchasing decisions and by anti-trust suits; etc. Of stakeholders holding multiple relational roles, some are fairly stable in terms of predicting which will dominate; others are less stable and much harder to predict.

It makes a difference whether individuals or organizations control their involvement in certain roles. Being an analyst or critic is clearly at the stakeholder's option. Being a customer, investor or employee usually is, but sometimes has involuntary aspects. Being a consumer of pollution by-products, however, or being a supplier in many situations often has a large involuntary component. Dissatisfaction with voluntary roles can lead to disengagement and withdrawal; the alternative in the case of involuntary roles has to include reaction and confrontation.

Relational roles have different time orientations, too. One problem inherent in most of the roles is that the occupants, like operating management within the firm, are constrained to think in terms of present relationships rather than future possibilities and needs. Thus, those within the enterprise concerned with strategic questions may have especially high interest in conservors, analysts, competitors and others who share a forward-looking orientation. Strategic thinkers inside must also keep an eye on potential stakeholders — new customers, new critics, etc. — as well as on those currently involved with the firm.

Out of their characteristics as persons and groups, out of the single and hybrid roles that they play, come the stances that stakeholders take *vis-à-vis* strategic decision-making in the firm. Since strategic awareness is probably lower in the populace at large than within many of the firms, many stakeholders simply continue as non-participants. Others may be content to express views on surveys and proxies, or through various ways to provide direct substantive inputs of ideas and opinions to the planning and decision-making process. There are some interveners whose challenge is not to specific plans or decisions, but to the autonomy and direction of the business system itself. These challengers, probably less numerous and less influential than many businessmen currently believe, might be labelled 'antipreneurs' as one businessman has done.[2] Still others may be able by assertion or by position in government and other regulatory groups to achieve power as referees, evaluating and ratifying or restricting strategic decisions.

3. Efforts at Intervention: Intermediaries in the Process

Strategic intervention can become a goal for either individuals or organizations; but although some individual voices like Ralph Nader's sound out with special vigour and power, most significant efforts at strategic intervention involve collective initiatives by organizations towards the enterprise. Successful intervention requires talent, resources and power to match what the enterprise itself can bring to bear. Thus, intermediaries between the stakeholder and the enterprise are an important part of the equation.

Whether by individuals or organizations, intervention usually has greatest potential for success if it can be made to seem to be on behalf of a broad constituency of stakeholders. This means that those that the enterprise is most aware of are likely to be claiming they represent many others. Such intermediary claimants for a voice in strategic management, though, are not always *representative* of broader constituencies. Many – to the confusion, frustration and sometimes damage of the enterprises they act against – are more properly described as *opportunistic*.

Intermediaries like those in the 'representative' column of Figure 1 take their leads primarily from consultations with the stakeholders they represent; and if those stakeholders are satisfied that intervention with the enterprise is not necessary, none is likely to be attempted. Intermediaries like those in the 'opportunistic' column of Figure 1 go looking for chances to intervene and for possibilities to rally stakeholders around their plans for intervention. Opportunistic intermediaries are in some cases purer instances of free enterprise – to satisfy egos, build power and earn profits – than the firms whose decisions they try to constrain or correct.

Some of these intermediary groups, like labour unions or even shareholders' groups, are not entirely external to the enterprises they deal with. Significant parts of their membership or constituent support may come from employees within the enterprise, so that they can act through a combination of external pressures for intervention and internal participation in both the political and analytic aspects of decision-making.[3]

In addition to the distinction that Figure 1 records between representative and opportunistic intermediaries for stakeholders, it is important to understand the different kinds of functions that either kind of intermediary can perform. The process of strategic intervention is very often a team effort involving different kinds of intermediaries.

With respect to kibitzing intermediaries, for example, communicators can both amplify and block their efforts. They can:

help kibitzers make their case and build support among stakeholders and within the enterprise;

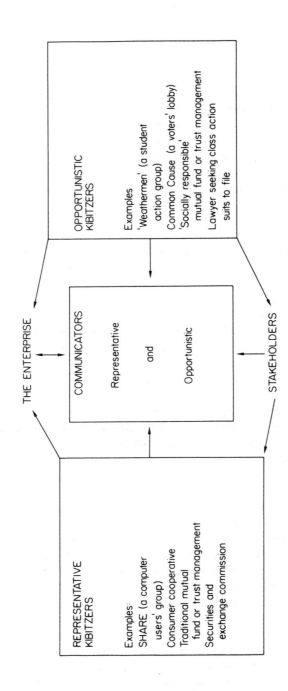

Figure 1. Primary lines of influence and interaction among intervening organizations.

help stakeholders carry a different message about their concerns and interests to the enterprise than an opportunistic kibitzer may be trying to convey;

help an enterprise build independent channels for dissemination of information and requests for support that a kibitzing intermediary, representative or opportunistic, may want to provide;

help enterprises and stakeholders to limit opportunistic excesses of kibitzers.

Kibitzing and communicating intermediaries provide ways of prodding referees into action under existing laws and regulations and of exerting influence in more flexible ways than laws and regulations may permit. Similarly, the referees serve both enterprises and stakeholders by removing some kinds of strategic intervention from a haphazard, *ad hoc* basis and establishing stable social guidelines and constraints so that enterprises do not have to be questioned and checked on each new decision.

Among the intermediaries, the communicators have an educational role; the kibitzers a probing and formative role; and the referees a stabilizing and routinizing role.

4. Challenges to Our Strategic Management Paradigms

I have not the space in this chapter, nor even with the space the confidence that I could suggest all of the ways and all of the reasons for modifying our paradigms of strategic management to include the reality of increasing external participation in the process. Rather than trying to offer answers, let me propose an agenda for exploration, an agenda that builds more than it should from my recent observations of business needs and less than it should from systematic review of the formal theory and analytic tools that might contribute to progress.

Too much of our current thinking about strategic intervention focuses on what enterprises should do and how they should respond when the initiative for intervention has already taken place. We have learned inside the organization that an important ingredient for the success of strategic planning is the effort that starts long before to build, train and motivate the organization to plan.

Preparatory work outside the organization is at least as important if businesses are to achieve the objective of making external demands for influence on strategic decisions more informed, more sympathetic to the 'business system' and more temperate in their impact on a firm's future options. What has to be done to build a greater awareness within management and stakeholders of the true dimensions of strategic issues in which they and the firm share interests? What is necessary to establish a higher level of knowledge and expertise about the problems that both enterprises and society face in making strategic decisions? How can one establish the levels of trust and credibility between firm and stakeholders that firms now understand they have to build between management and employees? How, against the realities of opportunistic action by many of the intermediaries with which the firms must deal, can channels of communication and influence be established with stakeholders to minimize the distortions and dangers that unchecked opportunism threatens?

Answering these questions poses challenges to traditional ways of managing.

One element in designing better paradigms is to find ways to broaden and diversify the daily person-to-person interactions that strategic managers have. Much to the disenchantment with business that threatens controversial strategic intervention comes not from people who are remote from involvement with business, but from employees, associates, neighbours and even members of their families who see options and consequences of decisions in different ways than the manager does. Other questioning coming from remote sources can be understood only if our basic premise about stakeholders — getting to know them first as whole persons rather than in terms of their visible relational roles to the enterprise — is right. The tradeoff in broadening these contacts is greater understanding in return for the diversion of scarce managerial time; the risk is that the approach to learn and to seek understanding will be interpreted as an invitation to kibitz, so that the pressures for outside participation will increase. Nevertheless, the record of the retail industry vs. the securities industry in keeping pace with changes in consumer views suggests that the investment is worth making.

A second element is the need to make stakeholders understand better how and why strategic decisions are being made, so that if they are satisfied that their interests are being considered they will not make or back spurious demands for interventions, and so that if they are motivated to intervene they will intervene in relevant and responsible ways. Greater stakeholder understanding, though, means 'opening the kimono' more: more willingness to have what the enterprise is doing and what it is planning to do reviewed and reported by journalists, students, historians, collectors of teaching cases for business schools and researchers. The gains in understanding and agreement by many stakeholders, especially to the degree that their views are now distorted by 'antipreneurs' as many businessmen fear, can be very great. Openness in any area of life is one of the key ingredients towards establishing stable attitudes of confidence and trust. Anticipatory reporting can also provide better protection against inevitable false or misleading charges that may be made than after-the-fact attempts at rebuttal.

But all this violates important business traditions. Privacy is not just seen as a privilege that society has granted to economic enterprises, but as a necessary ingredient for the operation of a competitive system, and as a necessary protection for encouraging managers and other employees to take risks that they might not venture if their actions were to be a matter for public scrutiny. Yet to the extent that misuse of the tradition of privacy is at the root of declining confidence and trust in letting businesses operate free of regulation and control, the tradition needs to be reconsidered. It is just possible that the best preservative of free or entrepreneurial enterprise in an increasingly interdependent and questioning society may be abandonment of our allegiance to private or secretive enterprise.

A third element in improving the preparatory climate for dealing with strategic intervention from outside the firm is the issue of repersonalizing the image that corporations present to the outside world. Again, as a matter of tradition and, to a degree, as a matter of law, corporations tend to choose low profiles on public issues. Even on disputes involving the conduct of a firm within an industry where stakeholders and opportunists may be mounting a major campaign for intervention, companies which have not been part of causing the problem will stay out of the debate and will not publicly take sides against the firm or firms which need to be forced into corrective action. Neutrality easily becomes interpreted as indifference or opposition; silence as insensitivity or incompetence.

If managers want to keep control over strategic decisions, they have to undertake the same kind of personal presentation of alternatives and some of the same kind of persuasion about their preferences outside the organizations they must do to keep control within. The work that the automobile and petroleum companies are now doing to regain strategic options on car design and pollution controls would have been much more effective if undertaken before pressures to pass laws had built up in Congress. Likewise, the multi-national corporations have been very slow in recognizing the need for strong public presentation of their position on direct overseas investment and on establishing manufacturing units overseas to supply domestic markets. These presentations must start more often than they do today from an understanding of the kinds of public knowledge and attitudes they are responding to.

As firms get closer to dealing with specific instances of intervention, they need better guidelines for handling the relationships and interactions that will be diffuse, political and non-hierarchical. Professors and reporters understand that they can get action against a badly performing employee by writing to the corporation president, but corporate managers do not often understand that you do not easily curb the errors or opportunism of reporters or professors by writing to the publisher or to the dean. Managers are hindered in their dealings outside by their overconfidence in the power of even superficial and loosely organized hierarchies; they are not well trained or well guided enough to seek instead centres and networks of influence.

They also need, in approaching specific situations, better ways to anticipate the kind of interaction that is likely to take place and the bases for disagreement or conflict that may emerge. Responsive action or attempts at conflict resolution, as research in this area demonstrates, depend greatly on the nature of the problem that is posed. It is particularly important, given current tendencies to resort early and easily to legal means for raising and resolving conflict, to seek alternatives that will respect the strategic needs of both the firm and of society better than reliance on legal proceedings is likely to.

A final problem which is real, but as yet badly defined, concerns the processes by which a firm uses media to keep direct relations with stakeholders and how, among both media and kibitzers, it defends itself against opportunists who will take advantage of the firm and stakeholders as well. The reality is that most media have to be opportunistic, as firms themselves are, to stay in business; for most are businesses, and with traditions of a free press which are important to maintain for other reasons, most are freer of public control than the enterprises they report about.

Their strategic interests in most cases depend more on giving an attention-getting, rather than balanced, view of the world if they are dependent on subscriber revenues, or on planning covering and sometimes emphasis to suit advertisers if they are advertiser-dependent.

There is extensive literature about the role that the press and media play in keeping government and business honest and on the role they can play generally in educating the public and helping to hold society together. There has not been the necessary research, so far as I can determine, to review the role of media as mediators in ensuring that stakeholders and enterprises work together rather than at cross-purposes at strategic levels in serving the long-term interests of society. The media have an important role in affecting stakeholder-enterprise interactions about strategic decisions, but to the extent that their influence increases, ways of evaluating their work and making them accountable for doing it will need to be strengthened.

5. Conclusion

This chapter represents a preliminary statement of problems, rather than a finished report of answers. It grew from a concern that we have only halfway developed the definition of what strategic management is all about. Strategic management has gained currency as a way to give enterprises greater leverage for progress or survival in a competitive, changing and unstable world. But managers in enterprises today must also respond to the concerns of all those outside the enterprise who have present or future stakes in the decisions it makes. Executives who understand what these stakeholders want can no more decide without consulting them and inviting their participation than they can plan on purely internal matters without consulting and inviting partiticipation from many of their employees. Strategic management, then, must wrestle with the desire of outside stakeholders for consideration and participation. It must be prepared, as well, to deal with more active outside challenges: initiatives by stakeholders on particularly important issues for strategic intervention. Responding to this broader view of strategic management means new efforts to map the domain of stakeholders in the enterprise and of the intermediary groups that provide linking channels of communication and influence. It means expanding the paradigms we have for strategic management and probably some fundamental changes, particularly towards openness about what heretofore have been private and internal operations, in the way that companies behave. Planners must get used to living in a kibitzer's world.

Notes

1. From Yiddish, a word well used by American card-game players to describe people who look on and offer unwanted advice or comments.

2. C. Howard Hardesty, Jr, in a speech to the American Mining Congress, where he was concerned with 'single-minded, persistent and totally myopic critics' of business.

3. The futility of trying to make sharp distinctions between the organization and its environment has been noted many times, but it is still not well built into our models for designing and managing organizations. It is a main theme from the time of Chester Barnard,

The Functions of the Executive (Cambridge, Harvard University Press, 1938) to an important recent paper by William Starbuck, 'Organizations and their environments' in M. D. Dunnette, Ed., *Handbook of Industrial Organizational Psychology*, Rand McNally, (forthcoming). A third source, looking at issues closer to the theme of this paper, is Jean Boddewyn, 'External Affairs: A Corporate Function in Search of Conceptualization and Theory' (NYU Schools of Business Working Paper, 73-16, 1973).

FEATURES OF STRATEGIC PLANNING IN HUNGARY

LÁSZLÓ HORVATH and LAJOS ZELKO

In this chapter we shall speak about some of the problems of strategic planning as they exist at the present time in Hungary. We do not have sufficient knowledge of the present situation in the other socialist countries to speak on their behalf, at least not in detail, about their problems in the field of strategic planning and strategic management. We feel, however, that the problems and approaches are quite similar, if not identical. Thus, what we say about Hungary should to a great extent be applicable to other socialist countries too.

1. The Main Characteristics of Social Ownership

First, we ought to speak about some of the basic factors which we think are substantially different in the socialist economies compared to those in the capitalist ones. We must emphasize, however, that what we are saying in this regard is our own understanding of the problems, and our conclusions must not be taken as representing the general viewpoint.

In Hungary, as in all of the socialist countries, the means of production — i.e. the fixed and working capital, together with the land and the natural resources — are socially owned. The major and most important part of the means of production is owned directly by society (state ownership), while a smaller fraction is owned by a group of people who usually also operate their means of production (cooperative ownership). Regarding the latter, government departments and the elected legislative institutions also preserve the right to interfere directly in the cooperatives' activities if this is dictated by the interests of society.

How does the social ownership of the means of production manifest itself? In the cooperatives, through the elected corporate leadership, or management. Furthermore, in deciding about basic policy questions usually all members of the cooperatives may, and are expected to, vote.

In the case of state ownership, all members of society are considered as owners. Their position as owners is reflected in their right to education, to work (that is why unemployment is officially considered as incompatible with socialism) and to participate in social legislation on different levels through the elections and by direct contributions (for example by making observations and putting forward suggestions during the process of working out the national plans). Furthermore, in principle, all adult members of society have the right and responsibility to take part in the continuous control of the companies, the different institutions and of the bodies of local and central government. And the broad and very active participation in this process of control is — we feel — the most striking proof of the fact that people really think of themselves as owners.

At the same time, the concrete and actual direction of the basic economic organizations — the enterprises and the cooperatives — as well as of other institutions rests with and is the responsibility of the managers of those organizations. The managers, who generally can be considered as experts in the field, have to take into account the opinion of the socio-political leadership and trade union organizations in making decisions, especially in personnel questions. On the other hand, this also means that although the basic responsibility for the activities of an organization rests on the director, or president, he and the management are able to partly share this responsibility with the above-mentioned persons.

The organizations usually do have a certain autonomy in deciding about their activities. The extent of this autonomy generally depends on the judgement of the party, and this judgement is basically influenced by one factor: what kind of division of the decision-making right between the organs central government and the managers of enterprises and institutions is considered the most effective and optimal from the point of view of society? For this reason the extent of the autonomy of the organizations may differ from time to time and from country to country. Indeed, the optimal distribution of the decision-making rights between the central organs and the management depends on many factors, and thus it may vary to a considerable extent. We think that the nature of social ownership allows and requires an attempt to choose the optimal solution in this regard, while this is not the case with private ownership.

This division of the decision-making power or rights between government organs on the one hand and companies or institutions on the other is expressed by the relation between the national plans and the activities and responsibilities of the economic units and institutions. In Hungary neither the short-range (one-year), nor the middle-range (five-year) national plans are considered as directives to the economic units. This is at present an apparently significant difference in relation to the other socialist countries.

And yet, the national plans are laws, enacted by parliament, and the fulfilment of these plans is considered as one of the most important indicators of a healthy national economy. But how can the national plans be fulfilled if they are not broken down into detailed directives on the level of the economic units?

First, it is obvious that in many cases the means of production — machinery, equipment, building facilities, and even manpower resources — are not interchangeable. Given these factors, most of the companies do have their boundaries or limitations concerning the expansion or production or the product scale in the short run. To implement considerable changes, usually longer time and capital investment are required. But the greater part of the profits, that is the investment funds, is centralized in the state budget. This way the most important investment projects are decided upon and are financed by the state. In addition, the economic units very often have to borrow and supplement their own funds in order to be able to make meaningful and really significant investments. The conditions attached to the loans in general ensure that the investment activities of the economic units are in accordance with the intentions of the central organs, that is, with the targets of the national plans.

Furthermore, regulations concerning the use of the funds provided to the companies are wide-ranging. They are more detailed with respect to wages and revenue-sharing, while leaving sufficient autonomy regarding research and development, as well as the definition of product scale and mix or the regions (e.g. the countries where the exports are directed).

The economic units (companies, cooperatives and some of the institutions) do have a certain freedom in their pricing policy too. Only a group of the products and services sell on prices fixed by the State Price Office (mainly raw materials, energy and transportation), while for a major portion of the products and services only price floors or ceilings or both are set, and for a third group of the products there is no control in general.

From the above-mentioned it is quite obvious that within the described limitations the economic units do have considerable autonomy. From the point of view of strategic planning for the companies, the degree of this autonomy is enlarged by the fact that — as we shall discuss in more detail later — they can sometimes influence the national plans also.

Another distinctive feature of the social ownership of the means of production is that nobody has the right to convert them into personal income. For this reason nobody can inherit them or the position of manager.

2. Aims of Companies

The factors described have a very important bearing on the values and aims of managements and collectives of companies or institutions.

Since in such an environment the interests of society, i.e. of the state, always have priority, the most important strategic aim of the management and of all the employees of a company should be to find and to establish the company's place and position in the long-range and middle-range complex national plans. (Middle-range national plans often cover five years, while the long-range plans differ according to the different fields within the economy and may cover periods of from 5 to 15 and even to 25 years.) In Hungary, which is a very small economy by present standards and mostly for that reason is a quite open one, it is very important for most of the companies to watch how their role in international cooperation and in the process of integration is envisaged.

It is extremely important for the management of companies and institutions especially to have good relations with higher political and government organs. This way in the process of working out the national plans they may be able to influence their main directions and final targets. By means of these good relations they may also obtain favourable treatment, for example get certain subsidies, investment funds and credits, or acquire advance knowledge of new changes in the economic regulators, and so on.

However, the management also have to live up to the expectations of local party and trade union organs as well as to the expectations of the laymen in the company or institution. Their expectations are more closely related to the personal income and to the fringe benefits the company can assure.

It is probably correct to say that without meeting all these requirements no management can successfully perpetuate itself for a long time. As the autonomy of the enterprises becomes more and more significant, strategic planning within companies is playing a greater and greater role in meeting those requirements.

3. How Long a Period Do Long-range Plans Cover?

Since the autonomy of enterprises has gradually increased from the early 1960's and was significantly extended in 1968, research work concerning long-range planning in companies began to receive more attention.

The first interesting results emerged in connection with the definition of the lengths of time long-range plans are prepared for. In the terminology of our economic literature the expression 'long-range' always meant a longer than five-year period, and sometimes it has meant a period of 20 or even 25 years.

The first supposition naturally was that the period covered by long-range plans should differ from industry to industry depending mainly on the life-cycle of the different elements and products of the system within the enterprises. Accordingly surveys were conducted concerning their nature with the following results.

(a) Employees on an average stay with a company for 12 years, with a probable standard deviation of ±2 years.

(b) The expectable life-time of machines and equipment in a company is 14 years, with a probable standard deviation of ±2.3 years.

(c) The product cycle of firms in the machine industry on an average is 11.2 years, with a probable standard deviation of ±3.3 years.

(d) The expectable time-period of changing technologies is presently an average of 9.1 years, with a probable standard deviation of ±3 years.

The most important factor, i.e. the product cycle, cannot be defined precisely, not even in fields characterized by the importance of the construction of the product, like the machine-producing industry. The reason for this is the fact that the notion of 'new' or 'outmoded' product cannot be scientifically defined. We can surmount this difficulty if, in the process of investigation, not individual products but groups of products manufactured by homogeneous technology are considered. More precisely, the notion of 'homogeneous technology' in the manufacturing of certain groups of products can be described in terms of the following factors.

The technical parameters of the products, the technology and structural materials needed to get different parameters.

Materials needed for the manufacturing of the products, their possible substitutes, and the way these materials are prepared and worked on.

Rational methods of production, and rational technologies of production of the given products.

Organizational methods ensuring the necessary changes or stability in the technical parameters of the products.

Circumstances concerning the sales, use or consumption of the products, the system of connected services and guarantees.

The 9.1 ± 3 years period applies for changes in the techniques as described. During this time significant changes may come about regarding the parameters or technologies of the products from the point of view of a company. The results of our studies show that these changes mainly depend on the following factors.

In long-range planning changes in techniques play a very important role. These changes spread gradually within an industry and from industry to industry. They are of international character and depend on the decisions of government organs or on the social system only to a small extent. These factors may have an inhibiting or a stimulating effect.

Changes in the aims of a company may also influence the product cycles of given groups of products. In the socialist economies these changes come within the jurisdiction of government organs, but the companies play a very important role in initiating and effecting the decisions.

The product mix and the techniques of a company are greatly influenced by the degree of its participation in the international division of labour. It may be necessary to stop producing certain products, but at the same time it may become possible even in small countries to develop the production of certain groups of products and to achieve a very important role in these fields even on a world-wide scale. If this happens, the large scale of production and the concentrated R & D efforts bring about great changes in the techniques and technology.

The technique and technology involved in the production of certain groups of products may be influenced to a great extent by social changes having a considerable effect on consumer behaviour. A good example of this might be a great state project to improve the housing conditions of the population.

The data reflect the situation in Hungary in and around 1970, with the exception of those referring to employees average stay with a company. Those data reflect the situation in and around 1964.

The conclusion from these data is that from the point of view of the typical enterprise a decade should be the period for which realistic long-range plans can be prepared. For such a period prognostics concerning changes in technology and demand for products can also be considered generally reliable.

4. Internal Conditions of Companies

As far as the internal operations and functioning of companies are concerned, we do not think that any important differences in the methods of studying and evaluating them can be pointed out compared to those generally applied and accepted. After an enterprise has once been established, certain cyclical stages follow each other with regard to one product or to a family of products (products made by the same technology).

Obviously, the different activities or functions take a different course in the consecutive stages (the progressive, the optimal, the degressive and the innovative stages) of the production-life of a product in a company, and these functions are not synchronous with each other. The following functions are usually mentioned.

Moderate extension of production with a continuous improvement of technique and technology, more effective organization and increase of productivity

Marketing Prognostics, regarding changes in technology

Research and development

To analyse these functions in regard to given products or groups is considered an indispensable strategy in the armoury of long-range planning.

It is especially important to examine in detail the effect of the different functions on the net income of the enterprises. After-tax income is not only becoming a very important factor in raising the wages and the fringe benefits of the employees; it may be even more important from the point of view of creating the necessary funds and of qualifying for the necessary credits in order to invest and thus keep the company technically competitive and capable of extension. To make a realistic appraisal of the significance of net income in the overall situation in Hungarian enterprises, it should be pointed out, however, that only a small fraction of investments are financed by using the funds of the companies or through competitive credit arrangements. The credit policy of the National Bank is highly selective, and in many cases the flow of credit is rigidly defined by the national plan. Nevertheless the long-range profitability of a company still remains a very important factor, affecting its long-range perspectives and the position of managements also.

5. Definition of Long-Range Plans

It is generally understood that the aim of long-range plans is in fact to design a system — and thus to design the future conditions of production and of the realization of the products — and for this reason the conditions, outside of the system, should already be set out when planning is taking place.

Long-range plans should probably be quite precise

(a) in defining the future structure of production,
(b) with respect to essential developments (investments) and the location of new production facilities.
(c) in designing the movement of cadres and the training of the labour-force.

Precision of the plans is probably less required:

(a) in the description of the economic position targets.

(b) in calculating the future profits.

(c) in defining the aggregate indices for the technical position and level.

(d) in the detailed functional plans.

It is generally accepted in our literature that the structure of long-range plans should be as follows:

plans of the main processes in the production of the leading products, plans of other, less important activities;

functional plans;

aggregate plans concerning the assets and the results (profits);

plans for the growth of overall company accomplishments.

6. Strategic Decisions

In order to be able to prepare long-range plans, the top management of the enterprise has to arrive at certain strategic decisions in advance. First of all, the management has to decide about the period covered by the long-range plan. It has already been pointed out that long-range plans in the socialist countries usually apply for longer time periods than in the capitalist countries.

Another significant distinction may be in their different position in relation to markets, and consequently in their marketing concepts. While in the capitalist countries companies strive to acquire bigger and bigger markets, possibly to weaken and finally to acquire their competitors, to diversify their activities and thus acquire a share in the markets of other industries, enterprises in the socialist countries cannot conduct such a marketing policy. They have their place in the hierarchy and priorities within the national plans. Competition among them is only a tool in the many-sided process of stimulating and forcing them to produce higher-quality products, to produce less expensively and more effectively.

Although the national plans define the scope of activities of the enterprises, they usually leave the management to make strategic decisions in the process of decision-making about the concrete product mix of the companies in the future. Those decisions may have very important consequences with regard to the future position and profitability of the enterprises.

The system of strategic aims has to be worked out too. We may classify these aims in the following groups.

(a) Aims connected with the existence of the company, among them the aim of continuous liquidity.

(b) Positional aims, for example the position of cadres, of the management, the younger generation of managers, future replacement of top managers and employees; *the size* of the enterprise compared to the size of the industry; position in the *field of technique and technology*; position in *economic potential*; position in the market.

(c) Aims of a social and human nature.

From the above it can be seen that the theory considers strategic decision-making or planning as a prerequisite for effective long-range plans, and thus for the effective operations of companies.

7. The Present State of the Art — in Practice

Economic and especially technological forecasting to our knowledge is much more developed in the Soviet Union and in the German Democratic Republic than in Hungary. At the same time, in Hungary it has become quite general to work out alternatives for the possible course of economic development. The dissemination on a national level of information about the results of prognostics and alternatives offers a good basis for enterprises for strategic planning. At the present time they usually make long-range plans, but in must cases the plans are not really based on strategic decisions yet. The methodologies in preparing the plans also differ greatly. Long-range planning in many cases is not done directly by the top management. In companies, too, the top managements prefer to acquire alternative concepts for development and try to choose the best ones from them.

FINANCING OF STRATEGIC ACTION

WILLARD T. CARLETON and JAMES V. DAVIS

1. Introduction

The fundamental proposition underlying and motivating this chapter is that strategic management and financial resources management do not bear a close enough relationship to one another – either in theory or in practice. In the academic literature one gets the distinct impression that, for example, financial resources will normally (or always) be available to support, profitably, a major new programme of market penetration. By the same token, strategic and behavioural considerations are never permitted to qualify or make ambiguous an otherwise 'tight' financial planning process.[1] The consequences of such high-level inadequate theorizing are serious, for they render some powerful intellectual tools at least partially non-operational in real management settings.

In this chapter we shall describe some of the ways in which financial policy guidelines typically are employed to constrain non-financial management choices. Next, we shall ask how efficient such devices are in coping with the generic problem of strategic management – planning for major changes in the firm's internal and/or external environment. By placing typical practices in a conceptual or modelling framework, we shall demonstrate that far more efficient possibilities exist. The overall thrust of the chapter is to suggest the directions in which contemporary financial management theory can be made operational for the needs of strategic planning.

2. The Setting of Financial Objectives

In developing the set of objectives and the set of decision rules to accomplish the objectives that comprise the firm's strategic plan, the firm's decision-makers will eventually come to describe the objectives in financial terms.

In selecting among the numerous financial descriptors that could be employed as objectives, managerial choices are limited by both internal pressures and external market forces. The desire to employ a few relatively simple measures for ease of communication is understandable. The imposition of perceived market constraints in the form of earnings growth rates needed to sustain or improve stock multiples or to assure the amount of credit available to the firm leads to the choice of other descriptors. Finally, loan indenture provisions frequently force attention to working capital position, debt service coverage and the like as objectives. Often there is no meaningful attempt made to integrate these various objectives and constraints into a coherent (i.e. economically meaningful) or even internally consistent whole.

In what follows we shall describe a method for improving the financial aspects of the strategic planning process by explicitly recognizing and dealing with the multiplicity of objectives and constraints inherent in the planning process. This can be accomplished in a manner acceptable to top management. First, however, we wish to examine some of the more popular financial descriptors and show why their single-valued use may lead to suboptimal results.

2.1 Target ROI

One of the most popular ways to describe the firm's set of strategic objectives is to summarize them in a target return on investment figure. The limitations of a target ROI may be substantial in terms of measuring the overall health of an organization. Since the target ROI will often be set above the current level of performance, the firm may be able to achieve the new objective only by substantially changing the risk characteristics of its portfolio of product-market entries, or by limiting the scale of its investment outlays (taking on only highest-yielding projects). This is so because in order to raise the ROI to the target level, product markets with ROIs and risk characteristics different from those the firm is already in will have to be entered successfully.

(The criteria by which the firm will select its portfolio of product-market entries are themselves unclear. The difficulties in establishing an appropriate balance between cash-generating and cash-using businesses, between entries that offer considerable growth and those that are entering the mature phase of their life cycle, are considerable. The limitations on management's ability to deal with diverse business situations reduce the opportunities to diversify away that portion of enterprise risk which is attributable to economic fluctuations. Considerable work remains to be done in this area.)

An alternative to the generation of new product-market entries, at least to a limited extent, is the continual reassignment of resources of various kinds to higher-yield segments of the firm. Adoption of this approach also changes the risk characteristics of the business, calls for a different managerial climate than exists in many firms, different management systems designs, etc. It is doubtful that a single measure will adequately describe this complex process.

The unconstrained pursuit of a target ROI will also affect aspects of the firm's financing strategy and capabilities in complex ways. The interest rates for short- and long-term indebtedness as well as lender-imposed side conditions may change as the perceived risk changes. Perhaps even more importantly, if the target ROI is selected without reference to implicit stockholder requirements and expectations its achievement may be accompanied by a depressed stock price or earnings multiple — with attendant consequences for acquisition strategy. Finally, while most students and practitioners of financial policy would agree that ROI targets are an important ingredient of good financial planning, imposition of an inappropriate ROI target as a single goal may ultimately lead to its use as a rhetorical or symbolic, rather than practical, objective.

2.2 Target EPS

The usefulness of setting a target EPS figure as a single measure of progress towards strategic objectives is also open to question. Unless care is taken, this goal may induce management to sacrifice opportunities with long lead times in favour of opportunistic entries or acquisitions with more immediate payoffs.

The desire to attain a previously announced figure may put substantial pressure on management to employ questionable accounting practices or engage in marginal diversification or financing tactics. The quality of earnings reported at various times by firms like Telex, Memorex, Great Southwest, Leasco and Occidental is suggestive.[2]

Aside from the obvious communication problems with individuals external to the firm, such practices may lead to unintended internal deception. There is some evidence that not all Penn Central officials were aware of the widening gap between reported net income and cash flow which was created by the booking of land development profits where little cash changed hands.

The emphasis on short-term earnings is reflected in avoiding dilution in earnings per share. A financial vice-president of TRW has been quoted as saying that 'the price of the acquisition must be such that it will not dilute earnings per share on a fully converted basis now or in the future'.[3]

2.3 Target P/E Ratio

Adoption of a target P/E ratio leads to the same problems. The pressure on acquisition-oriented companies to maintain a high P/E ratio can warp a firm in a number of important respects. The need to report 'predetermined' profits may make the sheer availability of a particular firm more important than synergy, the quality of the acquired management, or the prospects for long-term growth in profits.

A preoccupation with P/E ratios explains in part the recent increase in the number of firms buying back their own common shares. Such firms as Studebaker Worthington have been quite active in this regard. Whether this is the best use of excess liquidity, however, is a complex question.

As with the preceding two measures, the concept of a target P/E ratio is not equal to the task of adequately reflecting the various managerial objectives which make up a strategic plan. In the first place, P/E is a resultant of many forces, of which only a subset (EPS growth, rate of return on equity dividend and financing policy) can be completely or partially managed by the firm. Interest on capitalization rates fluctuates widely as a reflection of macroeconomic forces which are imperfectly understood (as well as forecasted). Finally, to the extent that the stock market's expectations for a firm reflect more than currently reported earnings, currently recorded P/E may be no more than an artifact (for example, the case of a firm with temporarily depressed earnings whose multiple rises from 15 to 40). In sum, we would argue that concern for P/E reflects a very legitimate management interest in stockholders' welfare — the value of their holdings. Stated as a summary objective, rather than in an explicit, longer-run context of intrinsic value, P/E is a non-operational objective.

3. Integration of Objectives Through Simulation — Current Practice

It seems clear that there is nothing inherently inappropriate about management concern for the kinds of financial descriptors discussed in the previous section. Quite the contrary: to the extent that strategic product, market and financial decisions are of consequence to the shareholders for whom they are undertaken, 'consequence' is recorded largely in terms of such descriptors. Our caution is directed against the pursuit of *any* unidimensional financial objective, especially one arbitrarily chosen. Once it is admitted that financial objectives are *irreducibly* multi-dimensional, however, it becomes imperative to view them in an integrative framework.

By far the most popular such framework is the computer-based budget compiler, or financial statement simulator. While these simulation models vary tremendously in scale and detail,[4] there are some features common to virtually all.

(a) 'Bottoms-up' approach. The inputs to these models include decisions and forecasts made at a variety of organizational levels within the firm, for example, divisional sales forecasts and desired capital structure. The computer is then used as an electronic clerk which adds up the effects of all these disparate inputs.

(b) Accounting rather than finance. The underlying frame of reference is a sources and uses of funds equation. All but one of the sources and uses are *inputted* to the computer, directly or indirectly; the last one is an output of the process indicating a net funds need or surplus for each year being planned.

These points are easily illustrated with the simulation model of a hypothetical firm; details are kept at a minimum in order to highlight important features. Consider the sources and uses of funds statement for Firm X, whose balance sheet is as below:

Firm X Balance Sheet

Current assets (CA)	Current liabilities (CL)
Fixed assets (FA)	Long-term debt (L)
	Equity (E)

Forming first differences, we have as our summary statement of financial flows between end of year t and end of year $t + 1$:

$$\Delta CA(t + 1) + \Delta FA(t + 1) - \Delta CL(t + 1) - \Delta L(t + 1) - \Delta E(t + 1) = 0. \quad (1)$$

Under the assumption that Firm X does not, as a matter of policy, ever sell new equity issues, the change in equity, $\Delta E(t + 1)$, must equal profits less dividends, or

$$\Delta E(t + 1) = PR(t + 1) - D(t + 1) \quad (2)$$

where $PR(t + 1)$ = after-tax profits and $D(t + 1)$ = dividends paid. Furthermore, profits are also describable as earnings before interest and taxes ($EBIT(t + 1)$) less interest ($iL(t + 1)$, where i = interest rate), all times 1 less the corporate income tax rate T:

$$PR(t + 1) = (1 - T)[EBIT(t + 1) - iL(t + 1)]. \quad (3)$$

If equation (3) is substituted into (2), and (2) into (1), we are left with the funds flow statement which forms the basis of a statement simulator:

$$\Delta CA(t + 1) + \Delta FA(t + 1) - \Delta CL(t + 1) - \Delta L(t + 1) - (1 - T)$$
$$\times \{EBIT(t + 1) - iL(t + 1)\} + D(t + 1) = 0. \quad (1)'$$

Note that up to this point we have merely been describing accounting equations which always hold true. In order to generate forecasts of future financial statements, all the elements of equation $(1)'$ have to be forecasted or planned, either explicitly or implicitly. The underlying driving forecast for most simulators is of sales. Inputting sales forecasts for all planning years together with ratios of the relevant operating expenses to sales results in derived $EBIT$ forecasts for each year. Next, capital requirements are also forecasted implicitly, predicated on sales and forecasted asset turnover ratios. Thus we have $\Delta FA(t + 1)$ produced as model output. Finally, current liabilities are usually expressed as a function of sales, so that $\Delta CL(t + 1)$ can also be known.[5]

The result of these inputs is that the funds flow equation becomes the algebraic sum of 'knowns' or 'knowables' ($\Delta FA(t + 1)$, $\Delta CL(t + 1)$ and $(1 - T)EBIT(t + 1)$, which are derived from sales forecasts) and unknowns ($\Delta CA(t + 1)$, $L(t + 1)$, $\Delta L(t + 1)$ and $D(t + 1)$, which are financial decision variables). How are these decisions (which by their nature reflect policy choices) produced as output of the statement generator? The answer is: by simple rules of thumb. Typically, the dividend decision, $D(t + 1)$, is inputted directly. If one does this, then equation $(1)'$ can be rewritten as:

$$\Delta CA(t + 1) - \Delta L(t + 1) + (1 - T)iL(t + 1)$$
$$= -\Delta FA(t + 1) + \Delta CL(t + 1) + (1 - T)EBIT(t + 1) - D(t + 1) \quad (1)''$$

or as

$$\Delta CA(t + 1) + \{(1 - T)i - 1\}\Delta L(t + 1)$$
$$= -(1 - T)iL(t) - \Delta FA(t + 1) + \Delta CL(t + 1)$$
$$+ (1 - T)EBIT(t + 1) - D(t + 1)$$

since $L(t + 1) = L(t) + \Delta L(t + 1)$. The right-hand side is the net 'knowable' financial source (if >0) or need (if <0) for Firm X during year $t + 1$. ($L(t)$ appears on the right-hand side because at the beginning of year $t + 1$ it is already known.) The usual rule of thumb is to allocate all of any net financial source to the current assets account, all of any net financial need to long-term indebtedness. More complicated rules of thumb can be employed, but they all share a common characteristic: they produce planned financial decisions independent (except in a very limited sense) both of the earnings outcome of the model and of one another.

Thus, to the extent that finance theory deals with choices (such as whether to increase dividends or retire debt), budget compilers contain little finance since they only trace out (simulate) the financial and operating consequences of choices already made.

The ever-widening use of statement simulators is testimony to their practicality. For purposes of this paper, however, they are valid but incomplete devices. In the first place, 'bottoms-up' modelling, by treating lower and higher-level management concerns jointly, can easily produce a 'trees *versus* forest' problem. In any iterative use of such a model, in which forecasts and decisions are varied to answer a series of 'what if?' questions, it is all too easy to focus on lower-level and less important inputs (for example, a single division's sales forecasts) to the exclusion of major corporate financial policies (for example, capital structure or dividends). Of course, financial models are created for many uses, including testing the sensitivity of operating results to different sales forecasts. On the other hand, most people seem to prefer to avoid being confronted by difficult choices — such as the tradeoffs among major financial decisions — and users of simulators can easily concentrate on forecasts to the exclusion of decisions. Additionally, the mere burdening of such a model with financial details is distracting to top-management planning committees concerned with major decisions — capital expansion, dividends and financing. More than one budget compiler has acquired details to the point of being describable as a corporate model, only then to be relegated to a planning staff as its toy.

The second difficulty with budget compilers is that they simply are not very efficient screeners of financial plans. This also is easily illustrated. Assume that Firm X tries to incorporate in its financial plans the following policy objectives (some of which may have originated with the firm, some with its creditors).

Maximum leverage, in the form of an upper limit on the ratio of long-term debt to equity of 100 per cent:

$$L(t + 1) \leqslant 1.0E(t + 1)$$

or

$$L(t) + \Delta L(t + 1) \leqslant E(t) + PR(t + 1) - D(t + 1)$$

but since

$$PR(t + 1) = (1 - T)[EBIT(t + 1) - iL(t + 1)]$$
$$= (1 - t)EBIT(t + 1) - (1 - T)iL(t) - (1 - T)i\Delta L(t + 1)$$

$$L(t) + \Delta L(t + 1) \leqslant E(t) + (1 - T)EBIT(t + 1) - (1 - T)iL(t)$$
$$- (1 - T)i\Delta L(t + 1) - D(t + 1)$$

or

$$\{1 + (1 - T)i\}\Delta L(t + 1) + D(t + 1) \leqslant E(t) - [1 + (1 - T)i](t)$$
$$+ (-T)EBIT(t + 1) \qquad (2)$$

with the decision variables on the left-hand side.

Minimum debt service coverage, in the form of a rule that $EBIT$ be at least five times as large as interest payments:

$$EBIT(T + 1) \geqslant 5iL(t + 1)$$

or

$$\Delta L(t + 1) \leqslant \frac{EBIT(t + 1)}{5i} - L(t). \qquad (3)$$

Minimum working capital ratio of 2:

$$CA(t + 1) \geqslant 2CL(t + 1)$$

or

$$\Delta CA(t + 1) \geqslant 2CL(t + 1) - CA(t). \qquad (4)$$

Dividends per share (hence total dividends, with no new equity) be at least as large as in the prior year:

$$D(t + 1) \geqslant D(t). \qquad (5)$$

Earnings per share (hence earnings) growing at least 10 per cent per year:

$$PR(t + 1) \geqslant 1.1PR(t)$$

or

$$(1 - T)[EBIT(t + 1) - iL(t + 1)] \geqslant 1.1PR(t)$$

or

$$(1 - T)i\Delta L(t + 1) \leqslant (1 - T) - [EBIT(t + 1) - iL(t)] - 1.1PR(t) \qquad (6)$$

with the expression simplified and the decision variable, $\Delta L(t + 1)$, on the left-hand side.

Finally, sources of funds equal uses, or equation $(1)''$ must hold:

$$\Delta CA(t + 1) + [(1 - T)i - 1]\Delta L(t + 1) + D(t + 1)$$
$$= -(1 - T)iL(t) - \Delta FA(t + 1) + \Delta CL(t + 1) + (1 + T)EBIT(T + 1).$$
$$(1)''$$

In order to attach numbers to these goals, or requirements, assume the following year t results and year $t + 1$ forecasted values:

$CA(T) = 100$	$T = 0.5$
$FA(t) = 900$	$i = 0.08$
$CL(t) = 50$	$EBIT(t + 1) = 225$
$L(t) = 450$	$C(t + 1) = 60$
$E(t) = 500$	$\Delta FA(t + 1) = 100$
$D(t) = 20$	

The consequences are:

$$\Delta CA(t + 1) - 0.96\Delta L(t + 1) + D(t + 1) = \ \ 40.5 \tag{1''}$$

$$1.04\Delta L(t + 1) + D(t + 1) \leqslant 144.5 \tag{2}$$

$$\Delta L(t + 1) \qquad\quad \leqslant 112.5 \tag{3}$$

$$\Delta CA(t + 1) \qquad\qquad\qquad \geqslant \ \ 20 \tag{4}$$

$$D(t + 1) \geqslant \ \ 20 \tag{5}$$

$$\Delta L(t + 1) \qquad\quad \leqslant 107.5 \tag{6}$$

Given that the above most accurately reflects Firm X's policy requirements, how is a statement simulator employed so as to give recognition to them? The most typical format, as suggested previously, is to fix $D(t + 1)$ arbitrarily, and perhaps $\Delta CA(t + 1)$ as well. Assume, for example, that $\Delta CA(t + 1)$ and $D(t + 1)$ are set at their lower limits (given by inequalities (4) and (5)) of 20. From the sources and uses equation, $(1)''$, incremental borrowing, $\Delta L(t + 1)$, will then be slightly more than 5. It can be seen that this amount is well within the limits given by inequalities (2), (3) and (6) of 124.5, 112.5 and 107.5, respectively. In effect, Firm X has planned current assets and dividends in a conservative fashion, so as to be 'safe' on its other goals. The treatment of boundary conditions on financial policies as targets is satisfying because it produces exact answers, but of course the benefits may be illusory inasmuch as an infinite number of $\Delta CA(t + 1)$, $\Delta L(t + 1)$, $D(t + 1)$ combinations will also be 'safe'. Worse yet, in more complex simulators involving several time periods, the failure to consider goals explicitly may produce simulation results which violate the goals — but without that fact being perceived.

In terms of the requirement of an integrative framework alluded to at the beginning of this section, financial statement simulators thus are partially successful. They do permit accounting integration of controllable objectives and forecasts — hence are quite powerful in tracing out the accounting consequences of hypothesized strategic decisions such as major acquisitions. What they do *not* do is provide a mechanism for assessing tradeoffs among financial objectives and constraints.

The operations researcher or academic in such a situation would instinctively call upon some constrained optimization technique. It seems to be the case, however, that those who construct computerized budget compilers usually eschew any attempts to let the programme seek decisions through optimization techniques such as linear programming. As Gerschefski noted:

The case-study approach [budget compiler], unlike linear programming, makes it possible to develop a hierarchy of objectives, with the weights of emphasis on these objectives left up to management. The model provides management with the information to help it decide what trade-offs must be made in determining weights of emphasis. (p. 64)

Unfortunately, an unguided 'hunt and peck' series of re-runs of the budget compiler may not easily (if at all) produce satisfactory financial plans. Moreover, such a process, conducted by a staff assistant with a highly-detailed model, runs the danger of producing a final plan which is either ignored by top management or else reflects too much of the staff assistant's own sense of policy emphases. This latter danger is a direct consequence of not embedding top management policy goals in the model itself. If financial planning methodologies are to be truly useful, they should invite the participation of top management by focusing on major financial decisions and providing some guidence in the 'hunt and peck' process. Budget compilers are powerful tools, but they have serious inherent limitations.

It would appear to be a natural step to incorporate into planning models both accepted criteria of normative finance theory (such as maximizing present value of owners' equity) and goals (or constraints) as described above. In fact, a number of commercial banks have done so, pioneering the way in developing large-scale linear programming models as aids to asset and liabilities management.[6] This innovation is as significant as that of the budget compiler. From the standpoint of model structure, however, this effort reflects a philosophy quite opposite to that of the budget simulators. Given a set of interest rate forecasts as the key input, the typical bank LP model selects a programme of asset purchases and sales, issuance of time certificates of deposit and the like for each of the planning periods. The selected programme is the one which maximizes profits while at the same time obeying management's preferences (inputted as constraints) regarding liquidity position, capital adequacy, and so forth. By requiring top management emphasis to be *inputted explicitly*, the LP procedure is then able to screen out undesirable (or even unattainable!) financial plans extremely efficiently. In fact, if the use of such a model is regarded as iterative — one still may wish to explore 'what ifs?' by varying, for example, minimum required liquidity ratios — then the procedure is one of deterministic simulation different from the budget compiler only in that for each run only best plans are produced.

The analogous situation for the Firm X goals described previously would exist if that company could make one of its goals overriding for purposes of speeding up the 'hunt and peck' process. With the relative value of, for example, $\Delta CA(t + 1)$, $\Delta L(t + 1)$ and $D(t + 1)$ thus treated quantitatively, the model would then find the best among possible combinations of these decisions.[7] Since each run is a simulation for given policy objectives, subsequent simulation runs could also be made under different policy mixes. The principal point in such procedures is that each run or solution utilizes all the constraints bearing on financial decisions *explicitly* and *jointly*.

Unfortunately, Gershefski's misconception that LP approaches to financial planning do not permit management to develop an 'hierarchy of objectives' is a widespread one. Operations research writings on linear programming models all too frequently focus on the mathematics of a problem, or on the characteristics of a particular LP solution. The fact that this tool can be a powerful aid to a manager by allowing him to evaluate the profit consequences of alternative (for example liquidity) policies gets lost in discussion of the apparatus. The misconception, further, is not easily removed if the model is so large as to require batch-processing computing. Then, as in the case of large budget compilers, more staff assistants and computer operators come between top management and the model. Result: slow answers to 'what ifs?', so that management loses interest in and control over the planning process; more details than management can absorb (trees *versus* forest again); finally, dismissal of the concept as 'black box' magic. Once again, the model becomes a staff toy — the fate of most bank LP models. Now it is true that bank LP financial planning models typically address themselves to a more restricted range of financial decisions and a shorter time span than most budget compilers. On the other hand, the facts that only a few banks utilize such models and that few industrial firms have demonstrated enthusiasm for optimization techniques in their financial planning suggest that implementation difficulties have been very real. Given the power of the linear programming framework to answer the same questions as budget compilers *and more*, it is at least an arguable hypothesis that misunderstanding and bad modelling strategies have been responsible.

4. Integration of Objectives Through Simulation — A New Framework

In this section we describe a modelling development which preserves the essential features of financial statement simulators, but broadens them so as to permit the multiple interactions between financial goals and constraints to be assessed directly.

In designing our financial planning model we had as our guiding principle that contemporary finance theory could only be usable if the mind-numbing effects of large model size, computer mechanics and the mathematics of linear programming were removed.[8] Accordingly, the following features have been incorporated.

(a) The structure of balance sheets, income and funds flows statements remains at the heart of the model. These are broken down into the smallest number of accounts consistent with intelligent focus on the key financial decisions top management has to plan for: capital investment, working capital, capital structure and dividends. Since top management's financial planning responsibilities are in this area, we do not want to allow tradeoffs among these decision areas to be obscured by a welter of lower-level details. We follow a 'top-down' rather than 'bottoms-up' approach. On the other hand, simulators are extremely useful as integrators of forecasts and lower management level decisions. We therefore treat as key *inputs* to our model those items which are the most critical *outputs* of most statement simulators: operating earnings (*EBIT*) and capital expenditures (ΔFA) through time. Our model and a company's budget compiler can thus be thought of as hierarchical structure: top-down policy model built upon the output of a bottoms-up forecasting model.

(b) Outputs of the model are the major financial decisions (dividends, working capital, financing) of the corporation over the planning years. These are determined simultaneously using linear programming techniques. Thus, for example, not only is the effect of 1972's planned dividends on 1972's working capital position accounted for, but also the effect of both on 1973's borrowing slash debt repayment is explicitly felt. An intuitive grasp of the interplay of such choices is made more possible by suppressing non-essential accounting details.

(c) No model's output can ever be more valid than its input. There are three kinds. The first comprises forecasts of the economic environment, including such matters as profit margins, interest rates and industry P/E ratios (or costs of equity capital). The second includes legal restrictions on financial decisions, such as given by the minimum 'times interest earned' provision in a loan agreement. The third incorporates management policy requirements such as minimum annual EPS growth rate, upper limits on debt to total capitalization, etc.[9] As a philosophical note, financial planning is a meaningful and difficult task precisely because the first two kinds of input (forecasts and legal constraints) cannot be ignored except at peril to the financial health of the firm. The third set of inputs reflects management's attempts to cope with the first two. For a given set of 'best guesses' as to future economic conditions, known legal requirements and top management policy requirements, the model produces a 'best' financial plan as solution to a linear programme, but for another set of inputs another 'best' plan also results. Again, the reason for holding details to a minimum is to encourage top management to explore, through a series of computer runs, what the likely tradeoffs are between major policy requirements. For example, what are the consequences over time of simultaneously holding down allowed dividend increases and reducing debt/equity limits? (See Figure 1.)

(d) The corporate objective we normally employ in the model is the conventional cost of equity capital one: the 'best' plan is the one which, while staying within the limits permitted by the three kinds of inputs, makes the present value of owner equity as large as possible.[10] In order to test the sensitivity of plans even to this objective, however, we have included other possible definitions of 'best', as, for example, maximizing cumulative earnings over the planning years. In terms of concerns expressed at the outset of this paper – that a *single* financial descriptor not be utilized as the target by which strategic decisions be evaluate 1 – our model perhaps requires additional explanation. What the programming framework does is to express *all but one* of management's requirements for financial descriptors in terms of minimum and/or maximum acceptable outcomes (for example, the EPS target becomes 'at least 10 per cent per year' instead of 'equal to 10 per cent per year'). The remaining requirement becomes the one which is maximized – but *only* to the extent that the result is consistent with achievement of the other objectives. Mathematically, the search for a financial plan which meets multiple objectives

Inputs

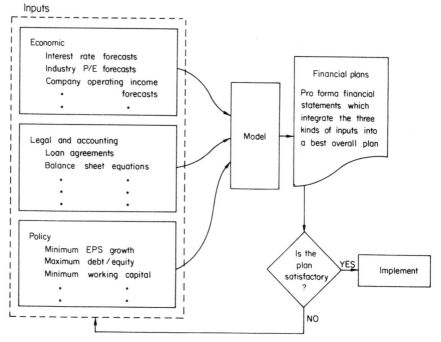

Figure 1. Structure of optimizing financial planning model.

could be equally well met if some other single objective were used to drive this constrained simulation.

(e) Ultimately, none of the above procedures will 'work' unless management can get answers to revised inputs rapidly, and in recognizable form. Therefore our model was programmed for a time-sharing computer with the option available of using a conversational mode. The user thus has to know virtually nothing about computers. His inputs are typed responses to such questions as 'Is a minimum annual growth rate in earnings per share required? The outputs are the familiar financial statements and ratio analyses. All the mathematics is 'black-boxed.' (See Figures, 2 and 3.)

We employ time-sharing deliberately, on the grounds that it can encourage the kind of iterative use most desirable for our (or any) policy model. On the other hand, the debate over time-sharing *versus* batch processing has been going on for some time, and nothing we say here will resolve the issue. We do quote, with approval, however, some recent thoughts by H. Martin Weingartner.[11]

Generally, the argument turns on whether high level personnel will ever sit down at the console of a time-shared computer and interact with the computer on their own, or whether the process will continue to depend on intermediaries. I believe this is a false issue. The real question is whether the decision-maker will interact with a *model*, with the model becoming an extension of his own information-processing capability; or whether he will utilize the output as he would a fast-turnaround batch processor. (p. 9)

Figure 2.

CDD INC

LONG RANGE FINANCIAL PLANNING MODEL

INPUT ALL RATIOS RATES AND PERCENTAGES IN DECIMAL NOTATION, AND BALANCE SHEET AND INCOME-STATEMENT ITEMS IN THOUSANDS OR IN MILLIONS OF DOLLARS OR SHARES.

SECTION 1

THIS SECTION REQUESTS INFORMATION FROM YOUR FINANCIAL STATEMENTS AS OF THE END OF YOUR LATEST COMPLETED FISCAL YEAR.

   1.01 INPUT THE LATEST COMPLETED FISCAL YEAR (E.G., 1970)?
1971

  INPUT BOOK VALUE OF:
   1.02 CURRENT ASSETS? 100
   1.03 BASE NET FIXED ASSETS? 800
   1.04 OTHER ASSETS? 100

     .   .
     .   .
     .   .

  INPUT:
   4.01 MINIMUM AVERAGE ADJUSTED 'TIMES INTEREST EARNED'
      RATIO? 5, 5, 5, 5, 5
   4.02 MINIMUM AMOUNT OF WORKING
      CAPITAL? 50, 55, 60, 60, 60
   4.03 MINIMUM WORKING CAPITAL RATIO? 1, 1, 1, 1, 1
   4.04 MAXIMUM CUMULATIVE DIVIDEND PAYOUT
      RATIO?.65,.65,.65,.65
   4.05 UPPER LIMIT ON LONG TERM DEBT TO EQUITY
      RATIO? 1, 1, 1, 1, 1

     .   .
     .   .
     .   .

  INPUT:
   3.01 NET FIXED ASSETS, ON THE BASIS OF NONDISCRETIONARY
      INVESTMENT, PLUS CAPITAL REQUIREMENTS TO
      SUPPORT FORECASTED
      INTERNAL SALES? 810, 820, 830, 840, 850
   3.02 OTHER ASSETS? 100, 100100, 100, 100, 100

If one thinks of a planning model's use as a one-shot affair, then it is difficult to quarrel with the advantages of a batch-processing format. If the best form of this activity is both iterative and interactive (for example, with the altering of constraints), then it seems to us that the hardware set up should be capable of providing answers while the manager is most interested in the problems. The question of who is to sit at the teletype is secondary.

Figure 3.

	1971	1972	1973	1974	1975	1976
INTEREST COVER/YEAR	5.98	5.20	6.06	9.54	11.16	13.06
ADJ AVE TIE		5.66	5.71	6.66	8.57	11.18
D/E: LONG TERM DEBT	0.60	0.86	0.85	0.83	0.78	0.71
TOTAL DEBT	0.70	0.92	0.90	0.87	0.82	0.75
WORK CAP RATIO	1.00	1.56	1.55	1.55	1.55	1.55
ANN DIV PAYOUT RATIO	0.45	0.44	0.45	0.41	0.42	0.38
EPS NO STK DIV	$1.29	$1.65	$1.89	$2.41	$2.70	$3.02
EPS WITH STK DIV	$1.29	$1.60	$1.79	$2.20	$2.40	$2.60
EPS FULLY DILUTED	$1.29	$1.60	$1.79	$2.20	$2.40	$2.60
DPS NO STK DIV	$0.60	$0.72	$0.85	$0.98	$1.13	$1.16
DPS WITH STK DIV	$0.60	$0.70	$0.80	$0.90	$1.00	$1.00
VAL/SHR NO STK DIV		$32.18	$34.61	$37.14	$39.77	$42.51
VAL/SHR INC STK DIV		$31.25	$32.62	$33.98	$35.33	$36.67
SHARES NO STK DIV	50.0	50.0	50.0	50.0	50.0	50.0
SHARES INC STK DIV	50.0	51.5	53.0	54.6	56.3	58.0
COST OF EQUITY		10.0%	10.0%	10.0%	10.0%	10.0%
ROI	25%	25%	25%	25%	25%	25%
TAX VAL NET FIX ASS.	$700	$866	$943	$1,034	$1,119	$1,197
EPS GROWTH RATE		24.3%	11.4%	23.3%	9.1%	8.3%
DPS GROWTH RATE		16.7%	14.3%	12.5%	11.1%	0.0%

5. Conclusion

Practical experience with our planning model thus far suggests that, aside from convenience, the following major benefits are available to a degree not possible with the other approaches to financial planning discussed earlier.

(a) Major prospective changes in the environment have a nasty way of impinging on both sides of the balance sheet, on the income statement and on the legal obligations of the firm. Mergers are, of course, the most obvious example. The effects are thus complex, and can only be evaluated by tools which preserve all of the ramifications. Budget compilers and sequential rules of thumb do not meet the test. We have found our model to be a very powerful analytical device for evaluating such complex 'what ifs?'.

(b) The strategy of building around the needs of the ultimate user — the top management financial planning group — yields handsome payoffs. Because of the perceived complexity of financial choices, there is often a tendency for major financial policies and targets to remain unquestioned and defended mostly by executive rhetoric. We have found our user-oriented model to be useful for the probing of simultaneous changes in policies.

(c) Computer experiments are, after all, cheaper than real world experiments. One of the most valuable results of our model's use is the occasional finding that — whatever corporate objective is employed — no plan is feasible. Nothing is more chastening than the realization that an asset, expansion plan and EPS growth requirement which look reasonable for a couple of years into the future may entail a financial condition still later which will require the rewriting of a loan agreement under distress.

Notes

1. See, for example, Ansoff, H. I. *Corporate Strategy* (Harmondsworth, Penguin, 1968), Hilton, P., *Planning Corporate Growth and Diversification* (New York, McGraw-Hill, 1970), Steiner, G. A., *Top Management Planning* (New York, Macmillan, 1969) and Ackoff, R. L., *A Concept of Corporate Planning* (New York, Wiley-Interscience, 1970).

2. Briloff describes some of the more memorable disasters. Briloff, A. J., *Unaccountable Accounting* (New York, Harper and Row, 1972).

3. Gillette, C. G., 'How buyer and seller look at a merger', in J. L. Harvey and A. Newgarden, *Management Guides to Mergers and Acquisitions* (New York, Wiley-Interscience, 1969), p. 97.

4. The plethora of models developed by First National City Bank of New York, a major innovator in this field, as well as George Gerschefski's efforts, come readily to mind. See Gerschefski, G., 'Building a corporate financial model', *Harvard Business Review*, July-August 1969, 61. Also, see Warren, J. M., and Shelton, J. P., 'A simultaneous equation approach to financial planning', *Journal of Finance*, xxvi, No. 5, December 1971, 1123.

5. In large models, sales forecasts, operating ratio forecasts and the forecasts of financial variables derived from these are usually generated in a decentralized — or 'bottoms-up' — fashion.

6. See Cohen, K. J., and Hammer, F. S., 'Linear programming and optimal bank asset management decisions', *Journal of Finance*, May 1967, 147; also Chervany, N. L., Strom J. S. and Boehlke, R. L., 'An operations planning model for the Northwestern National Bank of Minneapolis', in Schreiber, A. N. (Ed.), *Corporate Simulation Models, University of Washington*, 1970, 208–63; also, Komar, R. I., 'Developing a liquidity management model,' *Journal of Bank Research*, Spring 1971, 38.

7. The goals for Firm X — relationships $(1)''$, (2), (3), (4), (5) and (6) — are linear combinations of financial decision variables. If the financial objective which is accepted as most important for Firm X's planning is also describable of a linear combination of the decision variables, then linear programming can be used. In fact, as will be described below, goals such as maximizing present value of owner equity or maximizing cumulative earnings per share can be so described, although the algebra occasionally gets tedious. Consequently, and as will be seen, plans of companies like Firm X can easily be generated as financial statement simulations — but simulations in which all the policy objectives are recognized.

8. An early version of the model, programmed for demonstration purposes, is described in Carleton, W. T., 'An analytical model for long range financial planning', *Journal of Finance*, May 1970, 291. For practical application, that programme has been made both more general and tailored to corporation specification, and a number of minor technical errors have been corrected. The general framework remains the same, however. As a practical note, by far the greatest amount of computer programming effort has been devoted to making the model non-OR-user-oriented, as described below. We can testify that there is no such thing as a general-purpose, computerized corporate model, immediately useful to all firms!

9. It is useful to note again that the algebraic structure of the model is essentially the same as in Firm X's constraints, although more tedious because several years have to be described all at once.

10. This objective can be written as:

$$\frac{PV(0)}{N(0)} = \sum_{t=1}^{n} \frac{D(t)}{N(t) \prod\limits_{\tau=1}^{n} (1 + k_\tau)} + \frac{PV(n)}{N(n) \prod\limits_{\tau=1}^{n} (1 + k_\tau)}$$

where $N(t)$ = number of shares outstanding in year t; k_τ = period τ cost of equity capital (inputted directly or derived from a series of questions about industry P/E ratios, etc.); $PV(0)$ = solution value present value to be maximized; and $PV(n)$ = horizon year value (derived in terms of forecasted post-horizon — or long-term — opportunities). $PV(0)/N(0)$ is thus non-linear, because of the presence of $N(t)$ terms in the denominators, changes in which reflect equity financing — a decision variable. $PV(0)/N(0)$ can finally be encoded in the computer programme in the form

$$\frac{PV(0)}{N(0)} = \sum_{t=1}^{n} a(t)D(t) + a(n)PV(n) + \sum_{t=1}^{n} b(t)Y(t)$$

where $a(t)$ and $b(t)$ are fixed coefficients and $Y(t)$ = new equity in year t. This result is linear in the decision variables, which is what permits LP techniques to be exploited.

11. 'What lies ahead in management science and operations research in finance in the seventies', TIMS Interfaces, 1, No. 6, 5.

STRATEGIC IMPLICATIONS FOR ORGANIZATIONAL DESIGN

H. RAYMOND RADOSEVICH

1. Introduction

In the last decade, many organizations (particularly US industrial firms) adopted a managerial concern and subsequently a process for first, long-range planning and then, strategic planning. In many of these organizations, the process of planning strategy remained a top-management, primarily intellectual activity which produced 'plans' but little strategic activity. More recently, the concept of strategic management has been advanced by Ansoff (1972). This concept enlarges the managerial process of strategic planning to include the development of organizational and managerial capabilities to implement strategic activities.

Somewhat related concepts of innovation in organizations have been widely discussed in recent years. Writings by Shepard (1967), Drucker (1971), Labovitz (1971) and Maass (1972) are examples of the literature which describe the innovative organization and how it may be accomplished. These writings about innovation in organizations provide useful insights for elaborating the concept of strategic management but are incomplete for one very important reason. They virtually ignore the necessity of efficiently exploiting the current 'business' of the organization if it is to remain viable while reposturing itself to pursue innovations. Thus strategic management is concerned with both effectiveness (how much and what innovation is necessary to accomplish objectives) and efficiency (maximizing the value added to services and products returned to the environment in exchange for more resources).

In a rather simplistic explanation of the relationship between organizational strategy and structure in the US business firm, Chandler (1962) describes a sequential pattern of environmental changes causing revisions of strategy which result in new organizational structures. In the elaborate case studies in his book, Chandler reveals a very lengthy process of strategy revision and its accommodation in the reorganizing process. A successful management practice in the first half of the twentieth century was the sequence of: (1) initial definition of a new business, (2) organization of resources to pursue the new strategy and (3) the efficient, steady-state exploitation of the business whose product life-cycle was measured in decades. The sequence of substantially modifying strategy and then exploiting the new posture resulted in alternate periods of change and steady-state operations. In the last two decades, managements following the earlier practices discovered that the periods of steady-state operations seemed to be shrinking. The recovery of large investments made during periods of strategic change that are required to generate a new business potential became increasingly more difficult. Industries that operated a large-project mode invested heavily in development of new products and businesses and were surprised when the expected lengthy production runs never materialized. Many notable examples can be found in the post-war defence industries.

In this environment, managements became increasingly concerned with issues like shrinking product life-cycles, technological obsolescence and schedule and cost reductions of development. The panaceas became long-range planning and project or matrix organization structures.

For the last decade, writers have continued to document and predict increasing rates of change and turbulence in the environment. Well-known examples are Ansoff (1965), Drucker (1969) and Toffler (1970). The study of organization change has left the private domain of social scientists and imbued the literature of management. Empirical studies upon which management theories and concepts were developed were almost exclusively performed on change phenomena occurring in highly programmed organizational tasks. Findings there were very difficult to generalize to strategic change. Indeed, many of those who currently write on the topic of organizational change do not concern themselves with *what* is changing. Durant in the conception of General Motors managed a change process entirely different from the later one managed by Sloan. Before discussing organization structures which promote innovation, it is necessary to consider the different kinds of innovation or change which are needed in modern and future organizations.

2. Strategic Posture Vis-à-vis Exploitation Potential Innovation

There are many different dimensions of innovation which help diagnose the resultant impact upon the firm. The 'size' of the innovation is an obvious dimension and the one upon which the 'age of discontinuity' writings are based. Annual model changes in most manufacturing firms represent minor innovations which require relatively little managerial attention and minor modification of organizational capabilities. A new venture which redeploys a substantial portion of organization's resources in a new industry or 'business' is the 'size' of innovation with which strategic management is most concerned.

Within innovations that represent large discontinuities in the activities of an organization, a dichotomy exists in relationship to the organizational strategy. At one extreme of this dichotomy is strategic posture (S-P) innovation which results in new linkages to the environment and new potential for exchanges of resources for goods and services. That is, S-P innovation culminates in a substantially new strategic posture. Examples of this type of innovation would be the introduction of a radically new product line, the switch from physical product to service industries, or perhaps a national firm moving to a multi-national position. The leadership for such an innovation is typically entrepreneurial in nature, with great promotional skills. In the life of General Motors, Durant provided this kind of leadership.

The second type of innovation is exploitation potential (E-P) innovation where the strategy is set, the potential products, markets and technologies are in place, but innovation is necessary to ensure efficiency. The form E-P innovation may take includes changes in management systems, organization structures, process technology, or perhaps capital substitution for labour through automation. Most often E-P innovation is a combination of many of these factors. The management orientation or leadership style which fosters E-P innovation emphasizes a drive for routine, efficiency, and cost reduction. In the life of General Motors, the Sloan era took a virtually bankrupt organization with a good strategic posture and changed it to a financially viable, efficient operation within an initial period of relatively stable strategy. In his book, Chandler very meticulously describes the organizational needs, leadership skills, etc., for two distinct periods of organizational change. These two periods correspond to an initial S-P and a following E-P innovation.

3. Investment Vis-à-vis Divestment Innovation

Whether or not there is a limiting size beyond which organizations cannot be efficient is an issue raised periodically with respect to both public and private sector institutions. Yet for many industrial firms, volunteer organizations and government agencies, the growth ethos is consistently adhered to. Viability and self-perpetuation are almost synonymous with continuing growth. In dynamic, growing markets, stability represents declining market share and competitive position. However, in the environment most frequently predicted, a change of innovation ethos would seem to be more conducive to organizational health and viability. Decreasing product life-spans and further differentiation and segmentation of markets, as examples of environmental trends, suggest that organizational success will depend more upon rapid and constant redeployment of resources and strategic reposturing rather than accumulation of resources and growth.

Whether the organization intends to promote innovation as a basis for growth or in response to increased dynamics of the environment is an important question in terms of another dimension of innovation. This additional dimension of innovation recognizes that strategy can substantially be altered by dropping current activities as well as adding new activities. If an organization is going to promote wide-scale S-P innovation, the redeployment of resources may require initial and continuing divestment. Divestment innovation is one of the most difficult and poorly practised processes of organizational change. Few organisms are effective at voluntarily removing active portions of their anatomies, even if these portions are dysfunctional. Several firms, however, are starting to experiment in novel ways with this type of innovation.

In many of the large industrial firms of the United States, large portions of the resources are invested in mature product/markets. These firms are often characterized by the accumulation of large amounts of organizational slack in terms of cash reserves, personnel and even technology. A substantial improvement in the effectiveness of these organizations cannot depend entirely on investment innovation because the relative proportion of these new activities will still be small. Even if the investment innovation is highly successful, the inertia of the mature business when averaged in with the higher-performance new business will cause a very modest mean performance. By including divestment innovation, the great mass of lower-performance activities can be reduced and the resources committed to these activities redeployed towards greater organizational effectiveness.

Divestment innovation, to be true S-P innovation, must be carefully planned and managed to take place in a variety of forms. These forms include selling ideas, patents, physical facilities or entire businesses. Partial divestment may be accomplished by licensing, joint ventures, technical assistance, or even management assistance contracts. Considering all these alternatives, a much wider scope of divestment innovation can be defined to include activities and resources overlooked by most managements. Fronko (1971) describes the actions of a small, experimental group within General Electric whose perspective on divestment innovation includes several modes not commonly employed by other organizations.

The remainder of this chapter will address the structural issues involved in promoting innovation — both S-P innovation (including investment and divestment) and E-P innovation — while simultaneously exploiting the current business potential in as efficient a manner as possible.

4. Organizing Principles

The primary reason for organizing or bringing together entities which were previously disparate is to invoke economies of scale through division of tasks and specialization. Various 'organizing principles' have resulted in different forms of division or, in another sense, different ways of grouping subunits of the organization. The selection of the proper organizing principle is often viewed as the rudiments of the organization design process at each level of division. The 'proper' principle has in the past been predominantly selected on the basis of efficiency criteria. Table 1 presents some of these principles and examples of their respective advantages expressed in terms of efficiency criteria.

Ansoff and Brandenburg (1971) present a set of organization design criteria which includes the usual concern for steady-state efficiency. In addition, the set of design criteria includes three yardsticks for ability to innovate. These are strategic, structural and operating responsiveness. These criteria can be used to measure the effectiveness of the organization, to assist in the determination of

Table 1. Organizing principles with efficiency criteria

Organizing principle	Source of efficiency
Group by common functions	Large-scale-facilities economies of scale; 'full-line' distribution and sales; interchangeability of intragroup personnel
Group by common products (services)	Profitability delineation and control; standardization and interchangeability of components; minimized process delay for smaller capacity and inventories; product design modification for longer life-cycle
Group by common customer/market	Adaptability to specific customer needs; installation and servicing economies of scale
Group by geographic areas	Employment of intimate knowledge of local environment; transportation cost minimization
Group by projects	Motivation of professionals (results-oriented rather than profession-oriented); administrative ease in starting and terminating activities

whether or not 'the firm is in the right business'. To illustrate, a firm could be extremely efficient at making spats for men's shoes, that is, it may produce attractive, high-quality goods at the lowest possible costs. However, unless it could effect a major fashion revision, it would be so ineffective as to be of questionable viability. The ability of the firm to strategically reposture itself would be gauged using effectiveness criteria measuring responsiveness to the definition of new businesses, the conversion of production, distribution and sales operations, the restructuring of the organization, and the reorientation and reeducation of management to the new businesses. In the dynamics of the post-war industrial environment, new organization structures such as project and matrix forms involved and spread as management became concerned with 'responsiveness' or 'innovativeness' criteria. Gradually management has become increasingly concerned with another organizing principle, namely, group those activities together that are charged with being innovative or with redirecting the activities of the organization in response to changes in the environment, leaving as another distinct group those activities responsible for efficient exploitation of 'the current business'.

The segregation or division of the organization's resources on the basis of the innovation/efficiency principle is not radically new; however, the degree to which it is being applied by a growing number of *avant-garde* organizations is new. Basic and applied research groups have been physically isolated from current operations for decades, but only recently have entire divisions of firms been assigned responsibility for seeking, acquiring, implementing and integrating new businesses. The degree of segregation is dramatized by several structural alternatives which will be described later. An example is the 'future/present dichotomous' structure presented by Wills (1970) as being representative of an emergent form in British industry. In this example, the firm is divided into two distinct subunits. One is led by a 'future policy executive' responsible for planning and implementing future directions of the firm. The other is headed by a 'present policy executive' who is charged with planning and running current operations.

Obviously such an organizing principle would be pragmatically used by a minority of organizations at the present time. However, when the conditions for its proper use are examined, it becomes apparent that given the trends in the environment of most organizations, these conditions will be faced by a growing number in the future.

6. Conditions and Arguments for the Innovation/Current Operations Dichotomy

Innovation, particularly of the S-P type, is a resource-absorbing process. This is especially true for the managerial resources of an organization. Converting environmental contracts or linkages, organizational assets or processes from one form to another consumes resources without directly producing output which can be returned to the environment in exchange for more resources. It creates only the *potential* for this exchange process. An analogy may be made to the individual who pays a commission to his stockbroker to change his portfolio. The change process itself only incurs a loss (the commission) in exchange for a potentially greater return. (Hopefully the new portfolio will eventually return greater yields once the potential is exploited.) Why then should an organization seek a structure which will promote rapid, continual and effective innovation?

One answer lies in the dynamics of the organization's environment. Even in a reactive and defensive posture, it may be necessary to innovate to remain viable in an environment of large discontinuities. Such environments may result from dynamic, high technologies; short life-cycles; political instabilities; or consumer vagaries. From a proactive, aggressive position, such discontinuities may offer unique opportunities with at least short-run monopoly profits until uniqueness is lost. One condition, then, which suggests the use of the innovation/current operations organizing principle is large and frequent discontinuities in the environment of the organization.

A related condition is the existence of ambitious objectives and goals for the organization. If the objectives of the many constituencies represented in the organization — owners, managers, labourers and other participants, customers and beneficiaries — are demanding and the organization is intent upon satisfying them, productivity increases of the required size are rare without the introduction of substantial innovation.

Another related condition is the existence of non-productive or marginally productive resources. The greater the number of these resources and the more specialized they are, the more search and introduction of innovation is necessary in order to put these resources to use in new activities. To the extent that this is impossible, the more divestment innovation is needed in order to convert (through subsequent investment innovation) to more productive resources.

A common condition which requires the use of the innovation/current operations organizing principle is the existence of considerable organizational inertia against change. This inertia may be found in the form of top management approaching retirement, high capital intensity or heavy personal investment in particular expertise among professionals, to name a few. Other correlates to resistance to innovation can be inferred from the writings of Mansfield (1968) and Havelock (1969).

The arguments for use of the organizational segregation of innovation and current operations under the above conditions have been made by numerous authors. Examples may be found in Lorsch and Lawrence (1965), Radosevich and Hayes (1971) and Wills (1970). The arguments for differentiation are often based on the assumption of different organizational 'cultures' being most supportive of innovation *vis-à-vis* operations. Lawrence and Lorsch describe the

Table 2. Comparison of attributes: innovative units *vis-à-vis* operating units

Attribute	Innovative units	Operating units
1. Management problem-solving orientation	External (oriented to the environment), long-range time horizons	Internal (intrafirm), short-range time horizons
2. Activity characteristics	Unique, creative, self-described and directed	Repetitive, programmable (described by formal job descriptions)
3. Resource inputs	Highly-trained professionals, brain-intensive	Lower-skill personnel, capital-intensive (automation of processes)
4. Reward system basis	Self-actualization, intellectual curiosity, role autonomy	Economic, status associated with position and title
5. Management styles	Participative (information-controlled, joint decisions)	Reliance upon formal and position-based authority
6. Decision processes	Primarily intuitive modes with some *ad hoc* analytical studies	Analysable decisions with some explicit quantitative models
7. Risk attitudes	Take chances, tolerate some failures	Control uncertainties at low levels
8. Evaluation basis	Self and peer (professional) evaluation	Formal systems using standards defined by predetermined criteria
9. Technology used	Complex, near state-of-the-art, often advanced internally	Relatively simple, borrowed or converted from innovative groups or from outside the firm
10. Coordination basis	Face-to-face, two-way communication	Plans, memoranda, one-way directives

different cultures for research, sales and production in terms of the dimensions of departmental structure, orientation towards time, orientation towards others and orientation towards the environment. Wills differentiates the cultures on the important time dimension. Radosevich and Hayes differentiate the cultures in terms of the set of attributes displayed in Table 2. The main point of all of these arguments is that innovation and efficient operations cannot be housed in the same organizational units because the milieu which is most supportive of innovation would be unlikely to foster efficiency and routine in operations and *vice versa*.

In addition to the different cultures, the two types of activities are imbued with distinctly different kinds of expertise and require management processes peculiar to their uniquenesses. There exists a sort of Gresham's law which suggest that managerial concern for the programmed activities of current operations will drive out attention to innovative activities. The empirical study by Terleckyj (1963), verifies the intuitively plausible hypothesis that poor performance (for example, decreases in sales or earnings) results in cuts in innovation-oriented activities such as research and development after a lag of a year or two. Since innovation is a red-ink activity, it is commonly reduced in a crisis-stimulated, cost-reduction campaign, perhaps at a point in time when true innovation is most needed by the organization. Through segregation and the establishment of separate budgets and organizational entities for innovation, some shielding and stability of innovation is afforded during times of adversity.

7. Structural Alternatives for the Innovative/Current Operations Form

Those organizations which employ a structure having an almost total segregation of responsibilities for innovation and for efficiency in current operations are still few in number, although more are considering it every day. There are two basic forms most commonly employed for organizing as far as segregation is concerned and a slightly larger number of mechanisms for integrating the activities so that innovation is properly phased into current operations. It seems paradoxical that structures must be designed to emphasize both segregation and integration. However, if innovative activities have been successfully segregated during the incubation period, integration at a later stage when the commercial potential has been developed requires efficacious organizational transfer mechanisms to overcome the not-invented-here (nih) resistance syndrome.

One basic form for segregating innovation is shown in Figure 1 as representative of the structure employed by several industrial firms. This form is similar to the 'future/present dichotomous structure' referred to previously. The dichotomy is established at a very high level, frequently right below the chief executive officer, to divide the firm into one unit responsible for innovation or the establishment of the future business potential and another unit, usually considerably larger, that is responsible for the efficient pursuit of current business activities. In Figure 1, under the operating group executive, there often exists a divisional form based on different product markets. Occasionally the

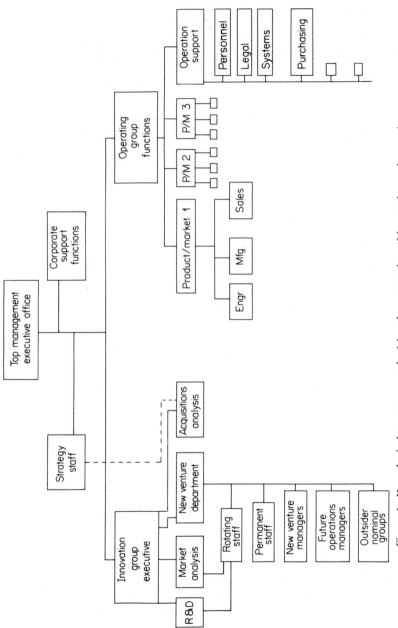

Figure 1. Hypothetical structure emphasizing the segregation of innovation and operating groups.

next level is grouped on a functional or geographic basis, but these structures present greater difficulty in transferring additional product market innovations into the operating group. Under a P/M divisional basis, divisional heads may accept and integrate an innovation if it is highly synergistic with their current operations. If an innovation is not sought by any of the current divisional heads, it simply becomes a new divisional entity, assuming the potential size is reasonable.

The innovation group interacts closely with the strategy formulation personnel (top management and staff) in this structure because the specific actions that are required to close any diversification gap defined in the formulation are to be planned and implemented in the innovation group. The strategy formulation process identifies the extent of innovation that is needed and provides broad guidelines for the search process. Specific alternatives generated by the innovation group are tested against the defined strategy and, in many instances, both the strategy and the innovation search process will be modified in a mutually adaptive manner.

A crucial initial decision process which significantly influences the activities of the innovation group is the 'make or buy' consideration resulting in an acquisitions programme, an internal development programme, or, most frequently, some combination. A staff for acquisitions analysis may be contained within the innovation group, particularly if acquisitions are likely to be closely integrated with other operations. Common alternatives are to include this analysis activity in the strategic planning staff or reporting separately to a top executive or committee. This is more likely to occur in the case of conglomerates or holding companies.

To foster internal development of new businesses, what used to be the corporate R & D function is joined by a market analysis group and a new venture group. Divisional responsibilities for technical development in the operating group are restricted to product and process improvement applications that are consistent with the substrategies of that division. That does not mean that new venture ideas never originate within operating divisions but rather that they are transferred to and nurtured in the innovation group unless they are highly compatible with divisional technology, customers, product lines, or unique managerial knowhow. In reorganization efforts to effect this type of structure, corporate R & D is often the predominant element in the innovation group. Experience with the structure suggests that over time the proportion of technical personnel is likely to decrease and their function will undergo considerable change.

There are several reasons for this. One is that there is much too much interorganizational duplication of R & D efforts. As a firm becomes more sensitized to its environment as a source of innovation ideas, it becomes aware that it is often cheaper and more effective to 'import' or transfer technology from outside rather than pursuing the scientific research activities. Foster (1971) suggests a methodology for employing a higher proportion of the scientific personnel in the transfer process rather than 'fooling with the test tubes' themselves. A tremendous amount of new technical knowledge is available in the public domain and can be discovered and transferred much more effectively if the search process is carefully guided by applications specifications which are derived from commercial analyses. One source of innovation is the market analysis group whose primary focus is the identification of unsatisfied needs in potential markets. The role of R & D then becomes one of identifying the appropriate technologies to apply. These may be developed or advanced internally, but more frequently they may be discovered at universities, research institutes or 'think tanks', government agencies, or even potential industrial suppliers. Experience in several venture groups has shown that this flow of innovation leads to new ventures with a higher proportion of commercial successes than when the flow is reversed. The reversed flow — a 'technical solution' or breakthrough developed first and then a market search for application — is characteristic of the process which occurs when R & D is not integrated with a marketing and commercial or venture analysis group in the innovative subunit of the organization.

The integration of the R & D group (technical solutions) and the marketing group (needs identification) within the innovation function is increasingly being accomplished by a 'ventures' group according to Jones and Wilemon (1972). They present a survey of the venture activities in the largest US firms. Slocum (1972) also describes a variety of venture activities and organizational configurations to accomplish them. The hypothetical structure in Figure 1 shows the venture department membership consisting of a rotating staff of technical and marketing personnel, a permanent staff of 'technique consultants', a group of new venture managers or 'organizational entrepreneurs', future operations managers who will eventually run those ventures that become commercial realities and non-members of the organization who temporarily assist in defining and analysing new ventures. These various groups contribute members to a venture team which is formed on a gradual basis as a venture idea passes sequential stages of analysis and the organization commits increasing amounts of resources to it. In terms of the usual structural charcteristics, the venture department is 'flat', has many temporary personnel assignments, and emphasizes interdepartmental communication.

The first personnel assignment to a venture is a venture manager. 'Assignment' may be a misnomer; in many instances, the venture manager selects the ventures he is excited about since this enthusiasm is considered important if he is to commit the energy necessary to guide it to fruition. In some instances the matching of venture manager to idea is made as soon as the potential venture is formally recognized by the organization so that he can develop early commitment to it. This is particularly important if the origin of the innovation idea is someone else who must convince a venture manager of its worth. The venture manager selects assistance from marketing and R & D on the basis of the most appropriate expertise to help him in a preliminary evaluation of market and technical feasibility. To develop the necessary autonomy for this evaluation, the venture manager must be assigned a budget to 'buy' this assistance in the analysis and development of the idea. Through the rotation of staff from R & D and marketing analysis into venture teams, the infusion of concern for corporate development needs is promulgated upon their return to their respective professional groups. If the initiation of venture action results from the discovery of a market need, the venture manager first seeks the addition of technical assistance to the team in order to find an answer to the need. If a 'solution' is discovered first, market analysis capability is added first to determine potential uses. The venture manager is responsible for interacting with the initial source of innovation to secure as complete a specification as possible and then developing the other half (the 'solution' or 'need') to a point of proven feasibility.

The permanent staff of the venture department acts as internal consultants on venture analysis methods, i.e. they are primarily trainers of the R & D and marketing professionals who are rotated through the department. They represent expertise in technology monitoring and forecasting, quantitative model development and statistical analysis, market research techniques, etc.

The future operations managers are selected from the operating group for the purpose of eventually assuming responsibility for the ventures when they reach the commercialization stage. The operations manager is temporarily assigned to the innovation group to perform a liaison funtion considerably before the actual transfer of any venture personnel or facilities to the operating group. He may serve as a broker for expertise from the operating group which is needed for venture start-up; for example, standard cost data or process technology may exist in a readily useable form within the operating group. He must join the venture group early enough to learn the technologies and markets that he must understand to build and run a successful competitive business. Because he will have the eventual responsibility of exploiting the business potential generated within the venture group, his is the final decision as to when the venture is ready to transfer, although the venture manager serves as an important adviser on this decision.

The venture department is also responsible for forming and using nominal groups of outsiders. These temporary organization members may be consultants on technology, analysts from venture capital firms interested in joint venturing, or representatives of potential suppliers and customers (particularly if the venture is aimed at industrial markets). Consumer market test panels might be included in this group. If the product is part of a larger system, outside experts on standardization or representatives of other component providers may be brought into the design process.

Obviously, to accomplish these activities, the innovation group structure must be 'flat', 'fluid' and creative. There is a great deal of personnel exchange, with people accepting a new role on the basis of project venture objectives and the conviction that they can contribute significantly. People must know and trust each other for open communication and common knowledge of where the expertise lies in the organization. Power and influence in decision-making must depend on expertise and contribution to the venture rather than formal hierarchical position. Many of these features are described in detail in the

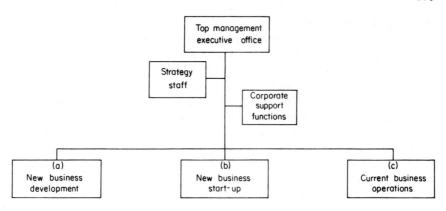

Figure 2. Hypothetical structure emphasizing the differentiation of strategy posture innovation and exploitation potential innovation. (a) Strategy – postured innovation: 'organizational entrepreneurs'. Activities: opportunity search; feasibility analyses; product design; market research; diffusion plans; acquisition and merger studies. (b) Exploitation potential innovation: 'organization builders'. Activities: life-testing; value analyses; process design; facilities design and construction; standard cost/pricing studies; labour market surveys; promotion and advertising plan; channel selection/sales organization; acquisitions integration; systems and procedures writing. (c) Exploitation of current business: 'running the shop'. Activities: budgeting and quota setting; scheduling and dispatching; monitoring performance of levels and flows; salary and promotion; product line modification.

writings on innovation in organizations which we identified in the first section of this chapter.

An alternative structure for the segregation of innovation differentiates between S-P and E-P innovation. Figure 2 shows a structural form currently being tried by several industrial firms. The differentiation and segregation of the two types of innovation is based on the different characteristics of leaders who are most successful at these distinct types of change-management activities. Chandler (1962, Ch. 6) describes the two types at considerable length. The 'organizational entrepreneurs', characterized by Durant at General Motors, are extroverts whose energies are directed towards interacting with the environment of the firm. This type is rarely found behind his desk. He is more often talking to potential customers, financial and supply sources, government regulatory representatives and managements of other firms for joint ventures of acquisitions. Much of the staff work, as suggested by the activities listed in Figure 2, is highly cognitive and creative. In contrast, the leaders of the E-P innovation activities are analytical, more introverted people epitomized by Sloan at General Motors, whose energies are most readily consumed in changing internal capabilities of the firm. The staff which supports the representative activities list in Figure 2 have some analytical duties, but these must be coupled with action-oriented change assistance as provided by specialists in organization development and industrial engineering, as examples.

8. Integrative Mechanisms

If the organization is structured to segregate and nurture innovation during its early stages through the provision of a distinct organizational entity and culture, the problems of transferring the results of innovative activities to steady-state operations are significant and require special transfer mechanisms. Quinn and Mueller (1963) suggest three necessary conditions to move technology across organizational transfer points. They describe the typical problems encountered when trying to assure the existence of these conditions. The problems are obviously closely related to the organizing principles used to define the groups between which transfer is necessary. The three necessary transfer conditions are *information* flow, *enthusiasm* for the results and *authority* for use. The problems in achieving these conditions include lack of common knowledge and language to facilitate communication, physical isolation, the complexity of innovative results, short-term management incentives and performance measures, overly long lines of formal authority and entrenched ideas and vested interests, the latter often being related to the ageing of key management personnel. Similar types of problems are discussed by Lorsch and Lawrence (1965). Examination of these representative problems suggests that transfer can more readily be accomplished between innovation and operating groups if the operating groups are organized on a product or market divisional basis. This is so because functional groupings typically exhibit greater intergroup disparities in knowledge and languages. When organizational units are formed around products or projects, there is usually a greater universal understanding of common problems, underlying technologies and organizational objectives. In addition, there is commonly a greater decentralization of authority and internalized enthusiasm for growth and new ideas.

To facilitate the transfer of innovations to operating groups, a number of mechanisms have been tried in industrial organizations. One of the most common, yet least successful, depends upon written proposals and results of feasibility studies which are disseminated to possible 'buyers' in the operating areas. This form of low-interactive transfer may exhibit severe communication problems if the innovation is complex or truly novel, and most certainly will transfer little of the enthusiasm and personal committment of the individuals who originated the idea, designed the prototypes and tested the feasibility.

Where continual transfer of innovations is sought, many firms have institutionalized a formal role which requires an individual to serve as the transfer agent. Such a role has been described by Litwin and Siebrecht (1967). Fisher (1970) reports a study which describes the different role expectations for the integrator from various organizational sources. He also compares characteristics of high and low performers in the role as rated by colleagues. High performers managed to fulfill conflicting expectations without appearing conciliatory. This is similar to the Lorsch and Lawrence suggestion for a skilful negotiator who represents a median set of values between the two groups. Successful integrators also exhibit assertiveness and initiative while at the same time being able to evaluate objectively and internalize those valuable contributions made by their colleagues. Fisher reports a greater orientation towards overall goals and strategies of the firm amongst the high performers. Significant self-esteem and confidence are also frequently described as important characteristics for these transfer agents, who must rely upon informal influence processes rather than formal authority, power and control of sanctions.

Another common transfer mechanism is the transfer committee or coordinating department. Lorsch and Lawrence (1965) contrast coordination departments in two firms and report that the more successful group represents a set of values that was more central between the conflicting values of the coordinated departments. (The less successful coordinating group had responsibility for market planning and sales coordination.) Thus a truly neutral position in terms of functional orientations is suggested. The more successful group also had a longer-time-horizon perspective and functioned in an organization with a lower degree of structure.

The coordinating committee transfer mechanism is used by several firms who are structured in the innovation/operations segregated form. In one instance, the committee is made up of permanent members from the second level of management, for example, the vice presidents of innovation, operations, planning and finance. In another case, the transfer timing is decided by a committee which has permanent members of the above sort but includes *ad hoc* members who are venture managers with ventures near fruition and divisional managers who may be interested in 'buying' the innovations. The charge of this committee is to facilitate the continual flow of innovations through the organizational pipeline. When joining particular sessions of the committee, venture managers are to provide information and infectious enthusiasm to push innovations down the pipe. Division managers, when serving as temporary committee members, are to pull the innovations from the pipe by providing personnel and financial resources to finalize transfer preparations, thus assuring that the innovation group doesn't hang on to its ideas and 'mother them to death'. Experience in this firm suggests that the committee has also been successful in facilitating divestment by assuring operations managers that new and more successful product-markets are available and will require continued used of their resources.

Other transfer mechanisms are used which physically transfer personnel, budgets, facilities and equipment and responsibility from the innovations group in one geographic area to an operating group located elsewhere. In some instances the venture manager is transferred and becomes the new product manager. However, as previously argued, the role requirements of these two positions are so distinct it is unlikely that many individuals can be highly successful at both. Therefore, it is suggested that an operations or product manager join the venture team at an early stage and serve as the nucleus of the physical transfer process.

There is a second type of transfer problem associated with the segregation of innovation groups. This problem is the transfer of organizational resources from the innovation group to the operations groups (or *vice versa*) whenever there are substantial changes in the amount of innovation that is needed by the organization. This problem has not been successfully addressed, unless the transfers are short-term, and represents a major deterrent to more widespread adoption of this organizational form. For example, technical resources from the innovation group who have been involved in the exciting design and testing of new products and services may be willing to do process modification studies in an operations group for several months. However, as previously discussed, the different organizational culture in the operations area would make a long-term assignment seem like eternal purgatory.

9. Conclusion

If the trends in the organizational environment of the post-industrial era continue to exhibit accelerated change in technologies, product and process introductions, consumer and social preferences and managerial practices, increasing numbers of organizations must be imbued with strategic management. Continuous generation and adoption of innovations will be a common norm which must be supported with appropriate organizational structures. In many instances these structures will resemble the dichotomous innovations/operations configurations discussed here. Evidence generated by numerous studies at the Harvard Business School and reported by Scott (1973) exhibits significant trends of top U S and European firms away from functional structures to the divisional form as their diversification increases. As the breadth and rate of diversification and redeployment of resources increases, the trends may well be to the innovation forms with which *avant-garde* firms are currently experimenting.

References

Ansoff, H. I. (1965). 'The firm of the future', *Harvard Business Review*, September–October, 162.

Ansoff, H. I. (1972). 'The concept of strategic management', *The Journal of Business Policy*, 2, No. 4, 2.

Ansoff, H. I. and Brandenburg, R. G. (1971). 'A language for organization design', *Management Science*, 17, No. 12, August, B-705.

Chandler, A. D., Jr. (1962). *Strategy and Structure*, Garden City, New York, Doubleday.

Drucker, P. F. (1969). *The Age of Discontinuity: Guidelines to Our Changing Society*, New York, Harper and Row.

Drucker, P. F. (1971). 'The innovative organization', *The Journal of Business Policy*, 1, No. 3. Spring.

Fisher, D. (1970). 'Entrepreneurship and moderation: the role of the integrator', In *Studies in Organization Design*, Ed. J. W. Lorsch and P. R. Lawrence, New York, Irwin, pp. 153–167.

Foster, R. N. (1971). 'Organize for technology transfer', *Harvard Business Review*, November–December, 110.

Fronko, E. G. (1971). 'One company's cast-off technology is another company's opportunity', *Innovation*, Number 23, August, 52.

Havelock, R. G. (1969). *Planning for Innovation*, Institute of Social Research, University of Michigan, Ann Arbor.

Jones, K. A., and Wilemon. D. L. (1972). 'Emerging patterns in new venture management', *Research Management*. November, 14.

Labovitz, G. H. (1971). 'Organizing for adaptation', *Business Horizons*, June, 19.

Litwin, G. H. and Siebrecht, A. (1967). 'Integrators and entrepreneurs', *Hospital Progress*, September, 67.

Lorsch, J. W. and Lawrence, P. R. (1965). 'Organizing for product innovation', *Harvard Business Review*, January–February, 109.

Mass, W. (1972). 'Making organizations adaptive to change', *Innovation*, No. 30, April 50.

Mansfield, E. (1968). *Industrial Research and Technological Innovation*, New York, Norton.

Quinn, J. B. and Mueller, J. A. (1963). 'Transferring research results to operations', *Harvard Business Review*, 41, No. 1, January–February, 49.

Radosevich, R., and Hayes, L. R. (1971) 'Management systems for organizational innovation', Institute for Strategic Management, Report Number 1, Vanderbilt University, December (in review).

Scott, B. R. (1973). 'The industrial state: old myths and new realities', *Harvard Business Review*, March–April, 133.

Shepard, H. A. 'Innovation-resisting and innovation-producing organizations', *The Journal of Business*, October, 1967, 470.

Slocum, D. H. (1972). *New Venture Methodology*, New York, American Management Association.

Terleckyj, N. E. (1963). *Research and Development: Its Growth and Composition*, New York, National Industrial Conference Board.

Toffler, A. (1970). *Future Shock*, New York, Random House.

Wills, G. (1970). 'The preparation and deployment of technological forecasts', *The Journal of Long Range Planning*, March, 44.

IV

The Strategic Manager

THE CHANGING MANAGER

H. IGOR ANSOFF

1. A Model of Management Education

Our concern in this chapter is with the manner in which education serves the managerial needs of organizations. A useful measure of the success of this service is the difference between the skills and knowledge of the practising managers and the needs of their organizations. The respective components of this difference are determined by a number of factors in the manner illustrated in Figure 1.

We shall use Figure 1 as the basic framework for the logic of this chapter. Attention will be focused on so-called purposive organizations which seek to satisfy identifiable goals through an exchange of resources with the environment. The business firm is a most conspicuous type of purposive organization, but so is the hospital, the university and service-rendering branches of the Government (Ansoff, 1972). The managerial needs of these organizations are determined in part by their institutional character and in part by the problems and opportunities presented by the environment. It is these needs that provide the 'demand function' to the educational institutions.

Although Figure 1 draws a distinctive boundary around educational institutions, the actual setting in which management education takes place is manifold. The setting ranges from on-the-job training of practitioners at one extreme, to intrafirm training programmes, to interfirm professional associations and to academic schools of business and management. Thus, we would lose a great deal of information if we were to assume that management education takes place only in academia.

The ability of the institutions to educate depends on the available managerial knowledge and on the societal knowledge which is relevant to management (for example, mathematical game theory, or applied psychology). Again, the spectrum of sources is very broad, ranging from an experienced manager, who is still the most valuable source of knowledge, to an abstract theory of organizational behaviour. These sources, as shown in Figure 1, are to be found within the user organizations, the academic ones, and in the larger society.

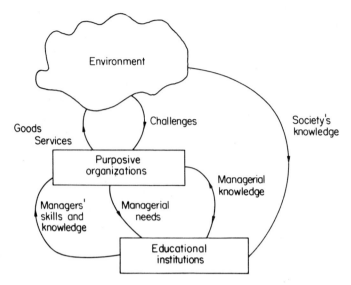

Figure 1. Dynamics of managerial knowledge. (State of management education) = (Managerial needs) − (Managers' skills and knowledge).

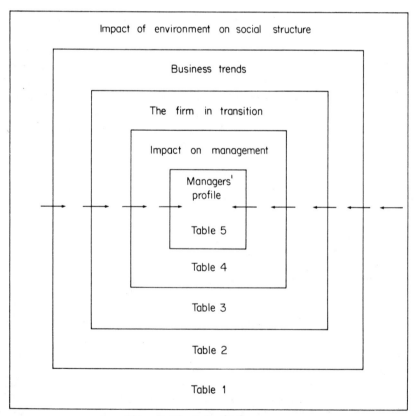

Figure 2. The logic of inference.

The ability of the institution to educate also depends on its cultural and social setting. Thus, education within the firm is biased towards pragmatism; in the university a business school is influenced by the theoretically biased research-oriented culture.

In summary, the future of management education will be determined by three interacting forces. One will be the needs of the user organizations, the second the educational technology, and the third the responsiveness of the educational institutions. In the history of management, organizational needs were the leading force. In response to these, technology evolved through trial and error and thus has lagged behind the needs. Institutions dedicated to education of managers have generally lagged behind advanced technology.

There is now a chance, albeit a small one, that the future technology will begin to anticipate the needs, and that under new institutional arrangements management education will become a demand generator instead of follower. There is a greater probability that the historical lag of education behind practice will persist. To shed light on the respective probabilities, we need to examine all three interacting forces.

2. The Changing Nature of Management

2.1 *The Logic of Inference*

For our purposes, the managerial needs of Figure 1 need to be expressed in terms of aptitudes, skills, values, perspective, and knowledge required of managers. These are related in a complex way to the tasks and the environment of management. We shall trace this relationship through a series of tables related in the manner shown in Figure 2.

The underlying assumption is that the managerial needs are traceable back to a series of converging environment influences. The furthest removed are societal trends which impact on the societal structure. This is symbolized by the outer ring and briefly described in Table 1. The next ring deals with the consequent

Table 1. The age of Discontinuity

Societal trends
> Arrival of the age of affluence
> Escalation of social aspirations from 'quantity to quality of life'
> Life-death potential of physical technology
> Ecological collision course
> Gap between physical and social technology
> Increasing inter-impact of organizations within society
> Decline of the growth ethic

Impact on social structure
> Loss of social centrality by the firm
> Pressure on the firm for social responsiveness
> Pressure on the public sector for efficiency and accountability
> Pressure on both for entrepreneurial response
> Convergence of challenges to private and public sector
> Search for new social architecture

Table 2

Business trends

    Emergence of three global marketplaces
    Increasing regulation and control of business behaviour
    Changing industry life-cycle patterns:
        Saturation of first-generation industries
        Emergence of second-generation industries
        Shrinkage of industry life-cycles

    Emergence of technology as a driving force:
        Proliferation of new industries
        Proliferation of new products
        Industry obsolescence through technology substitution
        Spectre of the 'R & D monster'

    Restructuring of demand:
        Relative growth of the service sector
        Growth of societal markets
        Consumerism
        Buying power of the non-earners
        Relative growth of luxury demand

    Changing human resource:
        Shift to white-collar workforce
        Disappearance of protestant work ethic
        Changing reward aspirations
        Professionalization of management

Table 3. The firm in transition

	Industrial 1950's		Transitional 1970's		Post-industrial 1990's
Social scope	Business under *laisser faire*	→	Business under societal constraint	→	Society in interaction with business sector
Geographic scope	National	→	International	→	Multi-national
Central theme	Profitability and growth		+ Strategic change		+ Optimum social utility
Time perspective	Historical	→	Extrapolation of history		+ Anticipation of future
Change	Controlled		+ Generated		+ Balanced
Work ethic	Hard work	→	Maximum leisure		+ Self-actualization
Power structure	Authoritarian	→	Participative		+ Political
Leadership	Consensual		+ Charismatic		+ Political + Statesmanship
Problem scope	Economic		+ Human		+ Political + Cultural
Problem type	Familiar Repetitive		+ Novel Episodic		+ Novel Episodic

Table 4. Consequences for management

Broadened business perspective
    From business to societal
    From uni-culture to poly-culture
    From uni-sovereignty to multi-sovereignty
    From uni-continent to multi-continent
    Need for broadened training
    Increased volume of management

Broadened public sector perspective
    Expansion of service to special constituencies
    Expansion of service to profitless industries
    New entrepreneurial freedoms
    Inadequacy of people-government dichotomy
    Inadequacy of business-government dichotomy
    Need for new organizational forms
    Need for new type of manager

Increased complexity of managerial activity
    Emphasis on organizational entrepreneurship
    Emphasis on facilitation, direction and control of change
    Coexistence of bureaucracy and adhocracy
    Growing complexity and decentralization
    Conflict between accelerated change and retardation of response
    Need for new systems, structures
    Increased volume of managerial work

Increased dependence of success on management quality
    Increased frequency and intensity of strategic change
    Accelerated incidence of novel problems and opportunities
    Increased size of single risk
    Need for improved training and technology

Changing people management
    Increased participation
    Redesign of work roles to match aspirations
    Erosion of authority based on ownership
    Shift to multi-constituency power structure
    Need for multi-constituency technology
    Increased volume of managerial work

Diffusion of managerial expertise
    Decision scope exceeds bounds of individual comprehension
    Increased dependence of decisions on technology
    Increased dependence on specialized expertise
    The spectre of technocracy
    Need for expertise in using experts

Growth in size of management
    Growing size of organizations
    Increased volume of managerial work
    Multi-contributor decision process
    Disappearance of minimum management ethic
    Need for cost-effective management of management

impact on the more immediate competitive environment of a particular class of purposive organizations. We describe this impact on the business sector in Table 2^2.

The third ring and Table 3 describe the changes in the characteristics of the firm under the influence of its environments. The ring next to the core, as well as Table 4, infer the consequences for the tasks and behaviour of management. Finally at the core of the diagram, we use Table 5 to describe the profile of the manager which will be needed to cope with the changing environment and the changing tasks. It is these characteristics that must be supplied by education if it is to be fully responsive *to managerial needs*.

Table 5. Evolution of the managers' profiles

Industrial 1950's		Post-industrial 1990's
World outlook		
Intra-firm	→	Environmental
Intra-industry	→	Multi-industry
Intra-national (regional)	→	Multi-national
Intra-cultural	→	Cross-cultural
Economic	→	Economic
Technological	→	Technological
		Social
		Political
Social values		
Surrogate owner	→	Professional
Committed to *laissez faire*	→	Committed to social value of free enterprise
Profit optimizer	→	Social value optimizer
Personal values		
Economic rewards + power	+	Self-actualization
Stability	+	Change
Conformity	+	Deviance
Skills		
Experientially	+	Acquired through
acquired	+	Career-long education
Popular leader	+	Charismatic + political leader
Participative	+	Political + charismatic
Goal-setter	+	Objectives-setter
Familiar problem-solver	+	Novel problem-solver
Intuitive problem-solver	+	Analytic problem-solver
Conservative risk-taker	+	Entrepreneurial risk-taker
Convergent diagnostician	+	Divergent diagnostician
Lag controller	+	Lead controller
Extrapolative planner	+	Entrepreneurial planner
Skill profile		
Generalist	→	Generalist—specialist + Professional specialist
World perspective		
Surrounding environment		Global environment
Semi-open system		Open system

In the past few years, a great many articles and books have dealt with the various steps of Figure 2. A selection of these are given in the References. It is beyond the scope and the intent of this chapter to analyse them in detail. Since there is a very large measure of consensus among the various authors, we shall confine ourselves to presenting the summary of conclusions and their implications for management education. (Beckwith, 1967; Bowen, 1949; Brickman and Lehrer, 1966; Carnegie Commission on Higher Education, 1971; Carroll, 1958; Clark, 1969; Drucker, 1969a,b; Gaber, 1964; Hodgkinson, 1970; Jungk and Galtung, 1970; Kahn and Wierner, 1969; Kerr, 1963; Kroll, 1970; Ansoff, 1965; 1973b; Toffler, 1970).

2.2 Trends Relevant to Education

Table 1 takes a broad societal perspective of the major trends in what is increasingly being called the emerging post-industrial era. Two important characteristics can be inferred from its perusal. The first, is that the word 'trend' frequently is a misnomer. 'Discontinuity' is a better descriptor of such developments as the escalation of social aspirations, the life-death potential of modern technology, decline of growth ethic, etc. All of these discontinuities require new dimensions of awareness, novel responses, new societal resource allocations (Drucker, 1969a).

The second characteristic, inferred towards the bottom of Table 1, is the convergence of societal challenges placed on the public and private sectors: the increasing demands on the private sector to behave entrepreneurially and efficiently, and the increasing demands for social responsiveness. This blurring of institutional demarcations suggests a convergence of managerial practices. It also signals the beginnings of a search for enrichment of social architecture, for 'intersect' organizational arrangements which combine and enrich the best characteristics of private and public organizations. It is in the development of this new social architecture that lie the as yet untapped frontiers of societal management (Ansoff, 1973b).

Table 2 summarizes the diverse predictions in the narrower perspective of the business sector. Here again, the dramatic impact of technology, shrinkage of industry life-cycles and shifts in values and work attitudes all call attention to impending discontinuities in managerial response.

Table 3 translates the business trends into the characteristics of the business firm at three points in time:(1) in the 1950's when the industrial era reached its pinnacle; (2) in the current transitional 1970's; and (3) in the 1990's when the post-industrial era will have arrived.

A summary glance at the first column gives an impression of the firm pursuing economic efficiency in an environment of strategic stability and under minimal societal constraints. As the firm moves into future, three basic trends occur: increasing interdependence with society, increasing incidence of environmental discontinuities, and increasing participation and influence of management and employees in the decision-making process of the firm.

A comparison of the columns in Table 3 suggests a point of central importance to management education: the post-industrial traits will not be a replacement of the industrial firm, rather they will be additives to he latter. The firm of the 1990's will thus be much more complex than its predecessor, and will be capable of a wider range of responses to challenges and threats.

The point is elaborated in Table 4. Management will continue its major concern with profitability but will do so in a very much wider social—political perspective. In its decision processes, management will have to cope with problems of ever-increasing complexity and rely increasingly on the advice of specialized experts.

Perhaps the most important point is the shift from the essentially uni-modal behaviour of the 1950's to the bi-modality of the 1990's (Ansoff, 1968). In the 1950's the major focus was on use of the firm's technology for successful exploitation of the firm's traditional markets. In the 1990's an equal concern will be on the shifts and changes in the technology and the markets of the firm in order to develop and maintain the potential for future exploitation. But this new emphasis will be an addition, and not a replacement of the older. Management will be devoting increasing energies to entrepreneurship and to organizational change, but it will continue its concern with profits subsequent to the change.

3. The Changing Manager
3.1 *The Generic Manager*

Table 4 is fairly easily translated into the profile of the post-industrial manager. The result is shown in Table 5. The first part describes the changes in social values and the perspective and the second the managers' personal values and the skill profile. The pluses before the last column are used to indicate that, as the preceding discussion suggests, the new traits and skills are additives to the old.

The referenced literature is fairly unanimous on the traits of the post-industrial manager described in the second column of Table 5. He is described as broad in outlook, an entrepreneurial risk-taker, a charismatic leader skilful in guiding complex organizations towards new directions and new departures and a skilful user of the new management technology.

He is contrasted with the industrial manager — a typical representative of the mass-production era: efficiency-minded, devoted to the concept that 'the business of business is business', skilful diagnostician and controller of operations, a popular leader who perpetuates and accelerates growth in its predestined directions.

The bulk of the literature pictures the new manager as the replacement for his predecessor. In the light of our preceding discussion, this product-substitution view appears to be overly simplistic, even if the new requirements call for an awesome range of skills and knowledge in an individual.

Given that the new requirements are to be added to the old ones, the new manager begins to loom as a latter-day Leonardo da Vinci.

Thus, it appears that to argue that the new post-industrial manager will replace the mass-production manager is to oversimplify both the problem and the solution. To get at the problem and the solution, it will be useful to trace the historical reasons for the oversimplification.

Historically, management grew from 'the bottom up'. As productive functions grew and became differentiated, each required special management attention. Managing each required a special understanding and experience in the peculiar logistics of the function. As a result, managers became specialized in production, marketing, finance, R & D, etc.

As the management pyramid grew, new levels of management appeared, not directly related to a particular logistic function. They were broadly classified into information-generating *staff* and information-using *line*. The specialization of the former occurred along his branch of knowledge (accounting, tax, industrial engineering). The qualifications of the line were seen to be a sum total of qualification of functional managers. Thus, to be a successful general manager, one had to know as much as one's functional subordinates (hence the practice of lateral job rotation in preparation for general management responsibility). A good test of a general manager was his ability to take over successfully the job of any of his subordinates.[3]

Towards the middle of the century, it became clear that something other than functional training identified a successful manager. It was increasingly perceived that management was a distinctive social—cognitive process that called for distinctive problem-solving skills, risk propensities, leadership and communication abilities, and that possession of these abilities, knowledge and skills was more important to a manager's success than his knowledge of a particular function. Managers from different parts of the firm appeared more alike than different from one another. Further, comparison of the firm with other purposive organizations suggested that management was generic not only across functions within a firm, but also across a whole class of purposive organizations (Ansoff, 1973b). To paraphrase a lady poet, 'a manager became a manager, became a manager'. The manager was seen as a 'man for all seasons', equally suited and able to perform as a manager of a refrigerator division in Arizona or of a multi-national computer company in France.

The development was an important one, for it shifted attention from the nature of physical work to the nature of the processes which guide the work. This opened the way to progress in the knowledge of management. As we shall presently discuss, the progress was both rapid and impressive.

When the post-industrial era began to demand new responses from management, the concept of a generic manager was already widely accepted. As it became clear that the generic mass-production manager lacked many of the new qualifications, it was logical to define a new generic post-industrial type. The 'Model-T' was to be succeeded by a 'Model-A'. The efficient manager of bureaucracy was to be replaced by a change-responsive 'adhocrat' (Toffler, 1970). But, as our analysis of Tables 1 to 5 shows, the 1950s' tasks of management are not being replaced, but enlarged and complemented; much of the equipment of the industrial manager will remain vital to the firm's success.

The firm will need new capabilities to introduce change, but also retention of the capabilities to exploit its consequences; it will need new risk-propensive attitudes in some activities of the firm, but also risk-controlling ones in others; it requires broadening of managerial perspective to include problems of society, but not at the risk of neglecting pursuit of profit. Thus, emergence of the post-industrial archetype is a sign not of replacement, but of an increase in the total range of managerial capability. Both change-generating and change-exploiting managers will be needed to do the job.

3.2 *Towards a Differentiated Manager*

What then is the probable shape of the future manager? One possibility would be an eventual reintegration of the two types of manager into one generic 'super-manager'. A second would be evolution of two generic archetypes: a change-generating entrepreneur and a change-exploiting profit market. A third alternative is further differentiation of the two archetypes into a variety of managerial roles, each focused on a particular aspect of the complex process of management. If this were to happen, the wheel of history would start on its second revolution. From the specialized functional manager we moved to the generic manager of the industrial era; from the two generic managers of the post-industrial era we would begin to move to a new type of specialization.

The historical evolution of the concept of managers is traced in Figure 3. Today we are at an important branching point in the scenario of the future of management education. Each alternative leads to different structures of managerial roles, different educational requirements and different institutional settings.

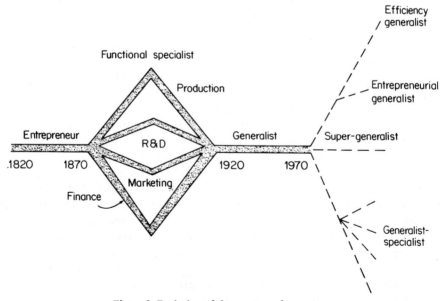

Figure 3. Evolution of the concept of a manager.

Having now lived with the dual-archetype solution for the past 12 years, and having contributed to designing a school for the change manager, I have concluded that the first alternative is an impossibility and that the dual archetype is an important transitional step to the ultimate differentiation of managerial roles.

My reasons for this conclusion are two. The first is that the increasing importance of cost-effectiveness in management will force differentiation of roles.

Management has already become 'big business'. If administrative expenses in a typical firm are added to the management components of functional overheads, close to one-third of total cost of doing business is incurred by management. Growing size, increased scope of decisions, increasing use of technology and computers — all these trends point towards bigger rather than smaller management. The 'least cost principle' that 'minimal management is best management', which is a relic of the industrial era, is dying hard, but it is clearly doomed to be replaced.

The replacement, of necessity, will have to be the cost-effectiveness principle. Large costs of management will not in themselves be bad so long as the effectiveness of management justifies the investment. Because of the hangover of the minimal cost principle, the search for effectiveness in management is relatively new, particularly when compared with effectiveness of production, which has been underway for some 70 years since Frederick Taylor.

It is reasonable to expect that, just as in production, division of managerial work will become an important contributer to cost-effectiveness and for some of the same reasons: the cost of training, the relative ease of maintaining proficiency, and the efficiency of repetitive operations.

A somewhat different reason for division of managerial work comes from a growing awareness that, even after a generic preparation, individuals do not fold into a standard mode of behaviour. Given the same managerial task, two individuals will use different styles and different problem-solving approaches. Within the concept of the generic manager, these deviations are viewed as undesirable. Thus, a manager who scores (1,9) on the Blake grid is presumed in need of help towards a better norm of behaviour.

If one looks beyond the generic concept, the same individual differences can be viewed as comparative advantages which can be best utilized by matching the individual to his role. Thus, in the process of 'getting things done through people', it is increasingly evident that some individuals are better at 'things' (task-oriented) and some are better at 'people' (process-oriented). A change-propensive risk-taking individual is frequently neither competent nor comfortable in guiding change-controlling efficiency-seeking activities.[4]

Thus, the trend towards differentiation of managerial roles can be made both on the grounds of costs and on the grounds of optimum match between an individual's native abilities and the requirements of the task. But the concept of specialization goes against the very underpinnings of American management culture, which correlates success with vesting authority and responsibility in a non-specialized general manager. The culture holds that it is only a generalist, who understands the total scope of management, who can make managerial suboptimization within the limits of his own job and with due concern for organization-wide implications of his action. When the continuing trend towards decentralization is added to this argument, a strong case can be made against specialization and in favour of broadly trained managers. Perhaps even in spite of the high costs and the non-optimal use of individuals, the best cost-effectiveness will lie in training a new generation of 'all-round' generalists.

This brings us to the second argument for differentiation of managerial roles. It is based on the fact that the demands on the new all-round generalist or even on the two archetypal managers will exceed both their capacity and comprehension. The physical overload is already evident at a number of managerial levels where concentration of total authority and responsibility in a single individual has become impossible due to the sheer overload of incoming work. Such overload has been the major reason for the emergence of the concept of the corporate office, which replaces the chief executive officer with a team of co-equals.[5]

Beyond physical overload, the breadth of vision and the depth of specialized skills required in key decisions also exceed the bounds of rationality and the learning capacity of a single individual. A future all-round manager would have something like the following attributes: the visionary risk-propensiveness and charisma of an entrepreneur, the instincts of a politician, the persuasiveness of a leader, the negotiation skills of a diplomat, the incisiveness of a controller and the logic and imagination of a planner. To deal effectively with experts he would have an adequate grounding in mathematics, economics, anthropology, political science, law, psychology, sociology, finance, accounting, international economics, physics, chemistry, biology and other natural sciences, and he would be highly skilled in using experts.

Save for Leonardo da Vinci, no historical person of genius occurs to me who could even begin to approach the span of aptitudes, skills and knowledge required of a post-industrial all-round general manager. Below the level of a genius, the requirements far exceed the capacity of even an outstanding individual, and the breadth of the problem-solving perspective is greater than the bounds of his rationality.

3.3 Characteristics of Differentiated Managers

The main points of the preceding section are summarized in Table 6. These points suggest a trend toward a *differentiated* manager, who is neither a specialist nor a generalist, as the most desirable of the three alternatives presented earlier. In the following pages, I will follow this branch of the scenario to describe the differentiated manager and then draw conclusions with respect to his education.

The future manager will be what psychologists call a T-shaped individual. He will be a generalist (the top of the T) in the sense that he will share with all other managers common understanding of the generic nature of a social guidance and

Table 6. Forces towards a differentiated manager

Shift from minimal management to cost-effective management

Differentiation of roles
  Growing size and cost of management
  Economies of division of work
  Efficiency of aptitude—task match
  Overload at 'natural' P—L foci

Differentiation of managers
  Knowledge and skills beyond learning capacity
  Problem scope beyond human rationality

---

control process called management: its generic problems, its generic processes, the dynamics of social processes, the cognitive dynamics of decision making. He will understand problems of leadership, of resistance to change, of the way people, systems, and structure add up to a managerial capability. He will have highly developed skills in problem solving and group decision making, and an expertise in using experts. He will be sensitive to the impact which his particular decisions and actions have on the total enterprise.

But his generalist knowledge will not be deep enough to equip him to deal single-handedly with the very complex, multifaceted managerial actions. In these, he will have a well-defined role utilizing his particular personal traits, special skills, and unique perspective. Thus he may have a distinctive expertise in incisive problem diagnosis, or he may contribute a strong sense of the political consequences of decisions. This narrower knowledge will be the stem of the T, and it will be the comparative advantage on which he will build his career. It may be focused on a specific environmental perspective, such as labour relations, or on a management process, such as planning, or on some social-political aspect of leadership, communication or coordination.[6]

The primary dimensions of his specialization are not likely to be along the division of physical work (functional areas), nor along institutional boundaries (business *vs.* health *vs.* educational management); these will be secondary distinctions. The primary specialization will be along the logic of managerial work and typical aptitude profiles of individuals. As an example, in a recent paper a colleague and I attempted to classify the top manager of the future. We called him a 'specialized general manager', and hypothesized six archetypal categories: leader, administrator, entrepreneur, statesman, planner and systems architect (Ansoff and Brandenburg, 1969). This first rough approximation to a classification will undoubtedly be replaced by more refined ones. It is not yet clear what dimensions will be the determining ones in the specialization. Table 7 presents several of them in the order of what I judge to be their relative likelihood.

The emergence of the 'specialized general manager' raises questions of the ultimate role of the specialist knowledge worker: the management scientist, the planner, the O D man, the accountant, the tax expert, etc. At one point in the

Table 7. Profile of the differentiated manager

Generalist Attributes

Skills: Social relations
Communication
Social influence
Planning
Ill-structured problem-solving
Expertise on using experts
Suboptimizing in relation to the total enterprise

Knowledge: Behaviour of complex organizations in complex societies
Generic problems of management
Generic process of management

Dimensions of Specialization

Dimension	Examples
Managerial problems	Entrepreneurial, political, cultural, operating, administrative
Managerial process	Planning, implementation, control, capability development
Cognitive profile	Risk propensity, tolerance to ambiguity, task motivation, gregariousness
Management technology	Systems design, data processing, humanistic psychology, operations research
Productive work	Production, marketing, finance, R & D
Scientific discipline	Economics, psychology, political science, systems theory
Professional technology	Corporate law, international law, accounting, tax, labour relations, industrial engineering

---

early development of management science, when its prospects for solving all managerial problems appeared bright, a suggestion was made that the distinction between a manager and a management scientist will disappear in time: every manager will become a qualified management scientist.

Our perspective suggests this to be an overoptimistic expectation. The demand on the new specialist-generalist will be such as to permit him a relatively short technical stem in his 'T'. His major specialty will be in the process of management itself (for example leadership) and not in the technical inputs to it. However, he will have a thorough understanding of the various disciplines, technologies, and specialized knowledge which contribute to management through his specialty. Thus, his stem will be 'long enough' to permit him to build a bridge between technocracy and management. He will know to test the relevance of the specialist's knowledge to a managerial problem, how to elicit necessary information, how to select the best problem-solving approach, and how to interpret the results. He will be an expert in using experts, and his entry on the scene will provide a pipeline through which expertise can flow into management. Rather than abolish the need for expert knowledge, the specialist—generalist will enhance the need for and the role of the specialist.

On the other hand, the historical crossover of erstwhile trained specialists into management is likely to become more difficult. So long as management was a practitioner's art, a talented specialist had an equal, or even better, chance alongside other aspirants for management responsibility. But, as training in management *per se* increases in scope and complexity, a specialist will need formal training to quality for a managerial role. As a result of this and of the enhanced opportunities, technical expertise is likely to become a distinctive career parallel to management, with distinctive progress ladders similar to those which already exist in research and development.

3.4. *Impact on Management Education*

Thus, there will not be *the* manager, but managers in the future. Each will have a broader perspective and knowledge than today's generalists and higher skills than many of today's specialists. Each will have a distinctive specialty which he will pursue through his career. Both the generalist's and the specialist's knowledge will be changing at a more rapid rate than today, threatening obsolescence on the job and requiring continuing attention to learning. Together, these trends will require substantial new departures in the approach to management education. Four probable departures are described below.

The first will be to develop two types of professional learning programmes with a degree of specialization within each. One will at the outset develop in all students the generic skills and knowledge of management and then allow each to choose a specialization path which best suits his abilities and interests (for an example of such a programme see the Masters Program Brochure of the Graduate School of Management, Vanderbilt University). The second programme for aspiring knowledge workers, will reverse the priorities. It will focus first on a broad understanding of various branches of managerial knowledge and their respective applicability, second on developing in depth a set of technical skills, and third on enough understanding of management to enable the student to interact and communicate with managers.

The second departure will focus the education process on knowledge and skills which remain relatively stable through a managerial career. Thus, an understanding of the socio—economic—political dynamics of the post-industrial era will serve the student longer than an in-depth understanding of food franchizing (which is an interesting manifestation of this dynamic); or a generalized skill in ill-structured problem-solving will last longer than a specific skill in cross-impact analysis.

This is not to suggest that situation-specific perishable skills and knowledge will become unnecessary, but given their rate of obsolescence, the manager will have to acquire and discard them as they occur. Thus, the third departure will focus attention on development of learning skills; an ability to sieze up rapidly and efficiently the social structure in an unfamiliar environment, the prevailing values, the cultural moves, and to select the appropriate mode of communication and style of leadership; an ability to confront a new body of knowledge and learn quickly its principle ingredients and its applicability; an ability, when confronted with a novel problem, to identify the key variables, to perceive their principal relationships, to bring to bear the relevant expertise and to select the most appropriate solution method. By comparison, the bulk of a manager's learning today is focused not on confronting novel environments, but on increasing his manipulative skills and knowledge in a few familiar environments. Thus, a major educational refocusing will be needed.

The fourth departure will be to spread a manager's education over his career span. The total volume of learning and its perishability will require a departure from today's practice: from both the episodic unconnected learning exposures for practising managers and the 40 years' worth of inoculation of management knowhow offered in today's masters level programmes. It is not yet clear what institutional arrangements will develop to handle this problem. It *is* clear that career-long learning will become a necessity in the post-industrial era.

References

Ansoff, H. I. (1965). 'The firm of the future', *Harvard Business Review,* Sept.–Oct.

Ansoff, H. I. (1968). 'The innovative firm', *Long Range Planning Journal,* 1, No. 2.

Ansoff, H. I. (1972). 'The concept of strategic management', *The Journal of Business Policy,* 2, No. 4, Summer.

Ansoff, H. I. (1973a). 'The next twenty years in management education', *The Library Quarterly,* 43, No. 4, Oct.

Ansoff, H. I. (1973b). Management on the threshold of the post-industrial era, *Challenge to Leadership, Managing in a Changing World,* New York, Free Press.

Ansoff, H. I. and Brandenburg, R. G. (1969). 'The general manager of the future', *California management Review,* 11, No. 3, Spring.

Beckwith, B. P. (1967). *The Next 500 Years,* New York, Exposition Press.

Bowen, H. R. (1949). 'Future of business education', *The Challenge of Business Education,* Chicago, University of Chicago Press, p. 36.

Brickman, W. W., and Lehrer, S. (Eds.) (1966). *Automation, Education and Human Values,* New York School and Society Books.

Carnegie Commission on Higher Education, (1971). 'Less Times, More Options: Education Beyond the High School', a special report and recommendations, New York, McGraw-Hill.

Carroll, T. H. (1958). *Collegiate Business Education in the Next Quarter Century,* Morgantown, West Virginia University Press, 3.

Clark, C. D. (1969). 'New directions in professional business education' *Preparing Business. Leaders Today,* Ed. P. Drucker, New York, Prentice-Hall, p. 245.

Drucker, P. F. (1969a). *The Age of Discontinuity,* New York, Harper and Row.

Drucker, P. F. Ed., (1969b). *Preparing Business Leaders Today,* New Jersey, Prentice-Hall.

Fiedler, F. E. (1973). 'The trouble with leadership training is that it doesn't train leaders', *Psychology Today,* Feb.

Gaber, D. (1965). *Inventing the Future,* New York, Knoff.

The Graduate School of Management, Vanderbilt University, Masters Program Brochure.

Hodgkinson, H. L. (1970). *Institutions in Transition,* Carnegie Commission on Higher Education.

Jungk, R. and Galtung, J. (Eds.) (1970). *Mankind 2000,* London, Allen and Unwin.

Kahn, H. and Wierner, A. J. (1969). *The Year 2000,* London, Macmillan.

Kerr, C. (1963). *The Uses of the University,* Cambridge, Massachusetts, Harvard University Press.

Kroll, A. M. (Ed.) (1970). *Issues in American Education,* New York, Oxford University Press.

Toffler, A. (1970). *Future Shock,* New York, Random House.

Notes

1. This chapter is an abbreviation of Ansoff (1973a).

2. Since education of managers for business is best developed, it receives our primary attention in this chapter. The question of applicability of business management to other purposive organizations has been treated in detail in Ansoff (1973b).

3. The fact that this atomistic perception has persisted till the present time is testified by the fact that in many business schools (including more than one of the world's leading ones) functional courses are followed by an 'integrative' one in which 'students apply what they learned to complex problems'. The implication is that there is nothing left to be learned once one has mastered functional knowledge.

4. A recent series of studies measured the relative success of 'task-motivated' and 'relationship-motivated' individuals in different managerial settings. The results point to a correlation of success to the match of the individual to the setting (Fiedler, 1973).

5. In the United States there is not yet enough evidence to show whether the corporate office is more or less effective than the single responsible executive concept. But in Europe, where the managerial culture has long been accepted as the concept of collegiality, a number of successful firms give evidence that the 'corporate office' can be made to work successfully.

6. The prototype of this generalist—specialist role exists in some collegially structured managements (e.g., DuPont Corporation). However, the structure today is limited to top management and the managers are 'defined', not trained, for their roles. In the future, they will be trained and the collegiality will spread downward through the organization.

ORGANIZATIONAL DESIGN, EMPLOYEE MOTIVATION AND THE SUPPORT OF STRATEGIC MOTIVATION

ROBERT A. ULLRICH

As we find ourselves rushing headlong, and sometimes being dragged unwillingly, into an era of unprecedented social and environmental change, managers are confronted with the problem of creating and maintaining interfaces with an environment that undergoes discontinuous change. Until the very recent past, the field of organizational behaviour tended to treat the problems of employee motivation and organizational change as related but separate areas of study. Given the rates of change evidenced in contemporary society, however, managerial concerns for steady-state efficiency must of necessity, give way to concerns for organizational efficiency under conditions of rapid and frequent change. Under these conditions, problems of increasing work motivation and decreasing employee resistance to change become inseparable. Perhaps in the not-too-distant future they will become identical by definition.

1. Current Perspectives on Motivation and Change

Considerable progress has been made to date in formulating, testing, and making direct organizational application of constructs of employee motivation and change processes. Works such as Herzberg (1967), Likert (1967), Tannenbaum (1962) and Bass (1970), to name a few, are distinguished by both their conceptual merits and their demonstrated applicability in contemporary organizational settings. Characteristically, each of the contributions mentioned above is based upon the assumption that employee productivity in both static and dynamic organinizational settings is increased when psychological dimensions of the employee's task are arranged such that basic and hitherto unfulfilled individual and group needs are met. No less characteristic of these studies is their assumed generality; that is, implicit in the prescriptions that arise from works of this sort is the notion that they are appropriate to work settings regardless of the technologies, organizational designs and organizational subcultures in which they are found. The lesson management is led to conclude from these and other studies is that increasing productivity and decreasing resistance to planned change can be accomplished by increasing or redirecting the motives of individuals within the organization.

Herzberg (1967) argues (with apparent good reason, but not without justifiable criticism) that factors intrinsic to the work itself (for example, achievement, recognition and responsibility) are significantly more likely to be sources of employee motivation than of dissatisfaction. Conversely, elements of the work setting that are extrinsic to the work itself (for example, company policy and administration, technical supervision and working conditions) are significantly more likely to be sources of dissatisfaction than of motivation. Management, therefore, is advised that improvements in extrinsic work elements will lead to a reduction in employees' dissatisfaction but to material increases in their motivation. Increased employee motivation is achieved primarily through increases in the availability of elements in the work setting that are intrinsic to the work itself.

Likert (1967) advocates what he calls the 'System Four' approach to management. System Four management is essentially an organizational design which serves to provide supportive relationships for its members, opportunities for group decision-making and group supervision, and the establishment of high-performance goals. In System Four organizations, both superiors and subordinates maintain high aspirations for the organization's performance. These aspirations, in fact, become established as the goals of the groups which make decisions and manage the organization. According to Likert, an organization that emphasizes support of the individual and his needs and allows for group management and decision-making *via* overlapping membership in the various strata of the organization's hierarchy (the linking pin function) provides the means by which the needs and desires of individuals can be met through the achievement of organizational objectives.

Research conducted by Tannenbaum (1962) and his associates indicates that there is an identifiable relationship between the type of influence processes found in an organization and the organization's effectiveness. Organizations in which top-, middle- and lower-level members all report that they have little influence over what goes on in the organization can be described as anarchistic. Authoritarian organizations are defined as those in which the level of influence exercised by the individual diminishes as one moves down through the organization's hierarchy. Conversely, democratic organizations are defined by Tannenbaum as those in which influence is inversely related to position in the hierarchy. Finally, organizations in which all members, regardless of their position in the hierarchy, report that they enjoy a high degree of influence over organizational affairs are classified as high total influence organizations. Tannenbaum goes on to demonstrate through studies conducted in numerous different settings that organizations which report high total influence are more effective in attaining their goals, regardless of how the goals differ from one organization to another, than are organizations falling into the remaining three categories.

Consistent with the orientation of Likert (1967), Bass (1970) argues that behavioural obstacles to the implementation of organizational plans can be reduced by moving portions of the planning process down into lower levels of the organization's hierarchy. In a study using a sample of 600 managers from six different cultures, Bass reports the managers' evaluations of their own performances when operating by their own plans and when operating by plans assigned to them by others. In an overwhelming majority of cases, managers report that their own plan is better, more flexible, easier to understand and makes better use of available manpower. Furthermore, they report having greater feelings of responsibility for the plans of their own design than for plans devised for them by others.

Where cooperative efforts between planners and doers are physically, economically or rationally unsound, Bass suggests that difficulties in implementing the results of planning can be ameliorated by: (1) building milestones into organization's plans that will enable those who are reponsible for a plan's implementation to develop a sense of accomplishment as these milestones are met, (2) discovering and resolving the reservations of non-planners concerning the plan's feasibility, (3) promoting commitment by allowing non-planners to modify non-critical elements of the plan and to provide planners corrective feedback, (4) building flexibility into the plan, (5) minimizing competition between planners and non-planners and (6) promoting understanding of the plan *via* effective instruction and communication.

The summaries of the works provided above are, indeed, too brief to do their originators justice. It is hoped, however, that they have served to illustrate some of the commonalities that pervade much of the literature in organizational behaviour. Underlying each of the organizational prescriptions is the implicit or explicit assumption that the affairs of an organization will be more readily discharged by employees who are provided opportunities to fulfill their needs for achievement, responsibility, recognition and the like; that providing the means for fulfilling individual and group needs will enhance the organization's ability to meet its objectives regardless of the technology or organizational system within which these goals are sought and regardless of the mental processes whereby the organization's goals and strategies are derived. These assumptions are of particular importance to individuals who formulate and implement organizational plans. Clearly, the groups that are delegated decision-making responsibility under System Four management, high total influence systems and even management by objectives (Odiorne, 1965) do not, in the last analysis, provide goals and strategic direction for the organization as a whole. Rather, they are seen as having the authority to choose from among alternative courses of action that are assumed to contribute to the attainment of pre-established goals and objectives. Hence, the assumption is reduced to the notion that, given organizational goals and a plan for their attainment, increasing employee motivation will increase the likelihood that these goals will be met.

One of the most elegant notions in the literature on motivation theory holds that productivity is a multiplicative function of motivation and ability. The question to be raised at this point is whether all elements of an organization are *able* to coordinate and control their activities through a planning process, for if it appears that a substantial number of an organization's members are unable, by virtue of the nature of their work, to direct their activities according to the plans of others, then one must argue that attempts to increase the motivation and commitment of the employees charged with the plan's implementation will, in these cases, prove futile.

2. Planning and the Problem-Solving Process

Central to the differentiation among membership roles in an organization is the nature of the problem-solving process required of successful incumbents of each role. Processes for solving problems can be differentiated according to the degree to which the problems themselves vary and to the extent that the search for problem solutions is logical and analysable.[1] In terms of variability, one can postulate that problems can be identified according to their location on a dimension that ranges from little variability with few exceptions at one extreme to great variability with many exceptions at the other. For example, in a large personnel department one individual may be responsible for tasks such as administering psychological tests to job applicants, tasks that do not vary greatly from one instance to the next and that give rise to few exceptions; while a second individual may be responsible for counselling employees who seek such assistance in connection with difficulties arising from their organizational or personal life. In the latter instance, the problems that confront the counsellor are subject to considerable variance. Similar dichotomies can be drawn by contrasting the problems encountered by individuals who work in accounting *versus* planning, production (especially in continuous process industries) *versus* research and development, and inventory control *versus* purchasing.

Obviously, the examples provided above are not pure examples in that the problems that fall into each half of the dichotomy can be further dichotomized according to whether or not logical, analysable approaches are available for their solution. Faced with a problem, an individual generally undertakes a process of search for feasible solutions. For certain classes of problems the process of search is logical in that it attempts to match the problems' characteristics with appropriate, learned solution steps. This being the case, the search procedure can be viewed as analysable. For example, automobile repair manuals provide the mechanic with logically sequenced procedures that can be followed in order to diagnose and remedy machine malfunctions. For other classes of problems, however, known solutions are unavailable to the problem-solver. Lacking manuals, programmes or formulae that facilitate a logical approach to the problem's solution, the individual is left to rely on problem-solving techniques that are based on the individual's experience, hunches, intuition and the like. In such cases, the process of searching for problem solutions is not analysable. Examples of problems for which solutions cannot be found via logical, analysable search include those that arise out of the need for innovation. Creativity, judgement and intuition frequently come into play as solutions are sought for problems in areas such as new product design, advertising and strategic planning.

Viewing problems according to both dimensions simultaneously allows us to identify four distinctly different problem categories. In doing so, it becomes possible to describe various differentiated work roles in complex organizations in terms of the category of problems that is most representative of the problems assigned to each role. Finally, by making adaptations to the work of Perrow (1970), it will be possible to make judgemental statements about the appropriateness of planning for the coordination of the work performed by these roles.[2]

Beginning in the lower right-hand quadrant of Figure 1, we find a class of problems that is described in terms of little or no variability and for which solutions can be obtained through a logical, analysable search process. Once identified, the solutions to these problems become rote. Clerks, order-takers, key-punchers, assemblers and the like deal with repetitive problems that have rote solutions. So mechanistic are these solutions, in fact, that most will be taken over by machines once what are at present technological difficulties are overcome. Key-punching, for example, will be subject to mechanization when optical scanning devices are refined to the extent that their economies are in line with competing personnel costs.

The quadrant numbered 2 in Figure 1 defines a class of problems that have programmable solutions. Since problem solutions can be developed using logical, analysable search procedures, coping with a large variety of different problems takes the form of developing programmed, step-by-step solutions for each problem, often making use of subroutines or techniques that are appropriate to a relatively large number of different programmes. An engineer, for example, who

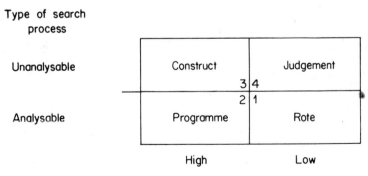

Figure 1. Problem characteristics and solution processes. Adapted from Perrow (1970).

custom designs centrifugal pumps for different users has a task for which a programmatic set of solutions exists. Although the design problem will change according to the material to be pumped, its temperature, rate of flow and the like, formulae and tables are at his disposal for the determination of appropriate structural modifications to the basic design. These formulae, moreover, constitute a set of subroutines that are appropriate to an entire class of design problems.

Quadrant number 4 contains a class of problems that vary little over time but lack solutions that can be determined via logical, analysable search. Judgement, intuition and experience weigh heavily in the solution of problems having these characteristics. It is, in fact, the repetitive nature of the problems that allows judgement to be built upon a collection of correlated but unexplained empirical data. The task of selecting manuscripts for publication is one that is repetitive and that requires considerable judgement. Although the decision-maker in this example may be provided with considerable data about the manuscripts under consideration and may have had considerable experience observing the 'kinds' of books that sell beyond the break-even point, he is for the most part unable to explicate the set of decision rules that apply to his eventual decision.

Finally, quadrant number 3 describes a class of problems that are subject to considerable variation and for which solutions cannot be derived through the use of logical, analysable search processes. Not being repetitive, these problems fail to provide the kinds of experiences that allow judgement to be formed, based on unexplained correlations of data. In attempting to develop solutions for problems with these characteristics, the individual generally relies on hypothetical constructs that serve both as paradigms for the various problems encountered and as general statements of cause and effect. Thus the psychiatrist is able to deal with unending variations of neuroses using personality constructs in the absence of laws of personality or behaviour. Establishing strategic plans and objectives and providing for their implementation are problems that utilize constructs in their solutions rather than judgement or programmatic sequencing of techniques, formulae and the like. In fact, most interorganizational problems, whether they are found in industry, government, academia or other segments of society, appear to be solved through the use of constructs.

The various activities that are carried out by complex organizations are coordinated by two major processes — planning and feedback. Planning, whether conducted by the 'doer' or by planners for the 'doer', can coordinate the work of an organizational unit when the work consists of solving problems that have solutions which can be derived through logical, analysable search procedures. Rote problems, as indicated by quadrant number 1 of Figure 2, can be planned for in considerable detail. Not only can we coordinate rote functions by specifying input and output criteria, we can also plan, if we choose, that exact nature of the activities that transform input into output. This, essentially, is the domain of time-and-motion study.

The problems described in quadrant number 2 are also subject to coordina-

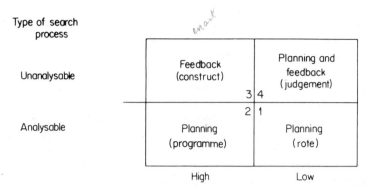

Figure 2. Problem characteristics and coordination processes. Adapted from Perrow (1970).

tion by planning. In this case, however, the degree of problem variation is great enough to render detailed planning overly complex. Hence, while overall planning and coordination are usually performed by others, much of the detailed planning left to the discretion of the organizational unit itself.

More complex situations are brought to light by quadrants 3 and 4. The problems described in quadrant 3 are solved by taking actions that are inferred from the hypothetical construct that defines the situation at hand. The eventual appropriateness (or inappropriateness) of these actions, then, is determined from the results which they produce. On the basis of these results, the problem-solver will be moved to derive more appropriate responses from his construct, to use the data gained from analysis of results to modify his construct prior to seeking a better course of action, or to do both. In any case, the problem-solver coordinates his activities (action-taking and construct-formulating) using the feedback that these activities produce. In a very real sense we have described a problem-solver who is similar to the artist whose progress in producing a painting is directed in part by the painting itself as it takes form. The major point to be made here, however, is that responding to feedback, rather than planning, is thought to be the appropriate means for coordinating activities similar to those defined in quadrant 3.

Quadrant 4 of Figure 2 represents a class of problems that are unique in that coordination is achieved through both planning and corrective feedback. Being for the most part routine, the problems described here are amenable to control *via* planning. This is true, however, only insofar as the judgemental process and the data which give rise to judgement remain fairly constant. In reality, discretion in the problem-solving process rests not with the planner but with the individual whose judgement provides the basis for action. As this individual's judgemental processes change or as changes occur in the data upon which judgements are made (as raw materials, employees, the environment, etc., change), his decisions will depart from the expectations of the planner. Another way of stating this is that, although the individual's activities can be planned for in a stochastic sense, they are, in the last analysis, determined by corrective feedback rather than the planning process.

In summary, we have described organizational problems in terms of four categories and have postulated, based upon the characteristics of problems in each category, that planning is appropriate to two problem categories, partially appropriate to the third and inappropriate to the fourth. If this is the case, then the aforementioned techniques for increasing employee motivation and decreasing resistance to change have limited applicability in producing an organizational environmement that is responsive to coordination by planning. However, it is premature at this point in the analysis under development to render further conclusions.

3. Reducing Problem Complexity Through Rational Behaviour

In order to bring the organization's activities further under the control of management so as to render them more efficient in a rational sense and, consequently, more amenable to control *via* planning, management is generally seen to undertake one of the following courses of action (Figure 3).

Problems for which programmable solutions exist (quadrant 2) can be assigned to individuals who perform rote solutions through what has been called differentiation (Katz and Kahn, , 966). Essentially, as programmatic solutions are developed, subroutines that are repetitive by virtue of their commonality to numerous other programmes are delegated to individuals in the organization who perform these routines as rote functions. The individual whose task it was to solve problems that had the characteristics described by quadrant 2, through differentiation, assumes the role of planner for individuals who execute discrete elements of the solutions.

By the same token, problems that require judgemental solutions can, through the development and application of modelling techniques, be transformed into

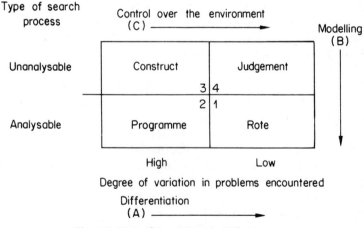

Figure 3. Means for problem simplification.

tasks requiring mainly rote operations. This, in essence, is what occurred in the area of inventory management subsequent to the 1950's. In earlier times, the function of maintaining inventory levels for thousands of line items required considerable experience with seasonal usage rates and trends. Clearly, reorder problems for each of thousands of line items could not be approached by inventory management personnel in a logical analysable manner. However, as inventory modelling techniques were developed through operations research and were met with advanced computer technology, it became possible to deal with each line item in inventory in a rote manner. Once computer programmes for inventory management were developed, not only were rote functions taken over by the computer, but necessary support activities for computerized inventory management such as key-punching, computer operation and the like came into being as rote operations. Finally, in order to cope with situations in which usage rates for particular items deviated from preestablished confidence intervals, logical, analysable procedures were established to determine the causes for deviation and to modify the computer programme accordingly.

Problems that are subject to considerable variation and for which logical, analysable search processes are unavailable tend to diminish the organization's ability to predict, plan and control its activities. In a sense, the situation described here can be thought to increase the entropy of the organizational system. For this reason, organizations attempt to restructure ill-structured problems as a means for self-preservation. Modelling, in this case, is inappropriate in that the variability of problems encountered renders the approach inefficient. Instead, the organization seeks to control the degree to which its problems vary. Attempts to influence consumer tastes, to control inputs through vertical integration and to 'socialize' employees are suggestive of the kinds of activities that are undertaken in order to reduce the variety of problems encountered. As variety is reduced, problem solutions increasingly lend themselves to judgement; and the inefficiencies which previously inhibited the application of modelling techniques are reduced.

The tendencies to simplify problems *via* controlling the environment, differentiating the organization and making application of modelling techniques are, of course, motivated by organizational concerns for steady-state efficiency. Yet, the accelerating rates of change that typify modern societies lead one to conclude that individuals and organizations will be increasingly confronted with problems that require solutions derived not through experience or formulae, but from constructs. To the extent that this is true, organizations which attempt to bring more and more of their problem-solving activities under the control of planning systems may, in fact, be failing to develop the organization of problem-solving capabilities that will be vital to survival in the future.

4. Reducing Problem Complexity Through Irrational Behaviour

Far more serious than the tendency mentioned above, however, is the propensity to bring problems under the control of planning systems through what appear to be irrational points of consensus within the organization.

Thompson and Tuden (1959) examine the various decision-making processes which organizations adopt in terms of the extent to which their members agree on two basic dimensions: (1) beliefs about the differential consequences of the several alternative courses of action which can be undertaken in attempting to achieve a particular goal, and (2) the evaluations of the potential outcomes (goals) of these courses of action on some scale of desirability. Decision-making regarding means implies that specific assumptions are made concerning the causal relationships between activities and their eventual results. Such assumptions about causation, in turn, imply knowledge of both historical and empirical evidence concerning relationships between means and ends as well as assumption about these relationships as they may exist in the future. The selection of goals, furthermore, indicates not a ranking of possible outcomes according to some inanimate schedule but the preferences that individuals and groups have for the various outcomes towards which their organization may strive.

In viewing organizations as decision-making entities, we can analyse the manner in which decisions are achieved by noting whether here is an agreement (consensus) among the organization's members on causal relationships and on preferences for specific outcomes, or whether there is disagreement (Figure 4).

Where decision-makers agree on the goals and means that are appropriate for the organization (or organizational subunit), the process of decision making becomes routine. Termed computation by Thompson and Tuden (1959), this *modus operandi* bears an overall similarity to the rote function mentioned above. On the other hand, where decision-makers disagree about both appropriate goals and means (quadrant number 3), the organizational anomie that results is alleviated when, through inspiration, innovation or a novel reinterpretation of reality, organizational members redefine the situation such that new goals or means emerge in a form that allows consensus to be developed. The most simple example of this phenomenon is provided by the instance in which organizational strife is overcome by developing solidarity around the presence of a real or fictitious external enemy that the leader has identified for his members. Quadrant number 4 describes a situation in which decision-makers

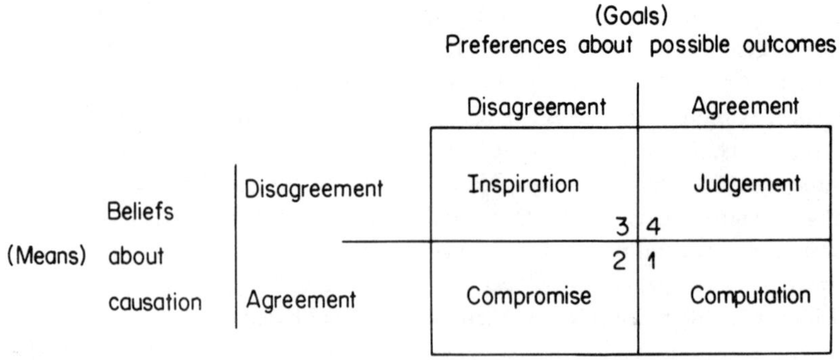

Figure 4. Organizational beliefs and problem-solving behaviour. Adapted from Thompson and Tuden (1959, p. 198).

disagree in their preferences for alternative means although there is consensus on organizational goals. This situation may come about because it is logically impossible to prove that a given course of action will provide for specific outcomes at some point in the future.

Faced with disagreement of this sort, decision-makers tend to rely on collective judgement. Indeed, there is evidence to suggest that in the face of uncertainty collective judgement is often superior to that of the individual (Sprott, 1969). Finally, one finds in quadrant number 2 a situation in which individuals agree on means but disagree concerning organizational goals. In a case such as this, collective judgement cannot resolve the disagreements indicated above, for the alternatives may be mutually exclusive in that the decision to implement one alternative course of action rules out the possibility of realizing outcomes associated with other courses of action. According to Thompson and Tuden, the appropriate strategy for selecting organizational goals in this situation is one of seeking compromise. Typical of bodies which attempt to achieve the selection of goals through compromise are those whose memberships are comprised of elected or appointed representatives, an example being the United Nations Security Council.

Thompson and Tuden propose that, while the situations they illustrate may occur with varying frequency, organizations as a rule tend not to be flexible but rather to adopt one of the four decision-making strategies as their dominant strategy and, furthermore, to base their structure upon the strategy chosen despite the fact that situations usually require differing strategies and structures. Thus in reacting to problems that are subject to considerable variance and for which solutions cannot be found *via* logical, analysable processes, some organizations may behave as if logical, well-structured solutions for these problems in fact exist. For example, it is obvious that students in a given college curriculum vary greatly in terms of their personalities and, significantly for our purposes, in terms of their learning styles and needs. In principle, each student ought to have access to the particular mode of instruction that best matches the manner in which he learns most efficiently. The learning problems encountered in the educational process, then, can be seen to vary extensively. Furthermore, solutions to these problems may be further removed from the realm of logical, analysable process than is generally held. By what method, for example, does one teach a student to become ethical, sensitive, rational or logical? Yet, the educational system, prior to the 1960's and to a lesser extent today, behaves as if all educational processes are programmable (in some cases, rote) and therefore amenable to detailed planning and extensive control. This, in fact, can be thought to have been at the heart of the student uprisings that occurred in the last decade. Frustrated by the bureaucratization of the learning process, students demanded, and in many instances won, the right to influence universities' decision-making processes. In terms of the models being developed here, they sought to make the educational system responsive to feedback and to break down existing beliefs that educational goals and means are known and therefore immune to question. The flurry of literature spawned by the movement (for example, Postman and Weingartner, 1971) served no purpose so much as that of questioning traditional educational goals and teaching methodologies. It is of great interest to note that initial responses to student demands were made in terms of curriculum revisions. Tinkering with the curriculum, the perennial indoor sport of faculties, left the goals and means of the university unchanged when, in actuality, these were the very issues being challenged. The ensuing attempts to provide students with unstructured learning situations, independent study and research opportunities and greater freedom of choice in selecting learning methods and objectives constituted more direct responses to the realization that, by virtue of the problem's characteristics, education in large measure defies control *via* planning. Parallel, though less dramatic, illustrations of this phenomenon in business and industry can be readily identified.

This is not to say that organizations should abandon arbitrary structures whenever arbitrariness is recognized. For instance, in the university example cited above, one can point to the fact that basic degree requirements are, historical precedence notwithstanding, arbitrary. The problem is that alternative requirements to those presently accepted would be equally arbitrary. While a degree is a symbol for a certain level of academic accomplishment, the relationship between the symbol and its referent rests, not on logic scientific principles of even hypothetical constructs, but on social convention. Business and governmental organizations are similarly fraught with policies and decision rules that are, in the last analysis, no more than conveniences. Yet they serve the necessary functions of limiting the organization's scope of activity and reducing the number of decisions, negotiations and arbitrations that arise from day-to-day activity and, in doing so, conserve the organization's energies. The major emphasis here, however, is on the necessity to examine goals, policies, procedures and the like, in order to determine whether or not problems have been irrationally defined by the organization to have those characteristics that make then appear most readily soluble.

5. Motivation and Resistance to Change

In the literature on motivation theory and organizational behaviour there is no assumption more questionable than the notion that human needs are basically insatiable. This line of thought leads to conclusions similar to the commonly held assertion that success in achieving aspired-to need satisfaction leads, in all cases, to increased aspiration levels for fulfilment of the need in question. Recent theory (Ullrich, 1972) holds that aspiration levels are integral to motives and are learned. Furthermore, an individual's experiences can be such that his aspiration for the fulfilment of a specific need becomes stabilized. Specifically, one of three relationships between the individual's current level of need fulfilment and his aspiration towards future levels of fulfilment for the need in question will be experienced as a result of the process to which allusion has been made here.

(1) For one reason or another various cues are *not* associated with increases in pleasure (or decreases in pain) such that an anticipatory goal response towards an increased level of need fulfilment is experienced. This is the point at which satiation occurs.

* (2) Undersatiation, on the other hand, can be said to occur when individuals aspire to rates of need fulfilment which are greater than the rates they experience.

(3) Finally, oversatiation can be said to occur when the level of need fulfilment experienced is in excess of the individual's aspirations concerning the level to which the need should be fulfilled. (Ullrich, 1972, p. 89)

These three relationships between need fulfilment and aspiration levels, together with perceptions of the environment, can be combined to produce the model illustrated in Figure 5.

In essence, the model states that for any given need, associated aspiration levels and perceptions of the environment in which need satisfaction is sought combine to produce identifiable goal-related behaviours. Where aspiration levels are in excess of current levels of need fulfilment and where the individual perceives that the aspired-to fulfilment is available in the environment at a 'reasonable cost', goal-directed behaviour occurs. Alternatively, if the individual's perceptions of the environment are such that he finds that the aspired-to goal is either lacking in the environment or available but only at what is felt to be a 'prohibitive cost', dissatisfaction will occur along with appropriate behaviours such as search for alternative sources of satisfaction, defensive behaviour, and the like. Finally, where the individual's level of aspiration for

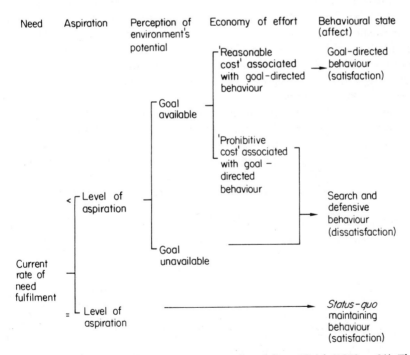

Figure 5. A model of behaviour in organizations. Adapted from Ullrich (1972, p. 91). The model presented here is a simplfied version of the original. The phenomenon of oversatiation, for example, has been excluded from consideration due to its apparent rarity in organizational settings.

need fulfilment is equal to the level of fulfilment that he presently enjoys, he will be motivated to engage in behaviour directed towards maintaining the *status quo*. Unlike goal-directed behaviour which seeks to realize increased need fulfilment through increased activity, *status-quo* maintaining behaviour that is undertaken by a rational individual may include attempts to reduce the amount of activity needed to preserve the *status quo*. By way of analogy we can say that the individual who is motivated to maintain the *status quo* will not attempt to maximize his total income. Rather, he will try to minimize the investment required to produce a fixed income. Research (Ullrich, 1972, p. 217) indicates that individuals, when motivated to maintain the *status quo*, experience levels of satisfaction that are not significantly different from those that accompany motives to increase levels of need fulfilment through goal-directed behaviour. The relatively high levels of satisfaction that accompany motives to maintain work relationships unchanged constitute major sources of resistance to change. Changes in the nature of the work itself and the surrounding work environment upset, so to speak, the economy of effort and reward that the individual is motivated to maintain.

One means for reducing this form of resistance to change lies in the organization's ability to raise the aspiration levels of its employees within the limits that it is prepared to meet. The tendency for some aspirations to stabilize is due, in part, to the individual's adjustment to a work environment in which greater aspirations are not justified in terms of the environment's potential to provide increased levels of need fulfilment. It is, after all, the poorly adjusted individual who continues to harbour aspirations that past experiences and realistic appraisals of the future show to be unattainable. Job enrichment and related techniques serve to restructure the individual's work and work environment such that hitherto unattainable sources of need satisfaction are brought within his grasp. The increased potential for need fulfilment serves as one of the cues that trigger changes in aspiration levels. Job changes that lead to job enrichment can be seen to arouse goal-directed behaviour. Conversely, changes to rote jobs that merely substitute one set of routine activities for another are most often met with resistance since they upset the worker's economy of effort.

One need that is thought to be fulfilled by job enrichment schemes that is not usually mentioned in the literature is the need for power (or autonomy). Job enrichment, as opposed to job enlargement, provides the employee with a substantial measure of control over the activities that constitute his job. Conceptually, the autonomy thus established serves to reduce resistance to planned change since the individual is able to influence, to some extent, the nature of the changes made. This degree of control allows not only for satisfaction of the individual's need for power, it also allows him to structure changes in the work setting in ways that contribute to the satisfaction of other needs. This, perhaps, serves as an explanation for the observation that participation in planning tends to facilitate the implementation of plans regardless of whether or not the employees in question perform rote functions.

For example, a study of sewing-machine operators indicates that planned change meets with the least resistance (as measured by productivity, levels of aggression and turnover rates) when workers are able to participate in the process of planning for change (Coch and French, 1966).

6. A Summary of Role Differentiation and the Planning Process

One idea that emerges from the discussion presented thus far is that employees' relationships to the planning process and, hence, the activities that can contribute to the successful implementation of formal plans, vary according to the characteristics of the problems that typify their roles in the organization. In earlier sections of this chapter distinctions were made among different classes of problems. Yet, jobs that consist entirely of problems belonging to one category are rare. More typical jobs deal with problems which belong to several categories.

Figure 6 illustrates work roles that are comprised of different problem assortments. Role No. 1 represents the functions of higher levels of management. While some activities consist of solving problems that require the application of programmatic solutions and judgement, the bulk of attention is devoted to problems that are solved through the application of constructs.[3] Dealing with personnel, for example, requires knowledge of at least naive constructs of personality and motivation. The concepts of management and management style, in fact, can be better defined as constructs than as principles or programmes.

In instances where an individual's work requires the integration of solutions that are derived from constructs, judgement, programmes and, to a limited extent, rote procedures, it is assumed that over time an internal consistency will develop such that the evolution of judgement and the selection of programmatic and rote solutions conform to the major constructs utilized by the individual. Although considerable variance will be found among the constructs entertained

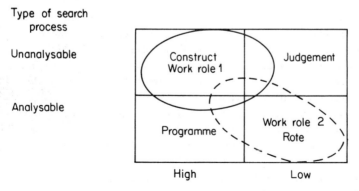

Figure 6. Role differentiation by problem mix.

by individuals who work in different segments of the organization, there is reason to believe that the thought processes of people who share responsibilities for common problems and similar educational backgrounds will tend towards conformity (Lawrence and Lorsch, 1967). Problems are encountered when activities are planned or undertaken by individuals entertaining one set of constructs in a manner that impinges on the activities of individuals who possess dissimilar constructs. Thus, a planning department may inadvertently develop a set of recommended changes for a segment of management that are fundamentally inconsistent with the constructs held by the managers in question. This observation, together with the notion that problems that are characterized by substantial variability and solutions that are derived from constructs are coordinated by feedback rather than planning gives rise to the following propositions.

(1) Participation in the planning processes by organizational members who have integrated their various problem-solving approaches with major work-related constructs facilitates the development and implementation of plans by virtue of the provision of opportunities to influence the development of plans that are consistent with the constructs they hold.

One of the findings of the Lawrence and Lorsch study (1967) is that effective organizations are characterized by interdepartmental differences, whereas less effective organizations tend to consist of people and structures that are more or less homogeneous across the organization. Thus participation in the planning process at the organizational level envisioned here should serve not to achieve consensus on constructs, but to allow planners to tailor their activities so that they are consistent with the constructs embraced by various segments of the organization.

(2) Since activities that are derived from constructs are coordinated by feedback, the participation of management in the planning process allows for the introduction of this feedback into the planning system.

Participation, in this instance, provides two avenues for improving the planning system. First, realization that certain activities cannot be planned for, in a formal sense, can trigger more appropriate responses from planners. For example, in the event that one is unable to plan the way in which a certain activity will contribute to organizational goals, it may be productive to constrain the manner in which such contributions are made. One is reminded here of Simon's observation that, 'If you allow me to determine the constraint, I don't care who selects the optimization criteria' (1964, p. 6). Second, feedback from operating units concerning the expected effects of various activities that are envisioned as part of an organizational plan can enrich the constructs utilized by planners.

Finally, what is indicated here is direct participation in the organization's planning process. Through organizational designs such as Likert's (1967) linking pin function, higher-level organizational members can be provided the opportunity to interact directly with the planning function. In dealing with resistance to change at lower levels of the organization, participation of this sort is generally uncalled for and could conceivably prove dysfunctional.

The second work role illustrated in Figure 6 represents the functions of lower-level ratios. While the ratios of the various kinds of problems encountered may vary from line to staff and from the shop floor to supervision, the roles, in general, differ from those found at higher organizational levels in terms of the extent to which constructs are called upon in the performance of duties. This is a major difference in that attempts to change the nature of functions performed at this level of the organization meet with resistance on occasion, but not with incompatibilities arising from conflicting constructs. Hence, a different form of participation in the planning process is appropriate for lower level employees. The nature of this participation is indicated in the following propositions.

(3) Since their job performance is not determined by internalized constructs, lower-level personnel experience motives to resist change that arise mainly from expectations that job changes will decrease, at least temporarily, their overall level of satisfaction.

Thus, we find that attempts to provide workers with influence over the manner in which changes will be made (but not over the nature of the changes themselves) result in decreased resistance to change. Presumably, the degree of autonomy thus established allows workers to implement change in a manner that is consistent with their needs and, in so doing, to attain a degree of satisfaction for their need for power.

(4) Motivational problems aside, the better the worker's understanding of anticipated job changes, the more skilful he will become in implementing these changes.

Allowing the worker to learn how and why changes will be made to his organizational unit provides him with a basis for understanding how variations in his own performance will affect the performance of other elements of the organization. More important, prior knowledge of the change process will enable the individual to mentally explore and rehearse various dimensions of his altered work role. There exists research evidence that suggests that observation (and reflection) can play as important a role in the learning of new skills as does practice (McCurdy, 1961). The increased productivity that is seen to attend job enrichment schemes (for example, Paul et al., 1969) can be attributed to more than increased worker motivation. In part, the degree of individual autonomy afforded to individuals through these schemes allows them to alter various aspects of their performance and, consequently, to learn their work role through experimentation. The increased knowledge of his work role and its variations not only allows the worker to operate more productively, it also equips him with skills and attitudes that enable him to alter performance during times of change.

References

Bass, B. M. (1970). 'When planning for others', in B. M. Bass and S. D. Deep (Eds.). *Current Perspectives for Managing Organizations*, Englewood Cliffs, Prentice-Hall, pp. 60–71.

Coch, L., and French, J. R. P., Jr. (1966). 'Overcoming resistance to change', in

H. Proshanski, and B. Seidenberg (Eds.), *Basic Studies in Social Psychology*, New York, Holt, Rinehart and Winston, pp. 444–60.

Hersberg, F., Mausner, B., and Snyderman, B. B. (1967). *The Motivation to Work*, New York, J. Wiley.

Katz, D., and Kahn, R. L. (1966). *The Social Psychology of Organizations*, New York, J. Wiley.

Lawrence, P. R., and Lorsch, J. W. (1967). *Organization and Environment: Managing Differentiation and Integration*, Boston, Division of Harvard University Graduate School of Business Administration.

Likert, R. (1967). *The Human Organization: Its Management and Value*, New York, McGraw-Hill.

McCurdy, H. G. (1961). *The Personal World*, New York, Harcourt, Brace and World.

Odiorne, G. S. (1965). *Management by Objectives: A System of Managerial Leadership*, New York, Pitman.

Paul, W. J., Robertson, K. B., and Herzberg, F. (1969). 'Job enrichment pays off', *Harvard Business Review*, March–April, 47, No. 2, 61.

Perrow, C. (1967). 'A framework for the comparative analysis of organizations', *American Sociological Review*, 32, 194.

Perrow, C. (1968). 'Technology and structural changes in business firms', in B. C. Roberts (Ed.), *Industrial Relations: Contemporary Issues*, New York, Macmillan.

Perrow, C. (1970). *Organizational Analysis: A Sociological View*, Belmont, Wadsworth.

Postman, N., and Weingartner, C. (1971). *Teaching as a Subversive Activity*, New York, Dell.

Simon, H. A. (1964). 'On the concept of an organizational goal', *Administrative Science Quarterly*, 9, 1.

Sprott, W. J. H. (1969). *Human Groups*, Harmondsworth, Penguin.

Tannenbaum, A. S. (1962). 'Control in organizations: individual adjustments and organizational performance', *Administrative Science Quarterly*, 7, 236.

Thompson, J. D., and Tuden, A. (1959). 'Strategies, structures, and processes of organizational decision', in J. E. Thompson, *et al.* (Eds.), *Comparative Studies in Administration*, Pittsburgh, University of Pittsburgh Press.

Ullrich, R. A. (1972). *A Theoretical Model of Human Behavior in Organizations: An Eclectic Approach*, Morristown, General Learning Corporation.

Notes

1. Adapted from Perrow (1970).

2. Perrow (1967; 1968; 1970) originated the analytical framework presented here as a means for categorizing technologies and the appropriate corresponding organizational structures. The same framework, it is felt, can be used to advantage to describe the classes of problems that confront various organizational decision makers and the forms of organization and control appropriate to the process whereby each class of problems is solved.

3. Rote functions are assumed to be delegated, for the most part, by management to lower levels in the organization.

ON THE PERSONAL DEVELOPMENT
OF THE STRATEGIC MANAGER

EDWIN M. BARTEE

It is one thing to be able to *think strategically* and it is another to be able to *act strategically*. This dichotomy represents the essence of the problem related to the personal development of strategic managers.

The problem may be further understood if we were to view an organization as a protective structure for its members against the high level of ambiguity and uncertainty that exists in the environment. This view would lead us to conclude that at least one reason people become members of organizations is to find a refuge and safety from the environment. The boundary conditions of the organization system serve as filters to protect its members from the high intensity of information that is prevalent outside the organization.

A part of this protection manifests itself in the form of tangible walls and physical structures that quite literally provide physical protection. Organizations also provide an opportunity for closer social relationships with other similar people which can serve to reinforce a need for social support and protection. A set of rules and norms also provide a greater predictability of behaviour within the functions of the organization. In each case, by comparison with its environment, the logical expectation would be that the necessity for an individual to take risks, to deal with conflict and to cope with ambiguity is significantly reduced within the organization as compared with an existence in its environment. It would logically follow, then, that as individuals become adapted to organizations and the insulation protection they provide, their tendency would be towards greater need for security and external protective mechanisms.

1. The Failure of Legitimate Learning Experiences

The temptation may be to suggest that the development of strategic managers is primarily a problem of learning new concepts of the right kind. The acquisition of cognitive knowledge is certainly a part of the issue, but does not deal with the critical problem of behavioural change. The primary issue here is one of *reinforced undesirable behaviour* rather than *insufficient knowledge.*

Learning new concepts will not influence the change in executive behaviour from an incremental style to an entrepreneurial style when the educational process used to learn them are inherently incremental in design. Our educational processes fall short because the institutions and individuals who operate and supply our educational systems suffer from the same dilemma as those organizations for which strategic managers are to be developed. Almost from the beginning we are exposed to a continual educational process that, by its design, reinforces incremental behaviour regardless of how entrepreneurial the cognitive information may be. For the most part, the typical formal learning process reinforces the following assumptions and behaviours.

(1) Legitimate learning is primarily a process of receiving prestructured and assimilated facts and data from an outside source. The individual behaviours that are reinforced are ones of passivity and dependence.

(2) Legitimate learning is almost totally an intellectual process of cognition and thought. The individual behaviours that are reinforced are ones in which *to know* is only *to know about*, with very little *knowing how*. This is particularly true for complex 'how's' that are involved in strategic management.

(3) Legitimate learning is only accomplished, for the most part, within well-structured, steady-state educational institutions. The behaviours that are reinforced are ones that perpetuate the steady-state processes that are prevalent within the educational environment.

If we accept these observations as true, it seems that there is little mystery as to why we do not have more managers behaving in an entrepreneurial manner. Also, given that the primary source of managers lies exactly within these 'legitimate learning' environments, it is not too difficult to become pessimistic in regard to future possibilities for an increase in the supply of entrepreneurial managers. It seems safe to assume that the conditions within our educational institutions will probably not change appreciably within the immediate future. And if this be true, it seems reasonable to assume that the problem of developing strategic managers is not one of education but of *reeducation*

2. The Process of Reeducation

What do we mean by reeducation? The first important aspect of the reeducative process involves not only learning but *unlearning*. The immediate and most difficult issue in this process is one in which an individual experiences basic behavioural changes. These changes in behaviour are many and complex, but they can be generalized in the following terms.

(1) Individual behaviour is changed from a basis *dependent* style to an evolving *interdependent* style.

(2) Individual behaviour is changed such that *knowing how* is legitimized as essential to a balance with *knowing about*.

(3) Individual behaviour is changed so that there is higher risk-taking behaviour and a higher tolerance for conflict and ambiguity.

Obviously, these are not objectives that are easily attained. They are probably not attainable at all unless the reeducative processes are developed as innovatively and effectively as possible.

A few obvious conclusions can be drawn concerning these processes. If re-education is to change behaviour towards an interdependent style, then it must obviously reduce the reinforcement of a dependent style. If 'knowing how' is to be balanced with 'knowing about', then the reeducative processes must give emphasis to experience-based learning. Also, if the behaviour is to change from a steady-state style to a high-risk style, the reeducative environment must be one in which high-risk style, the reeducative environment must be one in which high-risk behaviour is reinforced.

The reeducative process is inductive as well as deductive. The acquisition of knowledge in the inductive case is gained through the senses as a result of increased perceptual awareness, as opposed to a deductive process in which knowledge is acquired through conscious cognition as a result of intellectual reasoning. The reeducative goal is to gain a *balance* between these two processes. It is assumed that the contemporary human condition is one in which the deductive process is dominant. Therefore, to accomplish this balance, it is necessary to give heavy emphasis to inductive methods. Unfortunately, the reeducative process, because of this inductive emphasis, is often erroneously characterized as being inherently anti-intellectual and non-deductive.

How does this process relate to the development of strategic managers? What are some of the primary behaviours that we would expect from a qualified strategic manager? One such behaviour certainly would be the ability to function as an active and productive linkage between the organization and the environment. The implication for reeducation would therefore involve the structuring of the environment so that potential strategic managers could learn from it inductively.

3. The Phenomenology of Managerial Behaviour

Strategic managers are required to function effectively in ill-structured environments. If their personal style is one in which they have not exerienced any environments except well-structured ones, for the most part they will not be able to cope. Their response to the strategic personal environment will be one of threat. This will cause them to seek a reduction in the degree of *ambiguity* within the situation. To do otherwise would require them to deal with a level of *conflict* with which they are not able to cope. The degree of conflict would be a function of how much the managers expectations differ from the realities of their experiences. If their expectations are ones in which the environment around them (their experiences) is predictable, incremental and rational, they are certain not to have these expectations met in a futuristic, strategic environment. If they are required to function in such an environment, and their expectations are not met, they will then experience conflict. If their response to this conflict is one in which they are unable to modify their own personal expectations, then they have no alternative but to seek a different, more structured environment that matches their unchanging expectations.

If, however, they are capable of readjusting their expectations to fit the environmental situation, they would be able to tolerate the ambiguity, assume personal responsibility for modifying their own expectations, and therefore reduce the level of conflict for themselves so that they can effectively cope with the situation. The key difference between the two responses is characterized by the degree of dependency that the managers have on their external environment as compared to the dependency they have on their internally developed psychological processes. The reeducative experience is therefore one in which an individual is provided an opportunity to develop these internal psychological processes so that dependency upon external processes can be progressively minimized.

The reeducative process can be understood in terms of a *threat hierarchy* in which a manager's behaviour is characterized in terms of *psychological need, success criteria* and *chronological orientation*. These relationships are shown in Table 1.

Steady-state managers are obviously ones who tend to engage in the least threatening behaviour. That is, they are primarily preoccupied with current structural problems. Their basic need is to reduce ambiguity in their environment so that they can minimize personal conflict when their steady-state expectations are not met by this environment. One behaviour, but a more threatening one, would be to acquire certain cognitive skills that would increase the possibility of changing future environments so that they would better meet the managers' expectations. For individuals to assume responsibility for influencing the cognitive future, they must take greater risks. To assume such responsibility is to move in the direction of being a more effective strategic manager. However, the risk for these managers lies in the possibility of experiencing greater conflict in the future if their developed cognitive skills are insufficient to cope with the greater ambiguity.

There is obviously a limit to the degree of skills that can be acquired for meeting a constant set of expectations when the degree of ambiguity becomes great. When this limit is reached the logical recourse is to change expectations.

Our personal expectations can be cognitively understood, but they are socio-emotionally rooted in their development, and they are psychological in character (Kelly, 1955; Maslow, 1954). Our expectations of the future are formed as a result of our psychological experiences in the past. For a manager to learn how to cope with greater future ambiguity by changing personal expectations is a problem of developing a strategy for learning, that is, *learning how to learn*.

Managers who are learning how to learn are in a spectrum of development that is transactional in nature. That is, their life style is to commit themselves to a wider range of unfamiliar experiences, reflect upon these experiences, acquire the cognitive understanding necessary to internalize the behaviour, and repeat the cycle as an increasing act of individual commitment and less a dependency on their environment. The process of development that results from such learning can be characterized as follows.

(1) The strategic manager's set of future expectations is in a process of

Table 1. Managerial behaviour and its relationship to threat, ambiguity and conflict

Type of managerial behaviour	Manager's psychological need	Characteristics of behaviour		Manager's chronological orientation
		Success criteria for a manager's behaviour		
The manager is primarily preoccupied with current structural problems (least threat)	The manager is manifesting a need to reduce current ambiguity for himself	The manager is effectively discovering an environment that provides for structure and predictability that meets the manager's expectations		The manager is oriented from the past to the present in a cognitive sense
The manager is primarily preoccupied with the improvement of personal skills for solving future structured problems (greater threat)	The manager is manifesting a need to take responsibility for the reduction of future ambiguity for himself	The manager is effectively acquiring personal skills in problem-solving that allow him to influence the structure and predictability of future situations, so that the manager's future expectations are better met		The manager is oriented from the present to the future in a cognitive sense
The manager is primarily preoccupied with current interpersonal problems with other individuals at a socio-emotional level (greater threat)	The manager is manifesting a need to reduce current interpersonal conflict at a socio-emotional level	The manager is effectively resolving current interpersonal issues so that current problem-solving activity may effectively deal with the need for reduced ambiguity		The manager is oriented from the past to the present in a socio-emotional sense
The manager is primarily preoccupied with his personal development at a socio-emotional level (most threat)	The manager is manifesting a need to take responsibility for the reduction of interpersonal conflict at a socio-emotional level in the future	The manager is effectively acquiring a greater sense of personal self, differentiated from his external environment, so that he may more effectively cope with future interpersonal conflict		The manager is oriented from the present to the future in a socio-emotional sense

development and it is increasingly congruent with the changing multiple objectives of the environment and the developing strategies for choice between these objectives.

(2) The changing social needs of the strategic manager are increasingly satisfied by the ever-changing norms of conduct in the environment.

(3) The developing styles of interpersonal influence and control held by the strategic manager are increasingly consistent with the changing formal systems of authority and power in the environment.

(4) The changing ethical system of the strategic manager is increasingly consistent with the changing formal decision making processes in the environment.

What is significant to note in these processes is that strategic managers are far more than 'economic' in their make-up. They are also 'social beings' who seek satisfactions within their environment that are not only physiological but also psychological, sociological, political and legalistic in character. The 'economic model' is just not sufficient to adequately characterize the complex, dynamic task of developing strategic managers.

4. The Synthesis of Strategic Behaviour

Sir Francis Bacon once said, 'Those who have handled sciences have been either men of experiment or men of dogmas. The men of experiment are like the ant, they only collect and use: the reasoners resemble spiders, who make cobwebs out of their own substance. But the bee takes a middle course; it gathers its material from the flowers of the garden and of the field but transforms and digests it by a power of its own' (Bacon, 1960). It is clear that strategic managers are neither ants nor spiders, but bees. The material that they gather from their organizational 'gardens' and their environmental 'fields' is not merely collected and used, nor merely made into cobwebs. By utilizing a developed personal power of their own, strategic managers 'transform' and 'digest' this 'material' so that it represents a creative process of future-oriented change. The increasing personal development of these managers is apparent by their increasing tendency towards more effective risk-taking behaviour. For them to be willing to take such risks they must realize an increasing congruence between their personal goals and between their personal values, between their ideas and their feelings, and between their cognitive processes and their emotions. By realizing a greater personal congruency they are then able to take greater personal risks towards the influencing of change within their environment.

The pedagogy for the reeducative process and the synthesis of strategic behaviour consists of experience-based learning techniques. The general approach to this type of learning is as follows.

(1) A general conceptual orientation is obtained by the learner as a basis for the experience.

(2) The learner is then 'emersed' in the experience as an active, involved, fully participative person. The experience may be artificially structured as an

'exercise', or it may be a natural and real-time problem situation. The characteristics of the experience determine what can be learned from it.

(3) During and immediately after the involvement in the experience the learner receives feedback from an outside source. This feedback is designed to provide some continuous orientation to the cognitive world that relates to the experience and also provides a level of tension between the sensory and intellectual dimensions of the activity.

(4) After the learner withdraws from the experience, there is a period of reflection and assimilation. The experience is then internalized through the senses.

(5) This internalization stimulates an increase in perceptive awareness such that a cognitive dissonance is experienced. The individual responds to this condition by expressing a need for a new cognitive set to match the new level of awareness. It is at this point that theories and concepts are either created by the learner or deductively acquired from outside learning resources.

(6) The process of internalizing these newly acquired cognitive sets is a point of closure for the inductive method. These newly acquired intellectual states can serve as new orientations and the basis for a new experience with the cycle repeating.

The strategic problem is one in which a manager must explore the unknown and invent new approaches (heuristics) for the selection of future alternatives. To invent is to discover, and to explore is to pursue new situations and be able to make sense out of them. This cannot be done by someone who is accustomed to learning from well-structured situations that are primarily based upon knowledge of the past.

The methodology described above serves as a way in which the personal development of strategic managers may be accomplished so that *strategic behaviour* as well as strategic knowledge is learned. Past knowledge in the form of concepts and theories is not the material from which strategic behaviour can be learned but rather the orientation that is needed for *taking the first step*. This first step provides for the necessary intellectual awareness that is important for reducing the size of the conceptual world in a way that makes sense for the strategic problem at hand. It is the formation of the 'initial conditions' that are critical to the 'new situations'. An important part of this orientation would be the rules for a strategic search.

The second step is a critical one and proves to be the most difficult to execute in highly structured environments. The strategy opportunity space would contain the unstructured experiences that could serve as problem-centred learning opportunities. These situations are typically very complex and ambiguous, and to become 'emersed' in them to any significant degree requires a significant period of time to 'gain entry' into the task environment (Thompson, 1967). This process of gaining entry or 'making an intervention' is typically very time-consuming and is not generally understood by more traditional learning environments. It is only very recently that any body of knowledge has been developed on this process (Agryris, 1970). It is because of this lack of understanding that the entire reeducative process usually becomes dysfunctional in this second step. Typically, learners are seen to be 'wasting their time' when they are in the midst of the very difficult and intense struggle of gaining entry or making intervention into a problem situation. Another part of traditional learning environments that makes this step difficult to accomplish is the fact that instant evaluation is usually demanded of a situation which does not lend itself to immediate evaluation. When the initial experience is primarily one of gaining entry, then it is only possible to evaluate the effectiveness of that entry process. To attempt an evaluation of learning that is to be acquired within the task environment before this task environment is experienced is to create a disruption of the learning process.

In the third step the learner is to receive feedback from a learning resource who is outside the particular problem situation. In a specific strategic problem this feedback would provide continuing orientation in regard to the rules for strategy search, techniques of intervention and guidelines for choosing search directions. Developing strategic managers (the learners) would therefore be placed in desirable states of tension between their ongoing sensory experience and the outside feedback that they are receiving. Once the learners have successfully gained entry into the task environment, they are then able to acquire new sensory data that serve as material for the potential invention of new strategic alternatives. The possibility for evaluating this potential at this point is very low, if it exists at all.

The fourth step is concerned with the primary process of induction. The particular case was experienced in step two, and the generalization of this experience is first accomplished after the learners withdraw from it. The sensory data are internalized during a period of reflection and assimilation. In other words, the 'bees transform and digest the material by utilizing a developed personal power of their own'.

In the fifth step the developing strategic managers have reached a stage that will test their tolerance for personal conflict. As a result of the previous steps, the learners' levels of awareness and perception have been raised. Some of their past constructs about the world are no longer congruent with their newly internalized experiences and the developing expectations resulting from them. In the particular case of strategic alternatives, we would expect that some of the past alternatives would no longer be useful to these 'enlightened' individuals. Their response is to reduce the conflict by seeking new strategic alternatives that will be congruent with their new level of awareness. They will, therefore, become 'motivated' to develop the alternatives by creating their own, by acquiring different cognitive sets that were previously unknown, or by confirming the validity of existing alternatives. Step six serves as a terminal point to the general inductive process. The newly identified strategic alternatives can contribute to strategic change within the firm. They can also serve as new orientations for the replication of the reeducative learning process for the developing strategic manager.

References

Appelbaum, R. P. (1970). *Theories of Social Change,* Chicago, Markham.

Argyris, C. (1964). *Integrating the Individual and the Organization,* New York, Wiley.

Argyris, C. (1970). *Intervention Theory and Method,* Reading, Massachusetts, Addison-Wesley.

Bacon, Sir F. (1960). *The New Organon and Related Writings* (first published in 1620), Indianapolis, Bobbs-Merrill.

Kelly, G. A. (1955). *The Psychology of Personal Constructs,* New York, Norton.

Maslow, A. (1954). *Motivation and Personality,* New York, Harper and Row.

McClelland, D. C., and Winter, D. G. (1969). *Motivating Economic Achievement,* New York, Free Press.

O'Connell, J. J. (1968). *Managing Organizational Innovation,* Homewood, Illinois, Irwin.

Schein, E. H., and Bennis, W. G. (1967). *Personal and Organizational Change Through Group Methods,* New York, Wiley.

Thompson, J. D. (1967). *Organizations in Action,* New York, McGraw-Hill.

Vickers, Sir G. (1938). *Value Systems and Social Process,* New York, Basic Books.

V

Education
Selection and
Training

TOWARDS BETTER SELECTION AND PLACEMENT OF STRATEGIC MANAGERS

JAMES R. RAWLS and DONNA J. RAWLS

In any society, identification and grooming of management talent is critical to its continued development. In the United States, rapid industrial growth, continued expansion of investments and increasing consumer needs have interacted to create a true managerial elite. However, the need for capable managers now exceeds the supply, and, despite present economic conditions, the deficit appears to be growing (Bray and Moses, 1972; Campbell *et al* 1970; Guion, 1965; Megginson, 1967; Owens and Jewell, 1969).

The selection of potentially successful managers is becoming more and more complicated, due to the changing roles present day managers are expected to play. Organizations are now being forced to reorient themselves in order to respond more effectively to the changing demands from the environment. According to recent forecasts, problems of the future will include increasing foreign competition and a much greater need to penetrate foreign markets, accommodation to new values and aspirations of both management and the labour force, a redesigning of work roles in order to make them more satisfying, and an accelerating rate of death and birth of products and industries (Ansoff, 1973). As a result, managers are being forced to search for different response modes and to emphasize different behavioural dimensions in order to deal with these and other changing demands.

Present-day managers are being asked to play new roles and perform activities for which they often have little or no job-related background or experience. Furthermore, formal education very quickly becomes obsolete in such a rapidly changing technological society. Even when the manager attempts to update his training, the programmes that are offered are frequently not responsive to his present-day needs. In short, the criteria of managerial success are being redefined without accompanying support systems to enable the manager to attain success.

Thus, both the predictor and criterion sides of the selection equation are affected.

The preponderance of evidence seems to support the need for a new breed of manager. Recent trends appear to indicate that this 'new manager' must move towards more innovative handling of transactions between the organization and various environments characterized by ambiguity, uncertainty, inconsistency and increasingly high personal and organizational risk. This would seemingly require an increasingly large cadre emphasizing leadership that anticipates, channels and helps to create the forces of change. It would, thus, appear that a new creative, imaginative, entrepreneurial element will be required to cope with the rapidly changing environment. As Peter Drucker (1969, p. 43) put it:

Now we are entering again an era in which emphasis will be on entrepreneurship. However, it will not be the entrepreneurship of a century ago, that is, the ability of a single man to organize a business he himself could run, control, embrace. It will rather be the ability to create and direct an organization for the new. We need men who can build a new structure of entrepreneurship on the managerial foundations laid these last fifty years.

Recently, Howard Johnson (1968), the president of MIT, suggested that what management of the 70's needs most are individuals with entrepreneurial spirit and energy, who are innovative, who have the capacity for translating ideas into action, who are receptive to change and are initiators of change, who have high tolerance for ambiguity and uncertainty, and who have the will to risk.

A number of other authors, most notably Ansoff (1972; 1973), have suggested that this, in fact, is the case. While acknowledging the need for entrepreneurial input or strategic management, the term Ansoff prefers, he does not negate the import of the steady-state manager.

Ansoff (1972) describes the strategic manager of entrepreneurial manager as being driven by the desire to invent, to discover new markets and market techniques, to explore opportunities and to search for new ventures. He has risk-taking propensities; a positive attitude towards change; is goal-oriented (a self-actualizer); and is a divergent problem-solver, seeking to anticipate and forecast problems and opportunities. The operating manager or steady-state manager, on the other hand, is described as the administrator, as being concerned with the daily operating problems of the organization, and as focusing his efforts on developing a stable internal culture. He is a change-absorber, a cautious risk-taker and a convergent problem-solver. Strategic managers are described as charismatic individuals who use their skills to inspire others to accept change, while operating managers more often provide motivation for fellow workers to excel or improve over their past performance. Both types of managers are essential, although there is currently a need for a greater proportion of entrepreneurial managers.

On initial reflection it seems highly probable that the successful strategic manager and the successful operating manager may possess some of the same characteristics. Aside from exceptional cases, success in either management mode requires intelligence, general problem-solving ability (though they may possess different problem-solving skills and may choose to work on different kinds of problems) and ability to make decisions. In addition, success in both modes would more likely be associated with individuals who were aggressive, persistent, self-confident, dependable and emotionally mature. Skill in communications is essential, and leadership ability is also required for effective management in either mode (although Ansoff (1972) maintains that leadership styles differentiate the two types of managers).

The majority of selection research has, of course, been undertaken in order to identify successful managers in a global sense. There have been no studies to date that have attempted to identify potentially successful strategic managers as an isolated entity. The purpose of the present chapter is to speculate as to what characteristics one might look for in the 'new manager' and to suggest some ways and means which should assist in the identification and placement of individuals who would perform more effectively as strategic managers as opposed to operations managers. Let us begin by looking at the research findings that focus on the selection of successful managers in general.

1. Managers in General

The problem of identifying capable management personnel has received considerable attention in the past two decades. This has resulted, in part, from the recognition of the rather obvious fact that efficacious selection can contribute significantly to the effective and efficient functioning of organizations and to the satisfaction and productivity of individuals within these organizations. In addition, there has been, as was mentioned earlier, a growing concern with regard to the dwindling supply of competent managerial talent.

The selection research done to date has in all likelihood resulted in monetary savings of considerable magnitude. Moreover, it has probably eliminated numerous problems associated with placing an individual in a position that would make demands upon him beyond his ability to perform. A review of the management selection literature indicates that certain attributes rather consistently show up as being characteristic of the successful manager (see Table 1). For example, successful managers are fairly consistently found to be more dominant, aggressive, self-confident, independent, flexible, higher in need achievement and above average in intelligence. Furthermore, they have demonstrated rather consistent life patterns of successful endeavours, for example, successful peer and family relations, above-average scholastic achievement in high school and college, involvement in numerous extracurricular activities, active social life and attainment of positions of leadership in the organizations to which they belong.

The major criticism of these research efforts has been that managerial success has generally been gauged by very global criterion measures such as overall performance ratings by immediate superiors or certain indices related to salary, promotions, etc. The utilization of such broad-based criterion measures fails to take into consideration individual knowledge and skills that may be unique given certain functions and/or levels. Lacking these kinds of considerations, it has not been infrequent that individuals who have performed very well at one level in

Table 1. Managers in general

Dominant
Aggressive
Self-confident
High capacity for status
Desire for personal recognition
High energy level
Independent (self-reliant)
Self-reliant
Flexible (adaptive)
High frustration tolerance
Objective
Sociable
Extroverts
Cooperative and considerate
Leadership ability
Persuasive
Decisive
Take initiative (willingness to assume responsibility)
Masculine interest patterns
High need for achievement
High need for power
Emotionally mature (stable)
Above average intelligence (mental ability)
Higher scores on arithmetic and vocabulary tests
Verbal
Accept loss and hostility from others
Express hostility tactfully
Systematic in approach to problems
More likely to involve subordinates in decision-making
Take more time to make decisions
Perform more work in allotted time
Prefer activities involving independent thought
Prefer activities involving some risk
Reject activities involving technical pursuits and concentration on details
Enjoy contact with others in a leadership or dominant role
Prefer competitive physical and social recreations as opposed to aesthetic or cultural forms
    of recreation
Not very interested in social services or humanitarian activities
Primarily from business and proprietary classes while secondarily from professions and
    semi-professional classes
Happy early home life
Belonged to more organized early childhood groups
Assumed adult responsibility at an early age
Belonged to more high school, college and professional organizations
Involved in more extracurricular activities in high school and college
Successful in college both scholastically and in extracurricular activities
Take advantage of leadership opportunities
Hold numerous offices in social and professional organizations
Active in social activities as an adult
History of good health
Active in sports and hobbies
Above-average education
Continued to take advantage of emotional opportunities
Consistent life pattern of successful endeavours

one function are, in Peter Principle terms, promoted to their level of incompetence. The usual response to this situation is simply to eventually place such an individual outside the path of normal progress into some non-interfering, non-functional position. The obvious result is a gross misuse of the resources of previously demonstrated managerial talent, a loss that present-day organizations can ill afford.

Recent trends in management selection indicate a strong movement away from the use of global measures towards the utilization of more comprehensive systematic selection models that take into account individual, job and organizational variables. In so doing, the selection process encompasses the personal characteristics, training needs and organizational climate factors that foster managerial success (Bray and Moses, 1972; Campbell et al., 1970).

Since successful managerial performance results from an interaction of at least ability, personality, motivational and organizational factors, recent trends are most encouraging indeed. Moreover, given the current trends in management selection which emphasize career planning, placement and the utilization of selection instruments in pointing out individual training needs, current and future research should be much more responsive to present-day management needs. The directions now being taken should contribute significantly to identifying managerial potential earlier and to assisting organizations and individuals in optimally utilizing their human resources. An important outcome might be to channel the steady-state manager and the strategic manager into areas within the organization that would optimally utilize their abilities.

Although no research has yet been focused specifically on the selection of the strategic manager, some related research should have a direct bearing upon the selection of strategic managers. The first of these relates to studies focusing on the identification of entrepreneurs.

2. Entrepreneurs

According to the prevailing definition, an entrepreneur is one whose desire for independence has motivated him to establish his own firm. Often when entrepreneurs begin a start-up operation it is the result of negative factors associated with their previous corporate experiences. Elements like the following send entrepreneurs screaming for the corporation's exit (Dible, 1971): (a) inequities between major innovative contributions and financial rewards; (b) lack of recognition for innovative contributions in promotion and salary policies; (c) inadequate corporate communications from the generation of an idea to its fruition; and (d) interference with immediate reinforcement needs for personal achievement due to corporate red tape.

There are also elements outside the corporation that lure the entrepreneur to test his mettle (Dible, 1971). These include the following: (a) the desire to 'do his own thing'; (b) motivation to be his own boss; (c) the desire for personal fame; (d) motivation to obtain wealth; and (e) the desire for personal achievement or the sheer joy of winning.

In light of the entrepreneur's origin, it seems highly probable that many of the same characteristics possessed by entrepreneurs would also characterize the

Table 2. Entrepreneurs

Dominant
Aggressive
Self-confident
Optimistic
High capacity for status
Desire for personal recognition
High energy level
Independent (self-reliant)
Persistent (hard workers)
Flexible (adaptive)
High frustration tolerance
Extroverts
High need for achievement
Ego strength
Creative (imaginative, innovative)
High tolerance for ambiguity
Emotionally mature (stable)
Leadership ability (charismatic)
Decisive
Receptive to change
Ability to translate ideas into action
Risk-takers (but not gamblers)
Need for challenge
Enjoy situations in which they take personal responsibility for finding solutions to problems
Verbal
Communications skills
Early work history
Worked in smaller firms where they could view the whole organization
Hard-working
Guts (sheer determination)
Willing to work long hours
Do a lot of things
Desire immediate feedback
Cannot accept the leadership of others without reservation
Desire to be their own boss
Not recognized as being among the best managers
Desire to start their own business
Recognition of their own limitations and willingness to supplement their talents with others'
    abilities
Prefer experts to friends as working partners
Honest
Come from families with a tradition of independent business experience
Fathers were not authoritarian
Respect for father
Often bored with school
Low motivation for reading
Often do well with their hands
Like to travel
Intellectually curious
Good at putting things together and making new and better combinations
Willing to give up one bird in the hand to get two in the bush

---

strategic manager. Certainly, the profile of an entrepreneur should be much more like that of a strategic manager than a steady-state manager.

A review of the literature indicates that there are indeed, a number of personality and background factors that are characteristic of the successful entrepreneur. These can be seen in Table 2. The following exemplify the factors that have repeatedly shown up as being characteristic of the entrepreneur: dominance, aggressiveness, self-confidence, optimism, high energy level, independence, persistence, flexibility, creativity, and risk-taking propensity.

There is one finding that is of particular interest. The average age for all entrepreneurs is between the early and middle thirties. This seems about the time when there is a stirring of dissatisfaction with existing conditions, a certain amount of experience is acknowledged, and there still exists willingness to take a risk on something new.

3. Organizational Entrepreneurs

Interestingly, the individuals who are successful in heading up new ventures for corporations appear quite similar in several key characteristics to the entrepreneur who starts his own successful new business (Roberts, 1968). For example, the median age for new-venture managers is 36.

It has been felt for some time and is now supported by research that entrepreneurship is characterized by youth, or at least youthful energies. Yet, research on organizational entrepreneurship indicates that the corporations that have been studied showed a definite bias against younger managers taking on new-venture responsibilities. It should not be surprising, therefore, that many would-be organizational innovators leave major corporations to start their own businesses (Roberts, 1968). If organizations want to keep their organizational innovators from leaving, they are going to have to learn to identify them early and modify the organization's behaviour in the direction of being more responsive to the youthful innovators' needs.

Chandler (1962) lists the following attributes as being characteristic of the organizational innovator. They pay little attention to organizational structure; are extroverts; are brilliant salesmen; can 'charm the birds right out of the trees'; avoid tactical matters to concentrate on strategic matters; and are unable to appreciate the need to develop 'management in depth' and to define clear-cut lines of authority and communication (see Table 3).

In a recent article by John Komives (1972), the organizational entrepreneur is described as follows (see Table 3). He has a strong need for security *and* independence; needs to dominate the situation; is a moderate risk-taker; has respect for the entrepreneur *versus* the non-entrepreneur; is highly verbal, but usually does not do much reading; has a strong need for feedback; responds to the concrete rather than the abstract; and has a high energy level.

Although different variables were under study, when one compares the attributes of the entrepreneur in Table 2 and the organizational entrepreneur in Table 3, there are some striking similarities between the two. For example, all but one of the attributes Komives found to be characteristic of the organiz-

236

Table 3. Organizational entrepreneurs

Need to dominate the situation
High energy level
Need for security *and* independence
Highly verbal — usually do not do much reading
Moderate risk-takers
Strong need for feedback
Respond to concrete rather than abstract
Respect for the entrepreneur versus the non-entrepreneur
Extroverts
Brilliant salesmen
Could 'charm the birds right out of the trees'
Pay little attention to organizational structure
Avoid tactical matters to concentrate on strategic matters
Unable to appreciate the need to develop 'management in depth' and to define clear-cut
  lines of authority and communication

ational entrepreneur have been shown to be characteristic of the entrepreneur and are included in Table 2. In point of fact, there is additional evidence that the organizational entrepreneur and the outside or spin-off entrepreneur do look a good deal alike (Roberts, 1968).

4. Managers of Change

Some data recently collected in a study by Rawls and Ullrich (1973) also appear to be relevant to the identification of strategic managers. Subjects in the study were 48 graduate students who were about to enter or reenter both profit and non-profit organizations. As part of the investigation, three faculty members were asked to rate each student in the graduating class on the basis of how successful he or she had been in influencing or introducing change into the Vanderbilt Graduate School of Management system. A total of eight students were judged by all three faculty members as being highly successful in their influence attempts. These eight students were then compared with the other 40 students (see Table 4). On the Guilford—Zimmerman Temperament Survey the

Table 4. Managers of change

Dominant
Aggressive
Make their presence felt
High capacity for status
Flexible (adaptive)
Creative (imaginative, innovative)
Thick-skinned (objective)
High need for achievement
High need for power
High need for self-actualization
High in personal relations skills

'change agents' were significantly more 'thick-skinned' (Objectivity scale) and scored higher on the Personal Relations scale (tolerance of people and social institutions). On the California Psychological Inventory, subjects judged to be effective change agents scored significantly higher on the Dominance, Capacity for Status, Social Presence and Flexibility scales. Looking at the Ghiselli Self-description Inventory, change managers were significantly higher in Achievement Motivation, Need for Self-actualization and Need for Power, while scoring lower on Need for Security. Both groups had very high scores on Guilford's tests of creativity, with the change managers having the higher means of the two. The differences, however, were not statistically significant.

5. Strategic Managers

Previous sections of this chapter have suggested that there is a good deal of commonality between the characteristics of successful managers, entrepreneurs, organizational entrepreneurs, change managers and strategic managers (compare Tables 1, 2, 3, 4 and 5). These data, plus our present knowledge of strategic management job functions, indicate that certain attributes appear to be critical to the success of strategic management performance. Table 5 contains a tentative list of such characteristics. These include dominance, aggressivenes, self-

Table 5. Strategic managers

Dominant
Aggressive
Self-confident
High capacity for status
Desire for personal recognition
Optimistic
High energy level
Independent (self-reliant)
Take initiative (willingness to assume responsibility)
Persistent (hard workers)
High need for achievement
Flexible (adaptive)
Receptive to change
Creative (imaginative, innovative)
High tolerance for ambiguity
High frustration tolerance
Risk-takers (but not gamblers)
Leadership ability (charismatic)
Persuasive
Decisive
Organizational skills
Machiavellian tendencies
Faith in hunches despite some negative feedback
Accept loss and hostility from others
Prefer tasks involving some risk
Emotionally mature (stable)
Above average intelligence

confidence, high capacity for status, desire for personal recognition, optimism, high energy level, independence, persistence, flexibility, creativity, tolerance for ambiguity, frustration tolerance, risk-taking propensity, leadership ability, emotional maturity and above-average intelligence.

It may well be that this suggested list is incomplete, and there may also be characteristics that are unique to successful strategic managers. Obviously, this must wait for empirical verification.

On the other hand, the proposed list appears to be a good starting point for future selection research. Close analysis of the two modes or styles of management that have been discussed (strategic *versus* operational) seems to indicate that strategic management and operations management are not necessarily dichotomous dimensions, but probably exist in varying degrees within a particular manager. More specifically, simply because a manager is successful in a job requiring administration of steady-state operation does not mean that he would be unsuccessful in a strategic management function, and *vice-versa*. Moreover, some operations managers often perform strategic management functions quite effectively, and certainly the strategic manager must be effective in dealing with certain steady-state operations in order to be successful. Even so, it remains for empirical verification to discern those critical factors within the person and the organization that contribute to the successful performance of the strategic manager as opposed to the operations manager.

A first step in seeking empirical verification of purported differences is to identify organizations that provide the type of climate which attracts and nurtures a significant number of strategic managers. A second step would be to identify a sample of successful strategic managers and a representative sample of managers in general in the same organizations. A comparison of the two on the dimensions mentioned in Table 5 should then allow the isolation of critical factors that differentiate the successful strategic manager from managers in general. Further refinement should then come from a comparison of successful strategic managers and successful operations managers in the same organizations on the significant variables derived from step two. Finally, a study assessing organizational climate factors that attract, appropriately channel and provide reinforcement for success in both strategic and operational modes should be undertaken. Given these data, tentative selection, placement, training and incentive systems could be implemented that should, at the very least, decrease the likelihood of losing some of our more creative talent and increase the effective utilization of both strategic and operational managerial resources.

6. Recent Trends in Management Selection

Looking at the current trends in management selection, a number of things are taking place which should prove to be particularly helpful in identifying and developing the strategic manager.

There is a greater emphasis upon self-selection. Employers are increasingly being encouraged to look carefully at jobs that become vacant in order to determine whether or not they think they would prefer the open job to the position they presently hold. If they feel that their abilities and skills are in line with the requirements of the new job, and they feel they would be happier there, they may request that they be considered for the new position. Individuals who make such a request are then put through normal screening procedures for the open position.

It should be pointed out that certain precautions must be taken to ensure that the candidate is opting for a chance at a new job for the right reasons. For example, some may choose a less challenging, less satisfying job for more money. Others may attempt to escape from a position because of poor supervision, interpersonal conflict with peers, etc., but could obtain optimal satisfaction and make a maximum contribution in their present position should their problems be resolved.

However, with appropriate safeguards, this freedom of choice should prove to be very helpful to all concerned. It increases the opportunity for individuals (both strategic and operations managers) to chart their own courses. In so doing, there would seem to be an increased likelihood that managers would place themselves where their talents would be most suited.

This trend should also prove effective to some degree in dealing with the problem of the limited supply of managers. First, it would seem to be responsive to the criticisms of young people that the challenges of a business career are insufficient to meet their needs. Obviously, if this is to prove effective, organizations must provide challenging positions and then remove their biases against younger people taking on strategic responsibilities. Secondly, it might possibly cut down on the number of young creative individuals who leave major firms as a result of insufficient opportunities to make a contribution, develop their potential and see their ideas reach fruition within the corporation.

There is a movement away from the use of a single global criterion measure toward multidimension—multivariate criterion measures. It is encouraging to note that almost all management selection research has now ceased the continued and uncritical use of supervisory ratings as *the* criterion measure. Ratings by superiors have traditionally been included because it was assumed that the superior has the best overview of the situation and knows best how the manager's job behaviour contributes to the overall goals of the organization. However, there are a variety of other gauges that appear to be of significant importance (Lawler, 1967).

A rather large body of literature has now been accumulated on the ability of peer ratings to evaluate the performance of fellow workers. Peer evaluations are relevant because peers are in the best position to evaluate how a manager performs in terms of lateral relationships in working towards organization objectives. Further, peers often see the manager at times when his superior is not viewing his behaviour and, therefore, may witness aspects of his behaviour of which the superior is not aware. For the developing manager who has not yet attained a level to enable him to take on any strategic responsibility, but has the creative capacity to do so, such information provided by his peers could prove to be invaluable input for higher management.

A word of caution is in order with regard to the selection of the dimensions on which peers are to be rated. By definition, a creative idea is not normative, and creative individuals who produce innovations are often considered to be deviants. Similarly, change agents are often considered by their peers to be rebels and boat-rockers. Consequently, unless special attention is paid to the selection of dimensions upon which they are rated, these individuals may become victims of a negative halo effect and may be rated low, particularly on global measures. Under such circumstances, low peer ratings can have only undesirable effects. They may serve, for example, either to induce conformity or to discourage the individual from remaining with the organization. However, if appropriate behavioural dimensions are utilized in rating scales, and if these dimensions are viewed by the organization as positive attributes, peer ratings can be extremely useful. Examples of dimensions that could be useful in identifying the strategic manager are 'generation of innovative ideas' and 'receptivity to change.'

Ratings by subordinates are also relevant, since subordinates are able to determine the superior's impact on the human resources of the organization. The subordinate is also often in a position to observe more of his superior's behaviour than are either peers or superiors.

Self-ratings are relevant because the individual's self-perceptions are very important determinants of his behaviour. In addition, he has more information about his own behaviour than anyone else in the known universe.

Comparing these four different sets of ratings can often produce extremely valuable data. For example, if the superior's ratings of an individual are low, but the other three sets of ratings are high, a need for the supervisor to reassess his criteria for evaluating that person may be indicated .

At last, it appears that we are giving up our worship of *the* single criterion. Utilization of multidimension—multirater approaches is on the increase, and the results are quite gratifying.

Judgemental approaches like those previously mentioned are able to encompass factorially complex behaviours, behaviours which are typical of managerial performance. Most encouraging is the fact that when this approach is adopted, scales can be designed that are sensitive to managerial style variables. In addition, scales can be devised that provide information along such dimensions as creativity, risk-taking propensity, change agentry, etc. Obviously, this type of information could prove invaluable when making decisions regarding the placement of strategic and operations managers. Ideally, scales should be devised that would provide data across the whole domain of desired managerial behaviours.

There has been considerable effort invested recently in developing and refining selection instruments. For a variety of reasons, the production of selection tests in the traditional sense has been eclipsed by the attention given to the development of such techniques as management games, in-baskets, group interaction exercises and biographical information blanks. These instruments would appear to be especially amenable to adaptation along any or all dimensions that would tend to differentiate the strategic manager from the operations managers. In fact, simulations could be designed directly to that end.

There is another definite advantage in using this variety of instrument. That is, weaknesses and deficiencies can be identified that are highly relevant to performance of the tasks being simulated. As a consequence, the information produced can be designed into training programmes aimed at the manager's further development. In the case of the biographical information blank, not only would it enable identification of those who had demonstrated entrepreneurial skill in the past, but the information produced can pinpoint critical experiences lacking in an individual's background which can be provided for in training, so that the individual can be brought up to the experiential level of the more successful strategic or operations managers.

Much more attention is now being paid to placement and career planning. Instead of the one-shot screening-out procedures of the past, new selection systems are being incorporated with placement systems. The trend is towards multiple selection and classification. Moreover, there is an increasing consideration for the rights, sensibilities, needs and prior opportunities of examinees. One outgrowth of this is that selection procedures are much more informative in pointing up individual training needs. Thus, results can be communicated from a development point of view. Within this frame of reference, testing procedures are viewed much more favourably by examinees, and the results are much more meaningful for placement and career planning purposes. Consequently, the utility value is enhanced for both the individual and the organization.

There has been a major decrease in the use of assessment centres. A discussion of new selection procedures would not be complete without mention of the assessment centre approach. The simplest way to define an assessment centre is as a place where 'assessments' are made. 'Assessments,' in this context, represent the pooled judgements made by psychologists and several specially trained professional managers. While being observed for two or three days by psychologists and trained managers, candidates participate in management games, in-basket exercises, structured group experiences and leaderless group discussions. Candidates also take a number of paper-and-pencil psychological tests, a biographical inventory, and go through rather intensive interviews. Using a variety of criteria to evaluate each individual, it is the matter of multiple judgements based upon observations of performance in a variety of situations that is the crux of the assessment centre method (Wikstrom, 1967).

The assessment centre approach should prove very useful in assuring that strategic and operations managers are placed such that their talents are optimally channelled. In addition, on the basis of sheer volume of data alone, assessment centres should prove to be invaluable sources for concurrent and longitudinal validation studies on the selection and placement of strategic and operations managers.

7. Summary and Conclusions

It would appear that a new creative, imaginative, entrepreneurial manager is needed to cope with our very rapidly changing environment. In an effort to identify the characteristics of the strategic manager who must anticipate, channel and create these forces of change, the attributes of successful managers, entrepreneurs, organizational entrepreneurs and change managers were reviewed. On the basis of a comparison of these groups, a tentative list of attributes of successful strategic managers was derived. In looking at current trends in management selection, several suggestions were made that may prove helpful in the identification and placement of strategic managers, viz., self-selection; multidimension—multirater approaches; use of a variety of new selection instruments; emphasis on development, placement and career planning; and use of assessment centre approaches. In conclusion, there appears to be an urgent need to identify, properly place and develop potentially successful strategic managers, and the techniques to do so seem to be available. It remains now to get out of the armchair and into the data.

References

Ansoff, H. I. (1972). 'The concept of strategic management', *The Journal of Business Policy*, 2 (4), 2.

Ansoff, H. I. (1973). 'Management in transition', in *Challenge to Leadership: Managing in a Changing World*. New York, The Conference Board, Free Press.

Bray, D. W., and Moses, J. L. (1972). 'Personal selection', in P. H. Mussen and M. R. Rosenzweig (Eds.), *Annual Review of Psychology*. Vol. 23, Palo Alto, Calif., Annual Reviews, pp. 545—76.

Campbell, J. P., Dunnette, M. D., Lawler, E. E., and Weick, K. E., Jr. (1970). *Managerial Behaviour, Performance, and Effectiveness*, New York, McGraw-Hill.

Chandler, A. D., Jr. (1962). *Strategy and Structure*, Cambridge, MIT Press.

Dible, D. M. (1971). *Up Your Own Organization*, Santa Clara, Calif., Entrepreneur Press.

Drucker, P. F. (1969). *The Age of Discontinuity*, New York, Harper & Row, p. 43.

Guion, R. M. (1965). *Personal Selection*, New York, McGraw-Hill.

Johnson, H. W. (1965). 'Management for the 70's', *Dun's Review*, 91, 19.

Komives, J. (1972. 'Characteristics of entrepreneurs, with emphasis on the organizational entrepreneur', Unpublished manuscript, The Center for Venture Management, Milwaukee, Wisconsin.

Lawler, E. E., III (1967). 'The multitrait—multirater approach to measuring managerial performance', *Journal of Applied Psychology*, 51, 369.

Megginson, L. C. (1967). *Personnel: A Behavioral Approach*, Homewood, Illinois, Irwin.

Owens, W. A., and Jewell, D. O. (1969). 'Personnel selection', in P. H. Mussen and M. R. Rosenzweig (Eds.). *Annual Review of Psychology*, Vol. 20, Palo Alto, Calif., Annual Reviews, pp. 419—46.

Rawls, J. R., and Ullrich, R. A. (1973). 'A comparison of managers entering or re-entering the profit and non-profit sectors', Unpublished manuscript, Graduate School of Management, Vanderbilt University.

Roberts, E. B. (1963). 'A basic study of innovators; how to keep and capitalize on their talents', *Research Management*, 11, 24.

Wikstrom, W. S. (1967). 'Assessing managerial talent', *The Conference Board Record*, 4, 39.

DESIGN OF AN INTRAFIRM MANAGEMENT DEVELOPMENT PROGRAMME FOR STRATEGIC MANAGEMENT

KENNETH O. MICHEL

'The manager is the dynamic, life-giving element in every business. Without his leadership the 'resources of production' remain resources and never become production. In a competitive economy, above all, the quality and performance of the managers determine the success of a business, indeed they determine its survival. For the quality and performance of its managers is the only effective advantage an enterprise in a competitive economy can have.' (Drucker, 1954)

'Managers are responsible for charting the destiny of the firm and implementing the resulting strategies. The quality of that planning can be no better than the quality of managers who develop the plans. Satisfactory performance can result only from having qualified operating managers who control and implement according to quality plans.' (Cone and Kinney, 1972).

These two statements recorded 18 years apart by renowned 'students of the science' highlight the fact that the key role of the manager and the formulation and implementation of a business strategy are so intertwined that it is difficult to identify which is the warp and which is the weave. How and to what extent these two interdependent elements interact with each other determines the design, the strength, and the functional effectiveness of a business enterprise.

Accepting the fact that the success of a business is heavily dependent upon the quality and performance of its managers, it seems to make good sense for a business to increase the ability of its managers to respond effectively to constantly changing demands of the business. 'The increasing rate of change in almost everything about modern life puts an even greater demand on the manager for himself to change, develop, learn new things throughout his career in order to avoid his own obsolescence.' (Fickel, 1973).

Within General Electric we accept these premises and firmly believe in the value of an effective management development effort. 'Management development is a complex, life-long *learning* process for producing and accumulating the relevant know-how, skills, art, and attributes used by those individuals — the managers — who lead and control organization in our society.' (Drucker, 1954).

As Dr Saline further describes in his paper presented to the ASEE (Saline, 1973), the learning process for managers takes place in many ways: on-the-job experience; involvement with new assignments or new bosses; participation on task forces, study teams and committees; and assuming leadership responsibilities outside his or her job community organizations. churches or professional societies. Education is only *one* source for management development learning.

Even the education for the development of a manager has several sources: formal programmes offered by colleges and universities; seminars and conferences offered by professional societies and trade associations; self-study through commercially available packaged programmes or self-structured reading efforts; and intrafirm education programmes.

Although in the General Electric Company all of these avenues for learning are recommended to our people at various stages of their careers to accomplish specific developmental needs, our intrafirm education programmes are the predominant education sources for furthering management development learning other than the individual's formal degree study. This chapter will be concerned with the structure of an intrafirm education effort for the continuing development of strategic management.

If the objective of an intrafirm management education effort is to help its managers become continually more effective in the process of supplying direction and leadership to the business, there should be a rationale for the process of business, for the strategy which optimizes that process and the results it produces, and for the role of the manager in causing it to happen effectively. The rationale then becomes a guideline for structuring a meaningful education effort for a specific audience. This does demand that the designer of the education effort assume the responsibility for keeping the definition of 'meaningful' relevant both to the needs of the business and to the individual participant. The objectivity of continuing relevance can be more easily accomplished in intrafirm education than any other mode of education. The intrafirm course designer has the opportunity for continual contact with and feedback from operating managers and manpower planners who are constantly involved with the needs of the business and development needs of the individual. These are invaluable inputs to the accomplishment of an effective education experience.

1. A Rationale for Strategic Management

Figure 1 is an elementary representation of the business process. A strategy is the statement of how it is intended the elements of this process will interact in order to produce desired results. The job of the manager is to give the direction and the leadership to this process in order continually to increase its input-output efficiency.

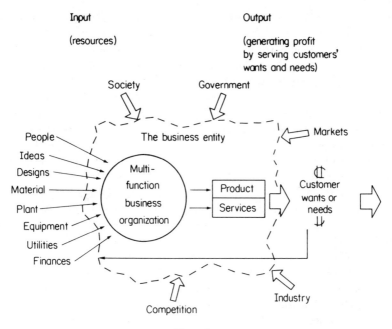

Figure 1

The inputs to the process are the resources of people, ideas, designs, material, plant, equipment, utilities and finances. The 'multi-function business organization' is the structure by which the subprocesses of creating and designing (engineering), producing (manufacturing), marketing and financing convert the resource inputs into the product, which can be hardware, services, or both. The product is made available through a distribution system to the customers, who will buy and pay for the product if they feel it satisfies their wants or needs. Payment by the customer for the product received recycles the resource of money back into the business process to cover the costs of operating the process and reinvest into expansion of the process or growth in its results. Any excess money is the profit which is paid to the owners or shareholders of the business entity and to the investors for the use of their capital.

The business entity is the legal body which operates as a one-product company, a multi-product company or a multi-business corporation.

Surrounding the business entity is the external environment. The elements of the external environment (society, government, markets, customers, industry, competition and suppliers) impact on the business in the form of opportunities or threats. An opportunity emanates from the elements of the environment as a political, economic, technological or social situation which presents a climate favourable to improving the input-output efficiency of the business process or favourable to the growth or expansion of the business process output. A threat emanates from the elements of the environment as a political, economic, technological or social situation which presents an unfavourable climate for improving the efficiency of the business process or for growth or expansion of its output.

A strategy is a statement of how what resources are going to be acquired and used to take advantage of which opportunities and minimize which threats to produce a desired result. Although strategy can be simplistically defined in one sentence with the aid of an elementary diagram, the complexity becomes extensive when formulating the strategy, planning the action which is intended to be followed and bringing about the action which will accomplish the results, even for a one-product business.

The role of management is to offer direction and leadership in making this complex business process function with ever-increasing efficiency under conditions of constant change. To accomplish this with any degree of effectiveness the managers must know the state of each of these elements at any one time. To do this each element must be analysed to determine how, why and to what extent it evolved through the past into its present state. The analysis supplies facts about the elements of the environment, the conditions of the resources and the effectiveness of the multi-function organization to cause the resources to interact to produce the desired results.

To this understanding of the present state of all of these elements and why they are in that condition, the managers must add their intuition, experience and judgement to develop assumptions about the future condition of the elements of the environment and their impact on the business. Similarly, they must develop assumptions about the future condition of the elements of resource and what needs to be added to or changed in resource competence to meet the challenges offered by the future state of the elements of the environment.

The managerial strategic decisions then must be made as to how, when and to what extent the resource commitment will be made to produce what results, when and to what extent and what are the chances of suceeding in the desired time-frame. As the time elapses, it is the responsibility of managers to implement the planned actions so as to produce the desired results as a minimum, at the planned costs as a maximum, within a narrow range of the predetermined risk, or chance to succeed.

Although all managers have a responsibility to direct and lead the interaction with strategy during all three phases of formulation, planning and implementation, there are three levels of strategic management with different characteristics and scope of responsibility within any business entity. For any individual manager the nature of his task and responsibility is directly related to where he is in these three levels of strategic management. As shown in Figure 2, the three levels are (1) investment strategy or corporate strategy, (2) business strategy and (3) functional strategy.

At the investment strategy or corporate strategy level the managerial decisions are investment decisions involving capital funds. The strategic considerations are broad in scope and concern themselves with the total business entity and its arenas of endeavour. The mission is to maintain the total organization as a viable business entity within an ever-changing macro-

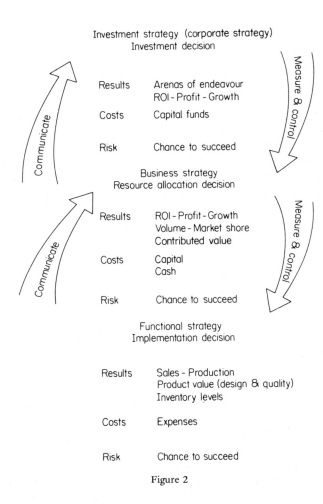

Investment strategy (corporate strategy)
Investment decision

Results	Arenas of endeavour
	ROI - Profit - Growth
Costs	Capital funds
Risk	Chance to succeed

Business strategy
Resource allocation decision

Results	ROI - Profit - Growth
	Volume - Market shore
	Contributed value
Costs	Capital
	Cash
Risk	Chance to succeed

Functional strategy
Implementation decision

Results	Sales - Production
	Product value (design & quality)
	Inventory levels
Costs	Expenses
Risk	Chance to succeed

Figure 2

environment. The measurable results desired are profit, return on investment, and growth which can be measured in earnings per share, price to earnings ratio of the stock, or the willingness of external investors to supply capital funds. A qualitative aspect of the business' viability is society's acceptance of the business entity as a good citizen. The time range of the strategic focus is several years into the future.

Below the investment level of strategic consideration is the business strategy level. This is the level at which leadership is given for the multi-function business organization. The decisions are principally those of resource allocation. The capital funds which are allocated as a result of the investment strategy level decisions are translated into the required input resources, identified in Figure 1. The scope of the strategic considerations at this level is related to the definition of the product market life-cycle curve and the response to the opportunities and threats posed within the context of a defined product/market life cycle. The measurable results at this level are return on investment, profit, growth usually in terms of volume and market share, and contributed value. The concerns for cost at this level are in terms of capital funds and cash. The time range for strategic focus at this level is generally one year, with the long-range consideration related to the characteristic of the specific product/market life cycle.

At the next level, the functional strategy level, the manager's responsibility is the direction and leadership of a functional subprocess within the framework of the multi-function business organization. Although the strategic decisions at this level are principally implementation decisions, of equal importance is the responsibility to make functionally oriented inputs to the business strategy and to formulate functional sub-strategies which will give optimum support to the business strategy. The results at this level are measured in terms of sales, production, value of product in terms of functionality of design, quality or reliability, inventory levels and income. The cost concerns at this level are in terms of expenses related to material, labour, and overhead. The time range of strategic focus is relatively short, one month to one year.

In the strategic formulation and planning stage, the output of efforts at the functional strategy level are vital inputs to the considerations at the business strategy level. Likewise, the outputs of the business strategy efforts are vital to the considerations at the investment strategy level. Forthright, viable and well-defined information must be communicated upwards in order for a business entity to formulate and plan cohesive strategies at all levels. To be effective, a manager at any level must understand what inputs are required at that level; what analysis and decisions must be made to generate the appropriate outputs at that level; and the quality, scope and clarity required of the outputs as they become inputs to the next level.

After the strategies have been formulated and the strategic plans have been agreed upon at all levels, the capital funds are allocated to the appropriate businesses at the business strategy level. Using the accepted business strategic plan as the guide, the resource allocation parameters are communicated to the functional strategy level managers. Their responsibility is to communicate the appropriate functional substrategy plan to all managers and subordinates in that function. As the business implements the accepted strategic plans, measurements and control are communicated downwards to give guidance in formulating operating decisions and initiation of contingency actions which may require deviation from the original strategy. In this phase of strategic management, it is the responsibility of the manager to monitor feedback, measure and control to keep the business process on the course of achieving desired results, within the parameters of the budgeted costs, preferably at no increase in risk. The success of the business during the implementation is dependent on the ability of the managers to make the appropriate tradeoff decision between variances in results, costs and risk.

The results and costs for any strategic management level as shown in Figure 2 become the criteria for measurement of the managers and their organizational components at that level.

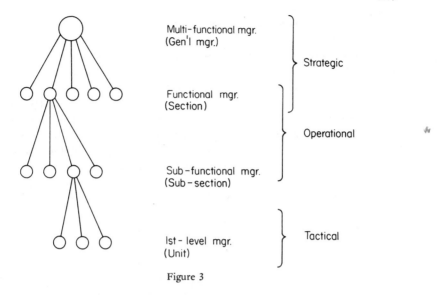

Figure 3

To complete the understanding of management's role in the operation of a business enterprise, the structure of management within the multi-function business organization (Figure 1) needs to be identified: These managers have the responsibility for organizing, directing and leading the subprocesses which translate the resource inputs of people, ideas, designs, material, plant, equipment, utilities and finances into product. Figure 3 visualizes the characteristics of their relationships and the focus of their tasks.

The role of the first-level manager has a tactical orientation. The responsibility is getting today's task accomplished. The knowhow and skills required are elementary fundamentals of manager's work, principally focused on management of people and heavy functional expertise.

The task orientation of the subfunctional level manager is principally operational. This level is the first manager of managers, and the responsibility is managing a subprocess which demands functional expertise. The time horizon is further out than just today's task. Goals are month-end accomplishments and objectives are year-end. The scope of the task becomes more business-process oriented and less people-process oriented.

The functional manager is the senior operational manager. Thorough knowledge of functional expertise and the total functional process is required of the manager at this level. A dual role emerges at this level of management because the functional manager assumes the responsibility for the first level of strategic management, the functional strategy level. The time horizon for results at this level is usually one year, and the scope of responsibility is both operational and strategic.

The role of the multi-functional manager is strategic. At this level, the perspective moves beyond a narrow functional expertise towards the understanding of the total business system or process. It is here that the responsibility rests for business strategic decisions. The interactions of all the functions and their impact on the total business must be understood, and leadership for accomplishing the strategic results is imperative.

2. A Career-Coordinated Approach to Education

As a manager progresses through the organization hierarchy in a business enterprise, there are different demands placed on his competence. At each level of responsibility the nature of the manager's role requires knowhow, skills, art and attitude which are broader in scope and different in time horizon and accountability. His expertise must shift from a strong functional orientation into

Table 1. Partial listing of educational activities for professional and managerial employees in General Electric

Position in Organization	Professional		General		Managerial	
Entry Level	AMSCC AEP FS	POMC EDC ERS	CDP PES			
Below unit level	SPC		K-T TDP	ICW CDP	FSC MSDC	GEMS
Unit	ERMC SPC	EOC	K-T ICW	CDP	MPC(EM) MPC(FTM) EMC	MSDC WP GEMS
Subsection	AMMS ERMC	MEC SPC	K-T ICW EO/MR	MORE CDP DSDC	MPC(EM) MDC EMC	IPW WP
Section	AMMS SPC	MEC	K-T ICW EO/MR	DSDC MORE	SPW GMC EWS	IPW WP
Department level and higher			EWS		SPW SPER	EWS

LEGEND

AEP, Advanced Engineering Program; AMMS, Advanced Marketing Manpower Seminar; AMSCC, Advanced Mfg'g Studies and Correspondence Course; CDP, Career Development Program; DSDC, Diagnostic Skills Development Seminar; EDC, Engineering Design Course; EMC, Experienced Manager Course; EOC, Engineering Operations Course; EO/MR, Equal Opportunity/Minority Relations Seminar; ERMC, Employee Relations Managers Course; ERS, Employee Relations Studies; EWS, Executive Workshops; FS, Financial Studies; FSC, Foremen/Supervisors Course; GEMS, GE Management Seminar; GMC, General Management Course; ICW, Interpersonal Communication Workshop; IPW, Implementation Planning Workshop; K-T, Kepner-Tregoe Problem Solving and Decision Making (GENCO, VERTEX); MDC, Manager Development Course; MEC, Modern Engineering Course; MORE, Management Operational Readiness Effort; MPC, Management Practices Course; EM, Experienced Managers; FTM, First-Time Managers; MSDC, Management Skills Development Course; PES, Professional Employee Seminar; POMC, Principles of Marketing Course; SPC, Specialized Professional Courses (all functions); SPER, Strategic Planning Executive Review; SPW, Strategic Planning Workshop; TDP, Talent Development Program; WP, Work Planning.

a broader area of strategic business expertise, and ultimately to a level of business statemanship

Indeed, the skills and activities which led to success in a manager's functional career — whether marketing, manufacturing, engineering, R & D, control, or finance — are usually those of specialization, of deep involvement in a narrow area. The specialist knows more and more about less and less.

In the medical and legal professions, specialization is the usual route to excellence and eminence. The manager, too, during the early phases of his career, follows this pattern; he establishes a track record by excelling in a particular speciality. But unlike the doctor and the lawyer, his career progression pattern is brutally shifted. Having earned his spurs as a specialist, the manager is given a new, a drastically different challenge, that of excelling as a generalist. Instead of knowing more and more about less and less, he now shifts to knowing less and less about more and more. (Uyterhoeven, 1972).

Our philosophy for management education at General Electric believes most of the learning takes in the 'on-the-job' environment, and the education programmes offer enhancement and enrichment of that experience.

The curricula are coordinated with the responsibilities the business demands of the individual at various stages of his or her career.

The professional curriculum focuses on developing know-how, skills, and art in a specific area of expertise. It helps to extend or deepen previous academic learning in a particular discipline and/or the expertise for a particular business function. For example, the designing of electronic circuits would be part of the professional curriculum as would sales training and shop operations. Areas of professional education relate to engineering, manufacturing, marketing, finance and employee relations. The general curriculum focuses on such areas as personal attitudes and awareness, human relationships, career development, and other process-oriented learning. The know-how, skills, art and attributes that can result from participation in the general curriculum are not restricted to specific areas of functional or academic expertise, nor to management work, *per se*. Rather, the know-how skills, art and attributes can be useful to specific individuals without regard to their particular work assignments.

The managerial curriculum focuses on business and the management of resources such as dollars, time and people to achieve business objectives. It helps to develop understanding about how a business operates in our society, business strategy and structure, strategic and operational planning, financial management and business operations. Considerable attention is given in the managerial curriculum to the total environment in which a business operates,

Table 2. The managerial curriculum

Course	Participants	Thrust
Managerial Skills Development (MSDC)	Selected below unit level	Developing managerial skills
Management Practices Course (MPC)	All unit managers	Managing professional employees
"Manager of Managers"	All subsection managers	Managing other managers
Manager Development Course (MDC)	Hi-po subsection managers	How a business works How managers make it work
General Management Course (CMC)	Hi-po section managers	How a business works Job of GM & his team
Executive Workshops (EWS)	Dept. level and higher	Selected aspects in operating a business

MONDAY		TUESDAY		WEDNESDAY	
Day 1	February 5	Day 2	February 6	Day 3	February 7
a.m.	Introduction (Ken Michel – GE) Concept of Strategy (Hugo Uyterhoeven – Harvard)	a.m.	Strategy Formulation: Vertical Integration (Ram Charan)	a.m.	Strategy Formulation: Interfirm Competition (Bill Guth – NYU)
p.m.	Strategy and Action for the Total Enterprise (Hugo Uyterhoeven) (Ram Charan – Harvard)	p.m.	Strategy Formulation: Impact of Environmental Change (Ram Charan)	p.m.	Strategy Formulation: Environment and Business Opportunity (Frederick Knickerbocker – Harvard)
Day 7	February 12	Day 8	February 13	Day 9	February 14
a.m.	Strategic Planning Process in GE (Ken Michel) Formulating Strategy for a Simulated Business (Dave Mehl and Dave Sims – GE)	a.m.	Integration of Corporate and Component Strategies (Mal Salter – Harvard)	a.m.	Funds Analysis Leasing and Debt Financing (Dave Hawkins)
p.m.	Planning for a Business Operation (Dave Mehl – Dave Sims)	p.m.	Financial Management: Fixed Assets and Depreciation (Dave Hawkins – Harvard)	p.m.	Investments in R & D Cash Flow and Taxation (Dave Hawkins)
Day 12	February 19	Day 13	February 20	Day 14	February 21
a.m.	Strategic Planning and Implementation (John Rosenblum)	a.m.	Strategy Implementation (Ram Charan) Strategy and Organization Leadership (John Rosenblum)	a.m.	Strategy and Planning for Results (Ram Charan)
p.m.	Planning for Strategy Implementation (Ram Charan)	p.m.	Continued (John Rosenblum)	p.m.	Summary Lecture (Ram Charan) Accounting and Business Strategy Walt Frese – Harvard)
Day 18	February 26	Day 19	February 27	Day 20	February 28
a.m.	Simulation Techniques for Strategy Evaluation (Paul Vatter)	a.m.	Economics and the Business Environment (Tom Hailstones – Xavier)	a.m.	Contemporary Issues in Economics (Tom Hailstones)
p.m.	Risk Analysis (Paul Vatter)	p.m.	Continued (Tom Hailstones)	p.m.	The Manufacturing Resource and the Business Strategy (Bob Hayes – Harvard)

	THURSDAY		FRIDAY		SATURDAY
Day 4	February 8	Day 5	February 9	Day 6	February 10

a.m.	Strategy Formulation: Multinational Competition (Knick Knickerbocker)	a.m.	Strategy Formulation: Dynamic Evolution of a Strategy (John Rosenblum)	a.m.	Strategy Formulation: Diversification Concept of Strategy Review & Summary (Hugo Uyterhoeven)
p.m.	Strategy Formulation: Dynamic Evolution of a Strategy (John Rosenblum – Harvard)	p.m.	Strategy Formulation: A New Market (Hugo Uyterhoeven)		

Day 10	February 15	Day 11	February 16		February 17

a.m.	Capital Management Intercorporate Investments (Dave Hawkins)	a.m.	Income Recognition & Management Performance (Dave Hawkins)		
p.m.	Inventory Pricing (Dave Hawkins)	p.m.	Implementation Planning (Bill Guth)		

Day 15	February 22	Day 16	February 23	Day 17	February 24

a.m.	Management Control: Technical & Behavioral Concepts (Dave Hawkins)	a.m.	Mergers & Acquisitions (Dave Hawkins, Dave Mehl, Ken Michel)	a.m.	Sequential Decision Analysis (Paul Vatter)
p.m.	Continued (Dave Hawkins)	p.m.	Decision Analysis & Probabilities (Paul Vatter – Harvard)		

Day 21	March 1				

a.m.	Impact of Manufacturing on the Business Strategy (Bob Hayes)			NOTE This advance planning sheet is furnished to GMC Participants for their convenience. The information, however, must be regarded as tentative, and will be confirmed only by the Daily Plans.

MONDAY		TUESDAY		WEDNESDAY	
Day 22	March 5	Day 23	March 6	Day 24	March 7
		a.m.	International Environment: Latin America (Warren Law)	a.m.	The Organization & the Individual (Kirby Warren)
p.m.	International Environment: Far East (Warren Law — Harvard)	p.m.	Strategy & Structure (Kirby Warren — Columbia)	p.m.	Integration of Functional Strategies (Bob Hayes)
Day 28	March 12	Day 29	March 13	Day 30	March 14
a.m.	Concept of Corporate Transformation (Ram Charan)	a.m.	Futurism and Business Planning (Ram Charan)	a.m.	To be announced
p.m.	Continued (Ram Charan)	p.m.	Continued (Ram Charan)	p.m.	Impact of Environment on "Big Business" Strategies — GE (Jim Baughman — Harvard)
Day 33	March 19	Day 34	March 20	Day 35	March 21
a.m.	Trends in Managing Human Resources (Mike Beer — Corning Glass; Mel Sorcher — GE)	a.m.	To Be Announced	a.m.	Legitimacy of the Corporation (Bob Estes — GE)
p.m.	Employee Relations in a Changing Environment (John Burlingame & Staff — GE)	p.m.	Leadership Management (Visit to West Point)	p.m.	Issues in Society (Mel Tumin — Princeton)
Day 39	March 26	Day 40	March 27	Day 41	March 28
a.m.	Strategy & Environment: Current Legal Issues in GE (Walter Schlotterbeck and Staff — GE	a.m.	Meeting Stakeholder Expectations (Bob Ackerman — Harvard)	a.m.	Emotional Health and the Executive (Harry Levinson — Harvard Medical School & Boston U.)
p.m.	Meeting Stakeholder Expectations (Margie Crimes — GE, Hal Hayes — GE, Tom Hilbert — GE)	p.m.	Job of the Middle Manager (Hugo Uyterhoeven)	p.m.	Preparation

THURSDAY	FRIDAY	SATURDAY
Day 25 March 8	Day 26 March 9	Day 27 March 10
a.m. Strategy Implementation: The Manufacturing Resource (Bob Hayes)	a.m. Business Strategy & Environment: Corporate Responsibility (John Matthews)	a.m. International Environment: Canada Summary Lecture (Warren Law)
p.m. Business Strategy & Environment: Public Expectations (John Matthews — Harvard)	p.m. International Financial Evaluations (Warren Law)	
Day 31 March 15	Day 32 March 16	March 17
a.m. GE International Strategies Implications for the Future (Jim Baughman)	a.m. Business and Government. A Working Partnership (Berkley Davis — GE, Harry Levine — GE)	
p.m. Strategy Review of Simulated Business (Bill Rothschild — GE) Views from the Executive Office (Herm Weiss — GE)	p.m. The Human Resource: Career Development (Bob Schuldt — GE, Walt Storey — GE)	
Day 36 March 22	Day 37 March 23	Day 38 March 24
a.m. Issues in Society (Mel Tumin)	a.m. Values and Management decisions (Bill Guth)	a.m. Perception and the World of the Manager (Bud Kilpatrick — Ohio State)
p.m. Values and Resource Management (Bill Guth)	p.m. Review of Simulated Business Operation (Dave Mehl, Dave Sims)	
Day 42 March 29	Day 43 March 30	
a.m. Values & Ethics (Ken Michel)	a.m. Getting It All Together (Billy Wireman — Eckerd College) Graduation	NOTE This advance planning sheet is furnished to GMC Participants for their convenience. The information, however, must be regarded as tentative, and will be confirmed only by the Daily Plans.
p.m. Joint Session (Speaker to be Announced)		

to human relationships and organization structure, and to developing and practicing some of the skills and judgement needed to do managing work.

The partial listing of educational activities for professional and managerial employees in General Electric is shown in Table 1. There is not, in general, a rigid prerequisite relationship among offerings. On the other hand, they are offered with important distinctions in mind as to needs and expectations, as well as to perspectives arising out of factors such as age, experience, level of responsibility, kinds of work, and potential of the participants. The common thread is that learning is a life-long process. To maintain the ability to learn new things and therefore to meet new challenges, the capacity to learn must be exercised. Each of the General Electric programs is itself a challenge. (Saline, 1973)

Presently, the managerial curriculum consists of a series of offerings which are sequenced into the manager's development programme at different stages of his or her career. Table 2 is a summary listing of present offerings.

In the design of a specific course, the challenge is not to find *enough* to fill in the array, but rather to sift out the flood of educationally 'tempting' subject matter and focus on 'what's worth knowing' and 'what's needed'. A practical way to develop the course content is to use the following six-step approach.

Step 1. Develop 'what's needed' charts for managers for each level in the organizational hierarchy.

Step 2. Develop 'what's worth knowing' charts for managers.

Step 3. Obtain inputs from manpower planners, operating and staff managers and executives, course participants and faculty.

Step 4. Distill possible educational offerings, including specific audience, objectives, methodology, etc.

Step 5. Assess the feasibility of offering specific learning experiences based on need, teachability, learnability and economics.

Step 6. Select (continue, add, modify, eliminate) offerings.

An example of a course curriculum which is coordinated to the career needs of the participants is Table 3. This is an eight-week programme that was designed to prepare the high-potential section manager (functional manager) to better understand the job of the next higher manager, the multi-function general manager.

In our concept for management education, it is believed that due to the nature of our rapidly changing world there are continually new challenges facing our managers. Continuing education is imperative for the continued growth and development of the leadership in a business enterprise. The very nature of the increasing complexity of the managers' responsibilities practically precludes their spending large blocks of time in 'school' situations, particularly at the executive level. In an effort to keep our managers abreast of the challenges of change and to offer educational support for coping with them we offer Executive Workshops. They are brief, two to four days in length, and sharply focused on one topic. The faculty are the best authorities that can be found from college campuses or business. The educational objectives are to equip the participant with understanding, techniques and processes that can be applied immediately back on the job. The topics for some of our recent workshops have been:

Strategic Planning Workshop
Strategic Planning Executive Review
Dealing With Risk and Uncertainty
Forecasting Workshop
Managing Current Assets

If indeed, as Drucker stated, 'The manager is the dynamic, life-giving element in every business', how can we not afford to give him the opportunity to be of the highest quality and performance.

'Mobility of challenge and of work must be matched by mobility of mind and of motivation.' (Fickel, 1973)

References

Andrews, Kenneth R. (1971). *Concept of Corporate Strategy*, Homewood, Ill., Dow-Jones, Irwin.

Drucker, P. F. (1954). *The Practice of Management*, New York, Harper & Row, p. 3.

Chandler, A. D., Jr. (1963). *Strategy and Structure*, Cambridge, Mass., MIT Press.

Cone, P. R., and Kinney, R. N. (1972). 'Management development can be more effective', *California Management Review*, **XIV**, No. 3, Spring.

Fickel, A. A. (1973). 'Notes of Management Education in General Electric', Paper presented to a delegation of USSR officials, February.

Saline, L. E. (1973). 'Education: one element in the management development process', Paper presented to the American Society for Engineering Education, April 1973.

Uyterhoeven, H. E. R. (1972). 'General managers in the middle', *Harvard Business Review*, March-April, p. 75.

Uyterhoeven, H. E. R. (1973). *Strategy and Organization: Text and Cases in General Management*, Homewood, Ill., Irwin.

Index